The Devil in Britain and America
By John Ashton
Edited by Anthony Uyl

Devoted Publishing
Ingersoll, Ontario, 2025

The Devil, in Britain and America
The Devil in Britain and America
By John Ashton
Edited by Anthony Uyl

'Nam ut vere loquamur, superstitio fusa per gentes oppressit omnium fere animos, atque hominum imbecillitatem occupavit.'
CICERO--De Divin., Lib. ii. 72.

Originally Published by:
Ward and Downey Limited. 12 York Buildings, Adelphi W.C. 1896.

The text of *The Devil in Britain and America* is all protected under Copyright ©2025 Devoted Publishing. The covers, background, layout and Devoted Publishing logo are Copyright ©2025 Devoted Publishing. This edition is published by Devoted Publishing a division of 2165467 Ontario Inc.

Contact us at: devotedpub@hotmail.com
Visit us on X (Formerly Twitter): @AnthonyDevPub
Published in Ingersoll, Ontario, Canada 2025

ISBN: 978-1-77356-562-0

Table of Contents

PREFACE 4
CHAPTER I 5
CHAPTER II 11
CHAPTER III 19
CHAPTER IV 25
CHAPTER V 29
CHAPTER VI 33
CHAPTER VII 37
CHAPTER VIII 45
CHAPTER IX 50
CHAPTER X 53
CHAPTER XI 56
CHAPTER XII 59
CHAPTER XIII 63
CHAPTER XIV 68
CHAPTER XV 71
CHAPTER XVI 77
CHAPTER XVII 81
CHAPTER XVIII 85
CHAPTER XIX 89
CHAPTER XX 93
CHAPTER XXI 98
CHAPTER XXII 103
CHAPTER XXIII 106
CHAPTER XXIV 111
APPENDIX 115
FOOTNOTES: 127

PREFACE

To my thinking, all modern English books on the Devil and his works are unsatisfactory. They all run in the same groove, give the same cases of witchcraft, and, moreover, not one of them is illustrated. I have endeavoured to remedy this by localizing my facts, and by reproducing all the engravings I could find suitable to my purpose.

I have also tried to give a succinct account of demonology and witchcraft in England and America, by adducing authorities not usually given, and by a painstaking research into old cases, carefully taking everything from original sources, and bringing to light very many cases never before republished.

For the benefit of students, I have given--as an Appendix--a list of the books consulted in the preparation of this work, which, however, the student must remember is not an exhaustive bibliography on the subject, but only applies to this book, whose raison d'être is its localization.

The frontispiece is supposed to be the only specimen of Satanic calligraphy in existence, and is taken from the 'Introductio in Chaldaicam Linguam,' etc., by Albonesi (Pavia, 1532). The author says that by the conjuration of Ludovico Spoletano the Devil was called up, and adjured to write a legible and clear answer to a question asked him. Some invisible power took the pen, which seemed suspended in the air, and rapidly wrote what is facsimiled. The writing was given to Albonesi (who, however, confesses that no one can decipher it), and his chief printer reproduced it very accurately. I am told by experts that in some of the characters may be found a trace of Amharic, a language spoken in its purity in the province of Amhara (Ethiopia), and which, according to a legend, was the primeval language spoken in Eden.

JOHN ASHTON.

CHAPTER I

Universal Belief in the Personality of the Devil, as portrayed by the British Artist--Arguments in Favour of his Personality--Ballad--'Terrible and Seasonable Warning to Young Men.'

The belief in a good and evil influence has existed from the earliest ages, in every nation having a religion. The Egyptians had their Typho, the Assyrians their Ti-a-mat (the Serpent), the Hebrews their Beelzebub, or Prince of Flies,[1] and the Scandinavians their Loki. And many religions teach that the evil influence has a stronger hold upon mankind than the good influence--so great, indeed, as to nullify it in a large degree. Christianity especially teaches this: 'Enter ye by the narrow gate; for wide is the gate, and broad is the way, that leadeth to destruction, and many be they that enter in thereby. For narrow is the gate, and straitened the way, that leadeth unto life, and few be they that find it.' This doctrine of the great power of the Devil, or evil influence over man, is preached from every pulpit, under every form of Christianity, throughout the world; and although at the present time it is only confined to the greater moral power of the Devil over man, at an earlier period it was an article of belief that he was able to exercise a greater physical power.

This was coincident with a belief in his personality; and it is only in modern times that that personality takes an alluring form. In the olden days the Devil was always depicted as ugly and repulsive as the artist could represent him, and yet he could have learned a great deal from the modern Chinese and Japanese. The 'great God Pan,' although he was dead, was resuscitated in order to furnish a type for 'the Prince of Darkness'; and, accordingly, he was portrayed with horns, tail and cloven feet, making him an animal, according to a mot attributed to Cuvier, 'graminivorous, and decidedly ruminant'; while, to complete his classical ensemble, he was invested with the forked sceptre of Pluto, only supplemented with another tine.

The British artist thus depicted him, but occasionally he drew him as a 'fearful wild fowl' of a totally different type--yet always as hideous as his imagination could conceive, or his pencil execute.

That the Devil could show himself to man, in a tangible form, was, for many centuries, an article of firm belief, but, when it came to be argued out logically, it was difficult of proof. The only evidence that could be adduced which could carry conviction was from the Bible, which, of course, was taken as the ipsissima verba of God, and, on that, the old writers based all their proof. One of the most lucid of them, Gyfford or Gifford, writing in the sixteenth century, evidently feels this difficulty. Trying to prove that 'Diuels can appear in a bodily shape, and use speeche and conference with men,' he says:[2]

'Our Saviour Christ saith that a spirite hath neither flesh nor bones. A spirite hath a substance, but yet such as is invisible, whereupon it must needes be graunted, that Diuels in their owne nature have no bodilye shape, nor visible forme; moreover, it is against the truth, and against pietie to believe that Diuels can create, or make bodies, or change one body into another, for those things are proper to God. It followeth, therefore, that whensoever they appear in a visible forme, it is no more but an apparition and counterfeit shewe of a bodie, unless a body be at any time lent them.'

And further on he thus speaks of the incarnation of Satan, as recorded in the Bible.

'The Deuill did speake unto Eua out of the Serpent. A thing manifest to proue that Deuils can speake, unlesse we imagine that age hath made him forgetfull and tongue tyde. Some holde that there was no visible Serpent before Eua, but an invisible thing described after that manner, that we might be capable thereof.... But to let those goe, this is the chiefe and principall, for the matter which I have undertaken, to shewe euen by the very storye that there was not onely the Deuill, but, also, a very corporall beaste. If this question bee demaunded did Eua knowe there was anye Deuill, or any wicked reprobate Angels. What man of knowledge will say that she did? She did not as yet knowe good and euill. She knewe not the authour of euill. When the Lorde sayde unto hir, What is this which thou hast done? she answereth by and by, The serpent deceiued me. Shee saw there was one which had deceiued hir, shee nameth him a serpent; whence had she that name for the deuill whome shee had not imagined to bee? It is plaine that she speaketh of a thing which had, before this, receiued his name.

'It is yet more euident by that she sayth, yonder serpent, or that serpent, for she noteth him out as pointing to a thing visible: for she useth the demonstratiue particle He in the Hebrew language, which seuereth him from other. Anie man of a sound mind may easilie see that Eua nameth and pointeth at a visible beast, which was nombred among the beastes of the fielde.'

The Devil seems, with the exception of his entering into persons, not to have used his power of appearing corporeally until people became too holy for him to put up with, and many are the records in the Lives of the Saints of his appearance to these detestably good people--St. Anthony, to wit. Of course he always came off baffled and beaten, and, in the case of St. Dunstan, suffered acute bodily pain, his nose being pinched by the goldsmith-saint's red-hot tongs. Yet even that did not deter him from again becoming visible, until, in the sixteenth and seventeenth centuries of our era, he became absolutely familiar on this earth.

But, according to all the records that we possess, his mission no longer was to seduce the saints from their allegiance, and, having become more democratic, he mixed familiarly with the people, under different guises. Of course, his object was to secure the reversion of their souls at their decease, his bait usually being the promise of wealth in this life, or the gratification of some passion.

He found many victims, but yet he met with failures--two of which are recorded here.

A NEW BALLAD.

SHEWING THE GREAT MISERY SUSTAINED BY A POORE MAN IN ESSEX, HIS WIFE AND CHILDREN, WITH OTHER STRANGE THINGS DONE BY THE DEVILL.

> A poore Essex man
>   that was in great distresse,
> Most bitterly made his complaint,
>   in griefe and heavinesse:
> Through scarcity and want,
>   he was oppressed sore,
> He could not find his children bread,
>   he was so extreme poore.
>
> His silly Wife, God wot,
>   being lately brought to bed,
> With her poore Infants at her brest
>   had neither drinke nor bread.
> A wofull lying in
>   was this, the Lord doth know,
> God keep all honest vertuous wives
>   from feeling of such woe.
>
> My Husband deare, she said,
>   for want of food I die,
> Some succour doe for me provide,
>   to ease my misery.
> The man with many a teare,
>   most pittiously replyde,
> We have no means to buy us bread;
>   with that, the Children cry'd.
>
> They came about him round,
>   upon his coat they hung:
> And pittiously they made their mone,
>   their little hands they wrung.
> Be still, my boyes, said he,
>   And I'le goe to the Wood,
> And bring some Acornes for to rost,
>   and you shall have some food.
>
> Forth went the Wofull Man,
>   a Cord he tooke with him,
> Wherewith to bind the broken wood,
>   that he should homewards bring:
> And by the way as he went,
>   met Farmers two or three,

Desiring them for Christ his sake,
    to helpe his misery.

Oh lend to me (he said)
    one loafe of Barley-bread,
One pint of milke for my poore wife,
    in Child-bed almost dead:
Thinke on my extreme need,
    to lend me have no doubt,
I have no money for to pay,
    but I will worke it out.

But they in churlish sort,
    did one by one reply,
We have already lent you more
    than we can well come by.
This answere strooke his heart
    as cold as any stone;
Unto the Wood from thence he went,
    with many a grievous groane.

Where at the length (behold)
    a tall man did him meet
And cole-black were his garments all
    from head unto his feet.
Thou wretched man, said he,
    why dost thou weep so sore?
What is the cause thou mak'st this mone,
    tell me, and sigh no more.

Alas, good Sir (he said)
    the lacke of some reliefe,
For my poore wife and children small,
    'tis cause of all my griefe.
They lie all like to starve,
    for want of bread (saith he);
Good Sir, vouchsafe therefore to give
    one peny unto me.

Hereby this wretched man
    committed wondrous evill,
He beg'd an almes, and did not know
    he ask't it of the Devill.
But straight the hellish Fiend,
    to him reply'd againe,
An odious sinner art thou then
    that dost such want sustaine.

Alack (the poore man said)
    this thing for truth I know,
That Job was just, yet never Man
    endured greater woe.
The godly oft doe want,
    and need doth pinch them sore,
Yet God will not forsake them quite,
    but doth their states restore.

If thou so faithfull bee,
    why goest thou begging then?
Thou shalt be fed as Daniel was
    within the Lyon's den.

If thus thou doe abide,
    the Ravens shall bring thee food,
As they unto Elias did
    that wandred in the Wood.

Mocke not a wofull man,
    good Sir, the poore man said,
Redouble not my sorrows so,
    that are upon me laid.
But, rather, doe extend
    unto my need, and give
One peny for to buy some bread,
    my Children poore may live.

With that he opened straight
    the fairest purse in sight
That ever mortal eye beheld,
    fild up with crownes full bright.
Unto the wofull man
    the same he wholly gave,
Who very earnestly did pray
    that Christ his life might save.

Well, (quoth the damn'd Spirit)
    goe, ease thy Children's sorrow,
And, if thou wantest anything,
    come, meet me here to-morrow.
Then home the poore man went,
    with cheerfull heart and mind,
And comforted his woful wife
    with words that were most kind.

Take Comfort, Wife, he said,
    I have a purse of Gold,
Now given by a Gentleman,
    most faire for to behold.
And thinking for to pull
    his purse from bosome out,
He found nothing but Oken leaves,
    bound in a filthy Clout.

Which, when he did behold,
    with sorrowe pale and wan,
In desperate sort to seeke the purse,
    unto the Wood he ran,
Supposing in his mind,
    that he had lost it there;
He could not tell then what to think,
    he was 'twixt hope and feare.

He had no sooner come
    into the shady Grove,
The Devil met with him againe,
    as he in fancy strove.
What seek'st thou here? he said,
    the purse (quoth he) you gave,
Thus Fortune she hath crossed me,
    and then the Devill said

Where didst thou put the Purse?
    tell me, and do not lye,

Within my bosome, said the man,
> where no man did come nigh.
Looke there againe, (quoth he)
> then said the Man, I shall,
And found his bosome full of Toads,
> as thicke as they could crawle.

The poore man at this sight,
> to speak had not the power,
See (q'd the Devill) vengeance doth
> pursue thee every hour.
Goe, cursed wretch, (quoth he)
> and rid away thy life,
But murther first thy children young,
> and miserable Wife.

The poore man, raging mad,
> ran home incontinent,
Intending for to kill them all,
> but God did him prevent.
For why, the chiefest man
> that in the Parish dwelt,
With meat and money thither came,
> which liberally he dealt.

Who, seeing the poore man
> come home in such a rage,
Was faine to bind him in his bed,
> his fury to asswage.
Where long he lay full sicke,
> still crying for his Gold,
But, being well, this whole discourse
> he to his neighbours told.

From all temptations,
> Lord, keep both Great and Small,
And let no man, O heavenly God,
> for want of succour fall.
But put their speciall trust
> in God for evermore,
Who will, no doubt, from misery
> each faithfull man restore.

'A TERRIBLE AND SEASONABLE WARNING TO YOUNG MEN.

'Being a very particular and True Relation of one Abraham Joiner, a young man about 17 or 18 Years of Age, living in Shakesby's Walks in Shadwell, being a Ballast Man by Profession, who, on Saturday Night last, pick'd up a leud Woman, and spent what money he had about him in Treating her, saying afterwards, if she wou'd have any more he must go to the Devil for it, and, slipping out of her Company, he went to the Cock and Lyon in King Street, the Devil appear'd to him, and gave him a Pistole, telling him he shou'd never want for Money, appointing to meet him the next Night, at the World's End at Stepney; Also how his Brother persuaded him to throw the Money away, which he did; but was suddenly taken in a very strange manner, so that they were fain to send for the Reverend Mr. Constable and other Ministers to pray with him; he appearing now to be very Penitent; with an Account of the Prayers and Expressions he makes use of under his Affliction, and the Prayers that were made for him, to free him from this violent Temptation.

'The Truth of which is sufficiently attested in the Neighbourhood, he lying now at his Mother's house,' etc.

Stepney seems to have been a favourite haunt of the Devil, for there is a tract published at Edinburgh, 1721, entitled 'A timely Warning to Rash and Disobedient Children. Being a strange and wonderful Relation of a young Gentleman in the Parish of Stepheny, in the Suburbs of London, that sold himself to the Devil for 12 Years, to have the Power of being revenged on his Father and Mother, and how, his Time being expired, he lay in a sad and deplorable Condition, to the Amazement of all Spectators.'

CHAPTER II

'Strange and True News from Westmoreland'--'The Politic Wife'--'How the Devill, though subtle, was guld by a Scold'--'The Devil's Oak'--Raising the Devil--Arguments in Favour of Devils--The Numbers of Devils.

In the foregoing examples we have seen the Devil in human form, and properly apparelled, but occasionally he showed himself in his supposed proper shape--when, of course, his intentions were at once perceived; and on one occasion we find him called upon by an Angel, to execute justice on a bad man. It is in

STRANGE AND TRUE NEWS FROM WESTMORELAND.

Attend good Christian people all,
Mark what I say, both old and young,
Unto the general Judgment day,
I think it is not very long.

A Wonder strange I shall relate,
I think the like was never shown,
In Westmoreland at Tredenton,
Of such a thing was never known.

One Gabriel Harding liv'd of late,
As may to all men just appear,
Whose yearly Rent, by just account,
Came to five hundred pound a year.

This man he had a Virtuous Wife,
In Godly ways her mind did give:
Yet he, as rude a wicked wretch,
As in this sinful Land did live.

Much news of him I will relate,
The like no Mortal man did hear;
'Tis very new, and also true,
Therefore, good Christians, all give ear.

One time this man he came home drunk,
As he us'd, which made his wife to weep,
Who straightway took him by the hand,
Saying, Dear Husband, lye down and sleepe.

She lovingly took him by the arms,
Thinking in safety him to guide,
A blow he struck her on the breast,
The woman straight sank down and dy'd.

The Children with Mournful Cries
They ran into the open Street,
They wept, they wail'd, they wrung their hands,
To all good Christians they did meet.

The people then, they all ran forth,
Saying, Children, why make you such moan?
O, make you haste unto our house,
Our dear mother is dead and gone.

Our Father hath our Mother kill'd,
The Children they cryed then.
The people then they all made haste
And laid their hands upon the man.

He presently denied the same,
Said from Guilty Murder I am free,
If I did that wicked deed, he said,
Some example I wish to be seen by me.

Thus he forswore the wicked deed,
Of his dear Wife's untimely end.
Quoth the people, Let's conclude with speed,
That for the Coroner we may send.

Mark what I say, the door's fast shut,
The People the Children did deplore,
But straight they heard a Man to speak,
And one stood knocking at the door.

One in the house to the door made haste,
Hearing a Man to Knock and Call,
The door was opened presently,
And in he came amongst them all.

By your leave, good people, then he said,
May a stranger with you have some talk?
A dead woman I am come to see;
Into the room, I pray, Sir, walk.

His eyes like to the Stars did shine,
He was clothed in a bright grass green,
His cheeks were of a crimson red,
For such a man was seldome seen.

Unto the people then he spoke,
Mark well these words which I shall say,
For no Coroner shall you send,
I'm Judge and Jury here this day.

Bring hither the Man that did the deed,
And firmly hath denied the same.
They brought him into the room with speed,
To answer to this deed with shame.

Now come, O wretched Man, quoth he,
With shame before thy neighbours all,
Thy body thou hast brought to Misery,
Thy soul into a deeper thrall.

Thy Chiefest delight was drunkeness,
And lewd women, O, cursed sin,
Blasphemous Oaths and Curses Vile
A long time thou hast wallowed in.

The Neighbours thou wouldst set at strife,

And alwaies griping of the poor,
Besides, thou hast murdered thy wife,
A fearful death thou dy'st therefore.

Fear nothing, good people, then he said,
A sight will presently appear,
Let all your trust be in the Lord,
No harm shall be while I am here.

Then in the Room the Devil appear'd,
Like a brave Gentleman did stand,
Satan (quoth he that was the Judge)
Do no more than thou hast command.

The Devil then he straight laid hold
On him that had murdered his wife,
His neck in Sunder then he broke,
And thus did end his wretched life.

The Devil then he vanished
Quite from the People in the Hall,
Which made the people much afraid,
Yet no one had no hurt at all.

Then straight a pleasant Melody
Of Musick straight was heard to sound,
It ravisht the hearts of those stood by,
So sweet the Musick did abound.

Now, (quoth this gallant Man in green)
With you I can no longer stay,
My love I leave, my leave I take,
The time is come, I must away.

Be sure to love each other well,
Keep in your breast what I do say.
It is the way to go to Heaven,
When you shall rise at Judgment day.

The people to their homes did go,
Which had this mighty wonder seen,
And said, it was an Angel sure
That thus was clothed all in green.

And thus the News from Westmoreland
I have related to you o'er,
I think it is as strange a thing,
As ever man did hear before.

In the old days the Devil was used as a butt at which people shot their little arrows of wit. In the miracle plays, when introduced, he filled the part of the pantaloon in our pantomimes, and was accompanied by a 'Vice,' who played practical jokes with him, slapping him with his wooden sword, jumping on his back, etc.; and in the carvings of our abbeys and cathedrals, especially in the Miserere seats in the choir, he was frequently depicted in comic situations, as also in the illuminations of manuscripts. He was often written about as being sadly deficient in brains, and many are the instances recorded of him being outwitted by a shrewd human being, as we may see by the following ballad.

THE POLITIC WIFE; OR, THE DEVIL OUTWITTED BY A WOMAN.

Of all the plagues upon the earth,
    That e'er poor man befal,
It's hunger and a scolding wife,
    These are the worst of all:
There was a poor man in our country
    Of a poor and low degree,
And with both these plagues he was troubled,
    And the worst of luck had he.

He had seven children by one wife,
    And the times were poor and hard,
And his poor toil was grown so bad,
    He scarce could get him bread:
Being discontented in his mind,
    One day his house he left,
And wandered down by a forest side,
    Of his senses quite bereft.

As he was wandering up and down,
    Betwixt hope and despair,
The Devil started out of a bush,
    And appeared unto him there:
O what is the matter, the Devil he said,
    You look so discontent?
Sure you want some money to buy some bread,
    Or to pay your landlord's rent.

Indeed, kind sir, you read me right,
    And the grounds of my disease,
Then what is your name, said the poor man,
    Pray, tell me, if you please?
My name is Dumkin the Devil, quoth he,
    And the truth to you I do tell,
Altho' you see me wandering here,
    Yet my dwelling it is in hell.

Then what will you give me, said the Devil,
    To ease you of your want,
And you shall have corn and cattle enough,
    And never partake of scant?
I have nothing to give you, said the poor man,
    Nor nothing here in hand,
But all the service that I can do,
    Shall be at your command.

Then, upon the condition of seven long years,
    A bargain with you I will frame,
You shall bring me a beast unto this place,
    That I cannot tell his name:
But, if I tell its name full right,
    Then mark what to you I tell,
Then you must go along with me
    Directly unto Hell.

This poor man went home joyfully,
    And thrifty he grew therefore,
For he had corn and cattle enough,
    And every thing good store.
His neighbours who did live around,

Did wonder at him much,
And thought he had robb'd or stole,
    He was grown so wondrous rich.

Then for the space of seven long years
    He lived in good cheer,
But when the time of his indenture grew near,
    He began to fear:
O what is the matter, said his wife,
    You look so discontent?
Sure you have got some maid with child,
    And now you begin to repent.

Indeed, kind wife, you judge me wrong,
    To censure so hard of me,
Was it for getting a maid with child,
    That would be no felony:
But I have made a league with the Devil,
    For seven long years, no more,
That I should have corn and cattle enough,
    And everything good store.

Then for the space of seven long years
    A bargain I did frame,
I should bring him a beast unto that place,
    He could not tell its name:
But if he tell his name full right,
    Then mark what to you I tell,
Then I must go along with him,
    Directly unto Hell.

Go, get you gone, you silly old man,
    Your cattle go tend and feed,
For a woman's wit is far better than a man's,
    If us'd in time of need:
Go fetch me down all the birdlime you have,
    And set it down on the floor,
And when I have pulled my cloathes all off,
    You shall anoint me all o'er.

Now when he had anointed her
    From the head unto the heel,
Zounds! said the man, methinks you look
    Just like the very De'el.
Go, fetch me down all the feathers thou hast,
    And lay them down by me,
And I will roll myself therein,
    'Till never a place go free.

Come, tie a string about my neck,
    And lead me to this place,
And I will save you from the Devil,
    If I have but so much grace.
The Devil, he stood roaring out,
    And looked both fierce and bold;
Thou hast brought me a beast unto this place,
    And the bargain thou dost hold.

Come, shew me the face of this beast, said the Devil,
    Come, shew it me in a short space;
Then he shewed him his wife's buttocks,

And swore it was her face:
    She has monstrous cheeks, the Devil he said,
        As she now stands at length,
    You'd take her for some monstrous beast
        Taken by Man's main strength.

    How many more of these beasts, said the Devil,
        How many more of this kind?
    I have seven more such, said the poor man,
        But have left them all behind.
    If you have seven more such, said the Devil,
        The truth unto you I tell,
    You have beasts enough to cheat me
        And all the Devils in Hell.

    Here, take thy bond and indenture both,
        I'll have nothing to do with thee:
    So the man and his wife went joyfully home
        And lived full merrily.
    O, God send us good merry long lives,
        Without any sorrow or woe,
    Now here's a health to all such wives
        Who can cheat the Devil so.

There is

    'A Pleasant new Ballad you here may behold
    How the Devill, though subtle, was guld by a Scold.'

    The story of this ballad is, that the Devil, being much amused with this scolding wife, went to fetch her. Taking the form of a horse, he called upon her husband, and told him to set her on his back. This was easily accomplished by telling her to lead the horse to the stable, which she refused to do.

    'Goe leade, sir Knave, quoth she,
        and wherefore not, Goe ride?
    She took the Devill by the reines,
        and up she goes astride.'

    And once on the Devil, she rode him; she kicked him, beat him, slit his ears, and kept him galloping all through Hell, until he could go no longer, when he concluded to take her home again to her husband.

    'Here, take her (quoth the Devill)
        to keep her here be bold,
    For Hell would not be troubled
        with such an earthly scold.
    When I come home, I may
        to all my fellowes tell,
    I lost my labour and my bloud,
        to bring a scold to Hell.'

    In another ballad, called 'The Devil's Oak,' he is made out to be a very poor thing; the last verse says:

    'That shall be try'd, the Devil then he cry'd,
        then up the Devil he did start,
    Then the Tinker threw his staff about,
        and he made the Devil to smart:
    There against a gate, he did break his pate,
        and both his horns he broke;
    And ever since that time, I will make up my rhime,

it was called "The Devil's Oak."'

But popular belief credited to certain men the power of being able to produce the Devil in a visible form, and these were called necromancers, sorcerers, magicians, etc. Of them Roger Bacon was said to have been one, and Johann Faust, whom Goethe has immortalized, and whose idealism is such a favourite on the lyric stage. But Johann Faust was not at all the Faust of Goethe. He was the son of poor parents, and born at Knittlingen, in Würtemberg, at the end of the fifteenth century. He was educated at the University of Cracow, thanks to a legacy left him by an uncle, and he seems to have been nothing better than a common cheat, called by Melancthon 'an abominable beast, a sewer of many devils,' and by Conrad Muth, who was a friend both of Melancthon and Luther, 'a braggart and a fool who affects magic.' However, he was very popular in England, and not only did Marlowe write a play about him, but there are many so-called lives of him in English, especially among the chap-books--in which he is fully credited with the power of producing the Devil in a tangible form by means of his magic art.

But the spirits supposed to be raised by these magicians were not always maleficent; they were more demons than devils. It will therefore be as well if we quote a competent and learned authority on the subject of devils.

Says Gyfford: 'The Devils being the principall agents, and chiefe practisers in witchcrafts and sorceryes, it is much to the purpose to descrybe them and set them forth whereby wee shall bee the better instructed to see what he is able to do, in what maner, and to what ende and purpose. At the beginning (as God's word doth teach us) they were created holy Angels, full of power and glory. They sinned, they were cast down from heauen, they were utterly depriued of glory, and preserued for iudgement. This therefore, and this change of theirs, did not destroy nor take away their former faculties; but utterly corrupt, peruert, and depraue the same: the essence of spirits remayned, and not onely, but also power and understanding, such as is in the Angels: y{e} heavenly Angels are very mighty and strong, far above all earthly creatures in the whole world. The infernall Angels are, for their strength called principalityes and powers: those blessed ones applye all their might to set up and aduaunce the glory of God, to defend and succour his children: the deuils bend all their force against God, agaynst his glory, his truth and his people. And this is done with such fiercenes, rage and cruelty, that the holy ghost paynteth them out under the figure of a great red or fiery dragon, and roaring lyon, in very deed anything comparable to them. He hath such power and autority indeede, that hee is called the God of the world. His Kingdome is bound and inclosed within certayne limits, for he is y{e} prince but of darknes; but yet within his sayd dominion (which is in ignorance of God) he exerciseth a mighty tyranny, our Saviour compareth him to a strong man armed which kepeth his castle.

'And what shall we saie for the wisedome and understanding of Angels, which was giuen them in their creation, was it not far aboue that which men can reach unto? When they became diuels (euen those reprobate angels) their understanding was not taken awaie, but turned into malicious craft and subtiltie. He neuer doth any thing but of an euill purpose, and yet he can set such a colour, that the Apostle saith he doth change himselfe into the likenesse of an angell of light. For the same cause he is called the old serpent, he was subtill at the beginning, but he is now growne much more subtill by long experience, and continuall practise, he hath searched out and knoweth all the waies that may be to deceiue. So that, if God should not chaine him up, as it is set forth, Revel. 20, his power and subtiltie ioined together would overcome and seduce the whole world.

'There be great multitudes of infernall spirits, as the holy scriptures doe euerie where shew, but yet they doe so ioine together in one, that they be called the divell in the singular number. They doe all ioine together (as our Saviour teacheth) to uphold one kingdome. For though they cannot loue one another indeede, yet the hatred they beare against God, is as a band that doth tye them together. The holie angels are ministring spirits, sent foorth for their sakes which shall inherit the promise. They haue no bodilie shape of themselues, but to set foorth their speedinesse, the scripture applieth itselfe unto our rude capacitie, and painteth them out with wings.

'When they are to rescue and succour the seruants of God, they can straight waie from the high heauens, which are thousands of thousands of miles distant from the earth, bee present with them. Such quicknesse is also in the diuels; for their nature being spirituall, and not loden with any heauie matter as our bodies are, doth afford unto them such a nimblenes as we cannot conceiue. By this, they flie through the world over sea and land, and espie out al aduantages and occasions to doe euill.'[3]

Indeed, 'there be great multitudes of infernall spirits,' if we can believe so eminent an authority upon the subject as Reginald Scott, who gives 'An inuentarie of the names, shapes, powers, gouernement, and effects of diuels and spirits, of their seuerall segniories and degrees: a strange discourse woorth the reading.

'Their first and principall King (which is of the power of the east) is called Baëll; who, when he is conjured up, appeareth with three heads; the first, like a tode; the second, like a man; the third, like a cat. He speaketh with a hoarse voice, he maketh a man go invisible, he hath under his obedience and rule sixtie and six legions of divels.'[4]

All the other diabolical chiefs are described at the same length, but I only give their names, and the number of legions they command.

Name	Legions	Name	Legions
Agares	31	Procell	48
Marbas or Barbas	36	Furcas	20
Amon or Aamon	40	Murmur	30
Barbatos	30	Caim	30
Buer	50	Raum or Raim	30
Gusoin	40	Halphas	26
Botis or Otis	60	Focalor	3
Bathin or Mathinn	30	Vine	none
Purson or Curson	22	Bifrons	26
Eligor or Abigor	60	Gamigin	30
Leraie or Oray	30	Zagan	33
Valefar or Malefar	10	Orias	30
Morax or Foraij	36	Valac	30
Ipos or Ayporos	36	Gomory	26
Naberius or Cerberus	19	Decarabia or Carabia	30
Glasya Labolas or Caacrinolaas	36	Amduscias	29
Zepar	26	Andras	30
Bileth	85	Andrealphus	30
Sitri or Bitru	60	Ose	none
Paimon	20	Aym or Haborim	26
Belial	none	Orobas	20
Bune	30	Vapula	36
Forneus	29	Cimeries	20
Ronoue	19	Amy	36
Berith	26	Flauros	20
Astaroth	40	Balam	40
Foras or Forcas	29	Allocer	36
Furfur	26	Vuall	37
Marchosias	30	Saleos	none
Malphas	40	Haagenti	33
Vepar or Separ	29	Phœnix	20
Sabnacke or Salmac	50	Stolas	26
Sidonay or Asmoday	72		
Gaap or Tap	36		
Shax or Scox	30		

'Note that a legion is 6666, and now by multiplication count how manie legions doo arise out of euerie particular,'

Or a grand total of 14,198,580 devils, not including their commanders.

How many of these fall to the share of England? I know not, but they were very active in the sixteenth, seventeenth and eighteenth centuries, especially in the seventeenth. They seem to us, nowadays, to have frittered away their energies in attending on witches, in entering into divers persons and tormenting them, and in making senseless uproars and playing practical jokes. Let us take about half a dozen of these latter. Say, for argument sake, that they are not very abstruse or intellectual reading; at all events, they are as good as the modern stories of spiritual manifestations, and are as trustworthy.

CHAPTER III

'The Just Devil of Woodstock'--Metrical Version--Presumed Genuine History of 'The Just Devil of Woodstock.'

THE JUST DEVIL OF WOODSTOCK.[5]

'The 16 day of October in the year of our Lord 1649, The Commissioners for surveying and valuing his Majesties Mannor House, Parks, Woods, Deer, Demesnes, and all things thereunto belonging, by Name Captain Crook, Capt. Hart, Capt. Cockaine, Capt. Carelesse, and Capt. Roe their Messenger, with Mr. Brown their Secretary, and two or three servants, went from Woodstock town (where they had lain some nights before) and took up their lodgings in his Majesties House, after this manner: The Bedchamber and withdrawing room, they both lodged in, and made their Kitchin; the Presence Chamber their room for dispatch of business with all commers: of the Councel Hall, their Brewhouse, as of the Dining room, their Woodhouse, where they laid in the clefts, of that antient standard in the High-Park, for many ages beyond memory, known by the Name of the Kings Oak, which they had chosen out, and caused to be dug up by the Roots.

'Octob. 17. About the middle of the night, these new guests were first awaked, by a knocking at the Presence Chamber door, which they also conceived did open, and something to enter, which came through the room, and also walkt through the withdrawing room into the Bed chamber, and there walkt about that room with a heavy step during half an hour; then crept under the bed where Captain Hart, and Capt. Carelesse lay, where it did seeme (as it were) to bite and gnaw the Mat and Bed-coards, as if it would tear and rend the feather beds, which having done a while, then would they heave a while, and rest; then heave them up again in the bed more high than it did before, sometime on the one side, sometime on the other, as if it had tried which Captain was heaviest; thus having heaved for some half an hour, from thence it walkt out, and went under the servants' bed, and did the like to them; thence it walkt into a withdrawing room, and there did the same to all who lodged there: Thus having welcomed them for more than two hours space, it walked out as it came in, and shut the outer door again, but with a clap of some mightie force; these guests were in a sweat all this while, but out of it falling into a sleep again, it became morning first before they spoke their minds, then would they have it to be a Dog, yet they described it more to the likenesse of a great Bear, so fell to examining under the Beds, where finding only the Mats scratcht, but the Bed-coards whole, and the quarters of Beef which lay on the floor untoucht, they entertained other thoughts.

'Octob. 18. They were all awaked, as the night before, and now conceived that they heard all the great clefts of the Kings Oak brought into the Presence Chamber, and there thumpt down, and, after, roul about the room; they could hear their chairs and stools tost from one side of the room unto the other; and then (as it were) altogether jostled; thus having done an hour together, it walkt into the withdrawing room, where lodged the two Captains, the Secretary, and two servants; here stopt the thing a while, as if it did take breath, but raised a hideous tone, then walkt into the Bed-chamber, where lay those as before, and under the Bed it went, where it did heave, and heave again, that now they in bed were put to catch hold upon Bed-posts, and sometimes one of the other, to prevent their being tumbled out upon the ground; then coming out as from under the bed, and taking hold upon the bed-posts, it would shake the whole bed, almost as if a cradle rocked; Thus, having done here for half an hour, it went into the withdrawing room, where first it came and stood at the bed's feet, and heaving up the bed's feet, flopt down again a while, until at last it heaved the feet so high, that those in bed thought to have been set upon their heads, and having thus for two hours entertained them, went out as in the night before, but with a great noise.

'Octob. 19. This night they awaked, not until the midst of the night, they perceived the room to shake, with something that walkt about the bed-chamber, which, having done so for a while, it walkt into a withdrawing room, where it took up a Brasse warming-pan, and returning with it into the bed-chamber, therein made so loud a noise, in these Captains' own words, it was as loud and scurvie as a ring of five untuned Bells rang backward, but the Captains, not to seem afraid, next day made mirth of what had past, and jested at the Devil in the pan.

'Octob. 20. These Captains and their Company, still lodging as before, were wakened in this night with some things flying about the rooms, and out of one room into the other, as thrown with some great force: Captain Hart being in a slumber, was taken by the shoulder and shaked until he did sit up in his bed, thinking that it had been by one of his fellows, when suddenly he was taken on the Pate with a Trencher, that it made him shrink down into the bed-clothes, and all of them, in both rooms, kept their heads, at least, within their sheets, so fiercely did three dozen of Trenchers, fly about the rooms; yet Captain Hart ventured again to peep out to see what was the matter, and what it was that threw, but then the Trenchers came so fast and neer about his ears, that he was fain to couch again: In the morning they found all their Trenchers, Pots and Spits, upon and about the rooms; this night there was also in several parts of the room, and outer rooms, such noises of beating at doors, and on the Walls, as if that several Smiths had been at work; and yet our Captains shrunk not from their work, but went on in that, and lodged as they had done before.

'Octob. 21. About midnight, they heard great knocking at every door, after a while, the doors flew open, and into the withdrawing room entred something, as of a very mighty proportion, the figure of it they knew not how to describe; this walkt a while about the room, shaking the floor at every step, then came it close to the bed side, where lay Captains Crook and Carelesse; and, after a little pause, as it were, The bed-curtains, both at sides and feet, were drawn up and down, slowly, then faster again for a quarter of an hour, then from end to end as fast as imagination could fancie the running of the rings, then shaked it the beds, as if the joints thereof had crackt; then walkt the thing into the bed-chamber, and so plaied with those beds there: Then took up eight Pewter-dishes, and bouled them about the room, and over the servants in the truckle beds; then sometimes were the dishes taken up, and throwne crosse the high beds, and against the walls, and so much battered; but there were more dishes wherein was meat in the same room, that were not at all removed: During this, in the Presence Chamber there was stranger noise of weightie things thrown down, and as they supposed, the clefts of the King's Oak did roul about the room, yet at the wonted hour went away, and left them to take rest, such as they could.

'October 22. Hath mist of being set down, the Officers imployed in their work farther off, came not that day to Woodstock.

'October 23. Those that lodged in the withdrawing room, in the midst of the night were awakened with the cracking of fire, as if it had been with thorns and sparks of fire burning, whereupon they supposed that the bed chamber had taken fire, and, listening to it farther, they heard their fellows in bed sadly groan, which gave them to suppose they might be suffocated, wherefore they call'd upon their servants to make all possible hast to help them; when the two servants were come in, they found all asleep, and so brought back word, but that there were no bedclothes upon them, wherefore they were sent back to cover them, and to stir up and mend the fire; when the servants had covered them, and were come to the chimney, in the corners they found their wearing apparel, boots and stockings, but they had no sooner toucht the Embers, when the firebrands flew about their ears so fast, that away ran they into the other room, for the shelter of their cover-lids, then after them walkt something that stampt about the room, as if it had been exceeding angry, and likewise threw about the Trenchers, Platters, and all such things in the room; after two hours went out, yet stampt again over their heads.

'October 24. They lodged all abroad.

'October 25. This afternoon came unto them Mr. Richard Crook, the Lawyer, brother to Captain Crook, and now Deputy-Steward of the Mannor, unto Captain Parsons, and Major Butler, who had put out Mr. Hyans his Majesties Officer: To entertain this new guest the Commissioners caused a very great fire to be made, of neere the chimney full of wood, of the King's Oak, and he was lodged in the withdrawing room with his brother, and his servant in the same room: about the midst of the night a wonderful knocking was heard, and into the room something did rush, which, coming to the chimney side, dasht out the fire, as with the stamp of some prodigious foot, then threw down such weighty stuffe, what ere it was (they took it to be the residue of the clefts and roots of the King's Oak) close by the bed side, that the house and bed shook with it. Captain Cockain and his fellow arose and took their swords to go unto the Crooks, the noise ceased at their rising, so that they came to the door, and called; the two brothers, though fully awaked, and heard them call, were so amazed, that they made no answer, untill Captain Cockaine had recovered the boldness to call very loud, and came unto their bed-side; then, faintly first, after some more assurance, they came to understand one another, and comforted the lawyer: Whilst this was thus, no noise was heard, which made them think the time was past of that nights troubles, so that, after some little conference, they applied themselves to take some rest. When Captain Cockaine was come to his own bed, which he had left open, he found it closely covered, which he much wondered at, but turning the clothes down, and opening it to get in, he found the lower sheet strewed over with trenchers, their whole three dozens of trenchers were orderly disposed between his sheets, which he and his fellow endeavouring to cast out, such noise arose about the room, that they were glad to get into bed with some of the trenchers; the noise lasted a full half hour after this. This entertainment so ill did like the Lawyer, and being not so well studied in the point, as to resolve this the Devil's Law-case, that he, next day, resolved to begone, but, not having dispatcht all that he came for, profit and perswasions prevailed with him to stay the other hearing, so that he lodged as he did the night before.

'Octob. 26. This night each room was better furnished with fire and candle than before; yet about twelve at night came something in, that dasht all out, then did walk about the room, making a noise, not to be set forth by the comparison with any other thing, sometimes came it to the bed-sides, and drew the Curtains to and fro, then twerle them, then walk about again, and return to the bed-posts, shake them with all the bed, so that they in bed were put to hold one upon the other; then walk about the room again, and come to the servants bed, and gnaw the wainscot head--and shake altogether in that room; at the time of this being in doing, they in the bed-chamber heard such strange dropping down from the roof of the room, that they supposed 'twas like the fall of money by the sound. Captain Cockaine not frighted with so small a noise (and lying near the chimney) stept out, and made shift to light a candle, by the light of which he perceived the room strewed over with broken glass, green, and some as it were pieces of broken bottles. He had not long been considering what it was, when suddainly his candle was hit out, and glass flew about the room, that he made haste to the protection of the Coverlets, the noise of thundering rose more hideous than at any time before; yet, at a certain time, all vanisht into calmness. The morning after, was the glass about the room, which the maid, that was to make clean the rooms, swept up into a corner, and many came to see it. But Mr. Richard Crooke would stay no longer, yet as he stopt, going through Woodstock Town, he was there heard to say, that he would not lodge amongst them another night, for a Fee of £500.

'Octob. 27. The Commissioners had not yet done their work, wherefore they must stay, and, being all men of the sword, they must not seem afraid to encounter with anything, though it be the Devill, therefore, with pistols charged, and drawn swords laied by their bed sides, they applied themselves to take some rest, when something, in the midst of night, so opened and shut the window casements, with such claps, that it awakened all that slept; some of them peeping out to look what was the matter with the windows, stones flew about the rooms as if hurled with many hands; some hit the walls, and some the bed's head close above the pillows; the dints of which were then, and yet (it is conceived) are to be seen, thus sometime throwing stones; and sometime making thundering noise; for two hours space it ceast, and all was quiet till the morn. After their rising, and the maid come in to make the fire, they looked about the rooms; they found fourscore stones brought in that night, and, going to lay them together, in the corner, where the glass (before mentioned) had been swept up, they found that every piece of glass had been carried away that night: many people came next day to see the stones, and all observed that they were not of such kind of stones as are naturall in the countrey thereabout; with these were noises like claps of thunder, or report of Cannon planted against the rooms; heard by all that lodged in the outer courts, to their astonishment; and at Woodstock Town, taken to be thunder.

'Octob. 28. This night, both strange and differing noise from the former, first wakened Captain Hart who lodged in the bed-chamber, who hearing Roe and Brown to groan, called out to Cockaine and Crooke to come and help them, for Hart could not now stir himself. Cockaine would faine have answered, but he could not, or look about, something he thought, stopt both his breath and held down his eye lids. Amazed thus, he struggled and kickt about, till he had awaked Captain Crook, who, half asleep, grew very angry at his kicks, and multiplied words till it grew to an appointment in the field: but this fully recovered Cockaine to remember that Captain Hart had called for help, wherefore to them he ran in the other room, whom he found sadly groaning: where scraping in the chimney he found a candle and fire to light it; but had not gone two steps, when something blew the candle out, and threw him in the chair by the bed side, when presently cried out Captain Careless, with a most pittiful voice, Come hither, O come hither, brother Cockaine, the thing's gone off me. Cockaine scarce yet himself, helpt to set him up in his bed, and, after, Captain Hart; and having scarce done that to them, and also to the other two, they heard Captain Crook crying out, as if something had been killing him; Cockaine snacht up the sword that lay by their bed, and ran into the room to save Crook, but was in much more likelyhood to kill him, for at his coming the thing that pressed Crook, went off him, at which Crook started out of his bed, when Cockaine thought a spirit made at him, at which Crook cried out Lord help, Lord save me; Cockaine let fall his hand, and Crook embracing Cockaine desired his reconcilement: giving him many thanks for his deliverance, then rose they all and came together, discoursed sometimes godly, and sometimes praied, for all this while was there such stamping over the roof of the house, as if 1,000 horse had there been trotting. This night, all the stones brought in the night before, and laid up in the withdrawing room, were all carried away again by that which brought them in, which at the wonted time, left off, and, as it were, went out, and so away.

'Octob. 29. Their businesse having now received so much forwardnesse, as to be neer dispatcht, they encouraged one the other, and resolved to try further, therefore they provided more lights and fires, and further, for their assistance, prevailed with their Ordinary Keeper to lodge amongst them, and bring his Mastive Bitch, and it was so this night with them, that they had no disturbance at all.

'Octob. 30. So well had they past the night before, that this night they went to bed confident and carelesse, untill, about 12 of the clock, something knockt at the door as with a smith's great hammer, but with such force as if it had cleft the door; then entred something like a Bear, but seem'd to swell more big and walkt about the room, and out of one room into the other; treading so heavily, as the floore had not been strong enough to bear it; when it came to the bed chamber, it dasht against the beds heads some kind of glasse vessell, that broke in sundry pieces; and, sometimes, it would take up those pieces, and hurle them about the room, and into the other room; and when it did not hurle the glasse at their heads, it did strike upon the tables as if many smiths, with their greatest hammers, had been laying on as upon an anvill: sometimes it thumpt against the walls, as if it would beat a hole through; then upon their heads such stamping, as if the roof of the house were beating down upon their heads, and, having done thus during the space (as was conjectured) of two hours, it ceased and vanished, but with a more fierce shutting of the doors than at any time before. In the morning they found the pieces of glass about the room, and observed that it was much differing from that glasse, brought in three nights before, this being of a much thicker substance, which severall persons which came in carried away some pieces of. The Commissioners were in debate of lodging there no more, but all their businesse was not done, and some of them were so conceited as to believe, and to attribute the rest they enjoyed the night before this last unto the Mastive bitch; wherefore they resolved to get more company, and the Mastive bitch, and try another night.

'Octob. 31. This night, the fires and lights prepared, the Ordinary Keeper and his bitch, with another man persuaded by him, they all took their beds, and fell asleep. But, about 12 at night, such rapping was on all sides of them, that it wakened all of them. As the doors did seem to open, the Mastive bitch fell fearfully a yelling, and presently ran fiercely into the bed to them in the truckle bed. As the thing came by the table, it struck so fierce a blow on that, as that it made the frame to crack; then took the warming pan from off the table and stroke it against the walls with so much force as that it was beat flat together, lid and bottom; now were they hit as they lay covered over head and ears within the bedclothes; Captain Carelesse was taken a sound blow on the head with the shoulder blade-bone of a dead Horse (before, they had been but thrown at when they peept up, and mist,) Brown had a shrewd blow on the leg with the back bone, and another on the head; and everyone of them felt severall blows of bones and stones through the bed clothes, for now these things were thrown as from an angry hand that meant further mischief; the stones flew in at the window as if shot out of a Gun, nor was the bursts lesse (as from without) than of a Cannon, and all the windows broken down. Now, as the hurling of the things did cease, and the thing walkt up and down, Captains Cockaine and Hart cried out, In the Name of the Father, Son and Holy Ghost, What are you? what would you have? what have we done that you disturb us thus? No voice replied (as the Captains said, yet some of their servants have said otherwise) and the noise ceast. Hereupon Captains Hart and Cockaine rose, who lay in the Bed-chamber, renewed the fire and lights, and one great candle in a candlestick they placed in the door, that might be seen by them in both the rooms; no sooner were they got to bed, but the noise arose on all sides more loud and hideous than at any time before, in so much (as to use the Captain's own words) it returned and brought seven Devils worse than itself; and, presently, they saw the candle and candlestick in the passage of the door, dasht up to the roof of the room, by a kick of the hinder parts of a Horse, and after, with the Hoof trod out the snuffe, and so dasht out the Fire in the Chimnies. As this was done, there fell, as from the sieling, upon them in the Truckle beds, such quantities of water, as if it had been poured out of Buckets, which stunk worse than any earthly stink could make. And, as this was in doing, something crept under the High Beds, tost them up to the roof of the House, with the Commissioners in them, until the Testers of the Beds were beaten down upon them, and the Bedsted-frames broke under them. And here, some pause being made, they all, as if with one consent, started up, and ran down the stairs until they came into the Counsel-Hall, where two sate up a Brewing, but were now fallen asleep; those they scared much with wakening of them, having been much perplext before with the strange noise, which commonly was taken by them abroad for thunder, sometimes for rumbling wind; here the Captains and their company got fire and candle, and everyone carrying something of either, they returned into the Presence-Chamber, where some applied themselves to make the fire, whilst others fell to Prayers, and, having got some clothes about them, they spent the residue of the night in singing Psalms and Prayers; during which, no noise was in that room, but most hideously round about, as at some distance.

'It should have been told before, how that when Captain Hare first rose this night (who lay in the Bed-Chamber next the fire) he found their Book of valuations crosse the embers smoaking, which he snacht up, and cast upon the Table there, which, the night before, was left upon the Table in the presence, amongst their other papers. This Book was, in the morning, found a handful burnt, and had burnt the Table where it lay; Brown the Clerk said, he would not for a 100 and a 100l. that it had been burnt a handful further.

'This night it happened that there were six Cony-stealers, who were come with their Nets and Ferrets to the Cony-burrows by Rosamond's Well, but with the noise this night from the Mannor-house, they were so terrified, that, like men distracted, away they ran, and left their Haies all ready pitched, ready up, and the Ferrets in the Cony-burrows.

'Now the Commissioners, more sensible of their danger, considered more seriously of their safety, and agreed to go and confer with Mr. Hoffman, the Minister of Wotton (a man not of the meanest note for life or learning, by some esteemed more high) to desire his advice, together with his company and prayers. Mr. Hoffman held it too high a point to resolve on suddenly and by himself, wherefore, desired time to consider upon it, which, being agreed unto, he forthwith rode to Mr. Jenkinson and Mr. Wheat, the two next Justices of Peace, to try what Warrant they could give him for it. They both (as 'tis said from themselves) encouraged him to be assisting to the Commissioners, according to his calling.

Sidenote: By which it is to be noted that a Presbyterian Minister dares not encounter an Independent Devil.

'But certain it is, that when they came to fetch him to go with them, Mr. Hoffman answered, That he would not lodge there one night, for £500, and being askt to pray with them, he held up his hands, and said, That he would not meddle upon any terms.

'Mr. Hoffman refusing to undertake the quarrel, the Commissioners held it not safe to lodge where they had been thus entertained, any longer, but caused all things to be removed into the Chambers over the Gatehouse, where they staid but one night, and what rest they enjoyed there, we have but an uncertain relation of, for they went away early the next morning; but if it may be held fit to set down what hath been delivered by the report of others, they were also the same night much affrighted with dreadful apparitions; but, observing that these passages spread much in discourse, to be also in particulars taken notice of, and that the nature of it made not for their cause, they agreed to the concealing of the things for the future; yet this is well known and certain, that the Gate-keeper's wife was in so strange an agony in her bed, and in her bed-chamber such noise (whilst her husband was above with the Commissioners) that two maids in the next room to her durst not venture to assist her, but, affrighted, ran out to call company, and their Master, and found the woman (at their coming in) gasping for breath: and the next day said that she saw and suffered that, which, for all the world, she would not be hired to again.

From Woodstock the Commissioners removed unto Euelme, and some of them returned to Woodstock, the Sunday sennight after (the Book of Valuations wanting something that was, for haste, left imperfect), but lodged not in any of those rooms where they had lain before, and yet were not unvisited (as they confess themselves) by the Devil, whom they called their nightly guest. Captain Crooke came not untill Tuesday night, and how he sped that night, the gate-keeper's wife can tell, if she dareth; but, what she hath whispered to her gossips, shall not be made a part of this our Narrative, nor any more particulars which have fallen from the Commissioners themselves, and their servants to other persons; they are all, or most of them alive, and may add to it when they please, and, surely, have not a better way to be revenged of him who troubled them, than according to the Proverb, tell truth and shame the Devil.

There remains this observation to be added, that on a Wednesday morning, all these Officers went away; And that, since then, diverse persons of severall qualities, have lodged often and sometimes long in the same rooms both in the presence, withdrawing room and bed Chamber belonging unto his Sacred Majesty, yet none have had the least disturbance, or heard the smallest noise, for which the cause was not as ordinary, as apparent; except the Commissioners and their company, who came in order to the alienating and pulling down the house, which is well nigh performed.'

As to the authenticity of the above, we are told in the Preface: 'And now, as to the Penman of this Narrative, know that he was a Divine, and, at the time of those things acted, which are here related, the Minister and Schoolmaster of Woodstock, a person learned and discreet, nor byassed with factious humours, his name Widows, who, each day, put in writing what he heard from their mouthes, (and such things as they told to have befallen them the night before), therein keeping to their own words.'

There was also a metrical account[6] of these strange doings, printed in the year in which they occurred; but although it exactly tallies with the prose as above, it is not written in so refined a strain.

The British Magazine for April, 1747 (vol. ii., p. 156) professes to give 'The genuine history of the good devil of Woodstock, famous in the world in the year 1649, and never accounted for, or at all understood to this time.' It is by an anonymous writer, who says he found it in some original papers which had lately fallen into his hands, 'under the name of authentick memoirs of the memorable Joseph Collins of Oxford, commonly known by the name of funny Joe,' and it puts forth that this said Joe, under the name of Giles Sharp, entered the service of the Commissioners as a servant, and with the help of two friends, an unknown trap-door in the ceiling of the bedchamber, and some fulminating mercury, played the part of the Devil; but as the document is not known to be in existence, and is only mentioned in the pages of a magazine a hundred years afterwards, the reader may attach whatever credit he pleases to it. At all events, it proves that something very extraordinary, according to popular rumour, did take place at Woodstock during the Commissioners' occupation.

CHAPTER IV

'The Dæmon of Tedworth.'

'THE DÆMON OF TEDWORTH.[7]

'Master John Mompesson, of Tedworth in Wiltshire, being about the middle of March, in the year 1661, at a neighbouring Town, called Ludgarshal, heard a Drum beat there, and being concerned as a Commission Officer in the Militia, he enquired of the Bayliffe of the Town, at whose House he then was, what it meant. The Bayliffe told him that they had for some dayes been troubled by that Idle Drummer, who demanded money of the Constable, by virtue of a pretended pass, which he thought was counterfeit. Upon this Information Master Mompesson sent for the fellow, and ask'd him by what Authority he went up and down the Countrey in that manner, demanding money, and keeping a clutter with his Drum? The Drummer answered he had good Authority, and produced his pass, with a warrant under the hands of Sir William Cawly and Colonel Ayliffe of Gretenham. These papers discover'd the knavery, for M. Mompesson knowing those Gentlemen's hands, found that his pass and warrant were forgeries; and upon the discovery, commanded the vagrant to put off his Drum, and charged the Constable to carry him to the next Justice of Peace, to punish him according to the desert of his Insolence and Roguery. The fellow then confest the cheat, and begg'd earnestly for his Drum. But M. Mompesson told him that if he understood from Colonel Ayliffe, whose Drummer he pretended to be, that he had been an honest man, he should have it again; but in the interim he would secure it. So he left the Drum with the Bayliffe, and the Drummer in the Constable's hands; who, it seems, after, upon intreaty, let him go.

'About the midst of April following, when M. M. was preparing for a Journey to London, the Bayliffe sent the Drum to his house; and, being returned, his wife told him that they had been much affrighted in the night by Thieves, during his absence; and that the House had like to have been broken up. He had not been at home above three nights, when the same noise returned that had disturbed his Family when he was abroad. It was a very great knocking at his Doors, and the out side of his House. M. M. arose, and with a brace of Pistols in his hands, went up and down searching for the cause of the Disturbance. He open'd the door, where the great knocking was, and presently the noise was at another. He opened that also, and went forth, rounding his House, but could discover nothing; only he still heard a strange noise and hollow sound; but could not perceive what was the occasion of it. When he was returned to his Bed, the noise was a Thumping and Drumming on the top of his House, which continued a good space, and then by degrees went off into the Air.

'After this It would come 5 nights together, and absent itself 3. Knocking very hard at the outsides of the House, which is most of it, of Board. This It did, constantly, as they were going to sleep, either early or late. After a month's racket without, It came into the room where the Drum lay, where It would be 4 or 5 nights in 7, making great hollow sounds, and sensibly shaking the Beds and Windows. It would come within half an hour after they were in Bed, and stay almost two. The sign of Its approach was an hurling in the Air over the House; and at Its recess they should hear a Drum beat, like the breaking up of a Guard. It continued in this Room for the space of two months; the Gentleman himself lying there to observe It: and though It was very troublesome in the fore part of the night, yet, after two hours disturbance, It would desist, and leave all in quietness: At which time perhaps the Laws of the Black Society required Its presence at the general Rendezvous elsewhere.

'About this time the Gentleman's Wife was brought to Bed; the noise came a little that night she was in Travail, but then forbore for three weeks till she had recover'd strength. After this civil cessation, it return'd in a ruder manner than before, applying wholly to the younger children; whose Bedsteads It would beat with that violence that all present would expect, when they would fall in pieces. Those that laid their hands upon them, could feel no blows, but perceived them to shake exceedingly. It would for an hour together beat, what they Call ROUNDHEADS and CUCKOLDS--the Tattoo, and several other Points of Warre, and that as dextrously as any Drummer. After which It would get under the Bed, and scratch there as if It had Iron Tallons. It would lift the children up in their Beds, follow them from one room to another; and, for a while, applied to none particularly but them.

'There was a Cock-loft in the House which had been observed hitherto to be untroubled; thither they removed their children, putting them to bed while it was fair day: and yet they were no sooner covered, but the unwelcome Visitant was come, and played his tricks as before.

'On the 5th of Novemb. 1662. It kept a mighty noise, and one of the Gentleman's Servants observing two Boards in the children's room that seemed to move, he bade It give him one of them, and presently the Board came within a yard of him. The Fellow added, Nay, let me have it in my hand: upon which it was shuft quite home. The man thrust it back, and the Dæmon returned it to him, and so from one to another at least 20 times together, till the Gentleman forbad his servant such Familiarities. That morning It left a Sulphurous smell behind It, very displeasant and offensive.... At night the Minister of the place, Mr. Cragge, and many of the Neighbours came to the House--and went to prayer at the Children's Bed-side, where, at that time It was very troublesome and loud. During the time of Prayer It with-drew into the Cock-Loft, but, the Service being ended, It returned; and in the sight and presence of the company, the Chairs walked about the Room, the Children's Shooes were thrown over their heads, and every loose thing moved about the Chamber; also a Bed staffe was thrown at the Minister, which hit him on the Leg, but so favourably, that a lock of Wooll could not have fallen more softly. And a circumstance more was observed, viz., that it never in the least roul'd, nor mov'd from the place where it lighted.

'The Gentleman perceiving that It so much persecuted the little Children, lodg'd them out at a Neighbour's House, and took his eldest daughter, who was about 10 years of Age, into his own Chamber, where It had not been in a month before. But no sooner was she in Bed, but the troublesome Guest was with her, and continued his unquiet visits for the space of three weeks, during which time It would beat the Drum, and exactly answer any Tune that was knock'd, or called for. The House where the Gentleman had lodged his Children, being full of Strangers, he was forced to take them home again; and, because they had never observed any disturbance in the Parlor, he laid them there, where also their old Visitant found them; but, at this time, troubled them no otherwise than by plucking them by the hair and night-cloathes.

'It would sometimes lift up the Servants with their Beds, and lay them down again gently, without any more prejudice than the fright of being carried to the Drummer's quarters. And at other times It would lie like a great weight upon their Feet.

''Twas observed, that when the noise was loudest, and came with the most suddain and surprizing violence, yet no Dog would move. The Knocking was oft so boysterous and rude, that it hath been heard at a considerable distance in the Fields, and awakened the Neighbours in the Village, none of which live very near this house.

'About the latter end of Decemb. 1662. the Drummings were less frequent, and the noise the Fiend made, was a gingling, as it had been of money, occasioned, as 'twas thought, by some discourse of an antient Gentlewoman, Mother to M. M. (who was one day saying to a Neighbour that talked of Fairies leaving money, that she should like It well, if It would leave them some to make amends for the trouble It made them) for that night there was a great chinking of money all the house over; but he that rose earliest the next morning, was ne're a groat the richer. After this It desisted from its ruder noises, and employed Itself about little apish Tricks, and less troublesome Caprichios. On Christmas Eve, an hour before day, one of the little Boyes arising out of his Bed, was hit on a sore place in his Heel by the latch of the Door, which the waggish Dæmons had pluckt out and thrown at him. The Pin that fastened it was so small, that 'twas for the credit of his Opticks that he pick't it out without Candle-light. The night after Christmas Day, It threw all the old Gentlewoman's Cloaths about the Room, and hid her Bible in the Ashes. In such impertinent ludicrous fagaries, it was frequent. After this the Spirit was very troublesome to a Servant of M. Mompesson's, who was a stout fellow, and of sober conversation.... His Master permitted him to give this proof of his courage, and lodg'd him in the next room to his own. There was John engarrison'd, and provided for the assault with a trusty Sword, and other implements of War. And, for some time, there was scarce a night past without some doubty action and encounter, in which the success was various. One while, John's bag and baggage would be in the enemy's power, Doublet and Breeches surprized, and his Shooes raised in rebellion against him; and then lusty John by Dint of Weapon recovers all again, suppresseth the insurrection of his Shooes, and holds his own in spight of Satan and the Drummer. And for the most part, our combatant came off with honour and advantage, except when his enemy outwatch'd and surprized him, and then he's made a prisoner, bound hand and foot, and at the mercy of the Goblin; till he hath got the opportunity of recovering his Diabolical Blade, and then our Champion is in good plight again....

'About the beginning of Jan. 1662 they were wont to hear a singing in the chimney, before It came down. And one night, about this time, Lights were seen in the House: One of which came into M. Mompesson's Chamber, which seemed blue and glimmering, and caused a great stiffness in their eyes that saw it. After this light, something was heard coming up the Stairs, as if it had been some one without Shooes. The light was also 4 or 5 times seen in the Children's Chamber; and the Maids confidently affirm that the doors were at least ten times opened, and shut in their sight. They heard a noise at the same time when the Doors were opened, as if half a dozen had entred in together. After which, some were heard to walk about the room, and one rusled as if it had been in silk. The like M. M. himself once heard.

'During the time of the Knocking, when many were present, a Gentleman of the company said, Satan, If the Drummer sets thee a work, give three Knocks, and no more, which It did very distinctly, and stopt. Then the Gentleman knockt, to see if It would answer him as It was wont, but It remained quiet. He further tryed It the same way, bidding It, for confirmation, if It were the Drummer, to give 5 Knocks and no more that night, which It did accordingly, and was silent all the night after. This was done in the presence of Sir Tho. Chamberlain of Oxfordshire and several others.

'On Saturday morning, Jan. 10. an hour before day, the Drum was beaten upon the out-sides of M. Mompesson's Chamber, from whence It went to the other end of the House, where some Gentlemen, Strangers, lay, playing at their door, and without, 4 or 5. several Times, and so went off into the Air.

'The next night, a Smith of the Village lying with John, they heard a noise in the room, as if one had been shooing of a horse there; and somewhat came, as it were, with a pair of Pincers, and snipt at the Smith's Nose, most part of the Night.

'One morning M. Mompesson rising early to go a Journey, heard a great noise below, where the Children lay, and, running down, with a Pistol in his hand, heard this voice, A Witch, A Witch, as they had also heard it once before; but, upon his entrance, all was quiet. Having, one night played some little pranks at M. Mompesson's Bed's feet, It went into another Bed, in which one of his Daughter's lay, where It passed from side to side, and lifted her up, as It went under her. At that time there were three kindes of noises in the Bed. They endeavoured to thrust at It with a Sword, but It very carefully avoided them, still skipping under the Child, when they were ready to thrust. The night after, It came panting like a Dog out of breath; upon which one took a Bed-Staff to knock, which was taken out of her hand, and thrown away with some violence. Upon this the company came up, and, presently, the room was filled with a bloomy noysome smell, and was very hot; though without Fire, and in midst of a very sharp and severe winter. It continued in the Bed, panting and scratching an hour and half, and then went into the next Chamber, where it knock'd a little, and seemed to rattle a chain. Thus it did for two or three nights together.

'After this, the old Gentlewoman's Bible was found in the Ashes open, the paper side being downwards. M. Mompesson took it up, and observed that it lay open at the third chapter of S. Mark, in which there is mention of the unclean spirits falling down before our Saviour; of his giving power to the 12 to cast out Devils, and of the Scribes' opinion, that he cast them out through Beelzebub. The next night they strewed ashes over the Chamber, to see what impressions It would leave. And in the morning, found in one place the resemblance of a great Claw, in another, of a lesser; some Letters in another, which they could make nothing of; besides many Circles and Scratches in the Ashes; all which, I suppose, were ludicrous devices, by which the sportful Dæmon made pastime with human Ignorance and Credulity.

'About this time, my[8] curiosity drew me to the House, to be a witness of some of those strange passages. It had ceased from It's pranks of Drumming, and ruder noises, before I came; but most of the more remarkable circumstances before related were confirmed to me there, by several of the Neighbours together, who had been present at them. At that time It used to haunt the Children; I heard It scratch very loudly and distinctly in their Bed, behind the Boulster. I thrust in my hand to the place where the noise seemed to be, upon which It withdrew to another part of the Bed; and, upon the taking out of my hand, It returned as before. I had heard of It's imitating noises, and therefore made the trial, by scratching certain determinate times upon the Sheet, as 5. and 7. and 10. which It did also, and still stopt at my number. After a while It went into the midst of the Bed, under the Children, and there panted like a Dog, very loudly. I put my hand upon the place, and felt the Bed bear up against it, as if something had thrust it up; but, by grasping, could feel nothing but the Feathers: and there was nothing under it. The motion It caused by this panting was so strong, that it shook the Rooms and Windows. It continued thus for more than half an hour, while I stayed, and as long after. I was certain that there could be no fallacy nor deceit in these passages, which I critically examined; and I am sure there was nothing of fear or imagination in the case; for I was no more concerned than I am at the Writing this Relation.

'But to proceed with M. Mompesson's own particulars.

'There came one morning a light into the Children's Chamber, and the voice, crying, A Witch, A Witch, for at least an hundred times together. M. M. seeing at a time some Wood move that was in the Chimney, when no one was near, discharged a Pistol into it; after which they found several drops of Blood on the Hearth, and in divers places of the Stairs.

There was a seeming calm in the House for 2 or 3 nights after the discharge of the Pistol; but then It came again, applying Itself to a little Child, newly taken from Nurse; which it so persecuted, that It would not let the poor Infant rest for two nights together, nor suffer a Candle in the Room, but would carry them away up the Chimney, or throw them under the Bed. It so scared this Child by leaping upon it, that for some hours, it could not be recovered out of the fright. Insomuch as they were inforced again to remove the Children out of the House. The next night, after they were gone, something about midnight came up the Stairs, and knockt at M. Mompesson's door; but he, lying still, It went up another pair of Stairs, to his Man's Chamber, to whom It appeared, standing at his Bed's foot. The exact shape and proportion he could not discover; but saw a great body, with two red and glaring eyes, which for some time were fixt steddily upon him, and, at length, disappeared.

'Another night, Strangers being present, It purr'd in the Children's Bed like a Cat; and at that time the Cloaths and Children were lift up from the Bed, and 6 men could not keep them down. Upon this they removed them from thence, intending to have ript open the Bed: but they were no sooner laid in another, but this second Bed was more troubled than the former. It continued thus 4 hours, and so beat the Children's legs against the Bed-posts, that they were forced to arise, and sit up all night. After this It would empty Chamber-pots into their Beds, and strew them with Ashes; and that though they were never so carefully watch't, It put a long piked Iron into M. Mompesson's Bed, and, into his Mother's, a naked Knife upright. It would fill porringers with Ashes, throw every thing about, and keep a noise all day.

'About the beginning of April 1663. a Gentleman that lay in the house had all his money turn'd black in his Pockets. And M. Mompesson, one morning, coming into his Stable, found the Horse he was wont to ride, on the ground, with one of his hinder Legs in his mouth, and so fastned there, that 'twas difficult work for several men, with a Leaver, to get it out. After this there were some other remarkable things; but my account goes no farther: Only M. Mompesson told me, that afterwards the house was several nights beset with 7 or 8 in the shape of men, who, as soon as a Gun was discharged, would shuffle away together into an Arbour.

'THE DRUMMER was tryed at the Assize at Salisbury, condemned to the Islands, and was, accordingly, sent away: but I know not how, made a shift to come back again. And 'tis observable, that during all the time of his restraint, and absence, the House was in quiet; but, as soon as ever he came back, the disturbance also returned. He had been a Souldier under CRUMWEL, and used to talk much of gallant Books he had of an odd Fellow's, who was counted a Wizard.'

CHAPTER V

'The Dæmon of Burton'--'Strange and Wonderful News from Yowel, in Surrey'--The Story of Mrs. Jermin--A Case at Welton--'The Relation of James Sherring.'

The next case (in chronological order) that I have met with is very similar to that of Mompesson, and, like that, shows the trivialities to which this species of Devil could descend, apparently, with no object.

'THE DÆMON OF BURTON.[9]

'There is a Farm in Burton, a Village in the Parish of Weobley, in this County,[10] which Mr. William Bridges, a Linnen-Draper in London, has in Mortgage from one Thomas Tompkins, a decay'd Yeoman man. This Farm was, about Michaelmas, 1669. taken by Lease by Mrs. Elizabeth Bridges, to commence from February then next; Soon after this Tenant was entered on the Farm, and lodg'd in the House, some Familiar began to act apish Pranks, by knocking boldly at the door in the dusk of the Evening, and the like, early in the Morning, but no body to be seen.

'After this, the Stools and Forms, though left in their proper places, were, every night set round the fire, which the Tenant perceiving, she set them next night under the Table, and next morning they were found set orderly about the fire as before, and a continual noise of Cats heard all night, but never seen.

'Afterwards, the Tenant having in a Room a heap of Malt, and another of Vetches, the two parcels were found next morning exactly mingled together, and put into a new heap.

'Another time she had baked a Batch of Bread, and laid the Loaves over night on a Table; next morning the Loaves were all gone, and, after search made, they were found in another Room, hid in Tubs, and covered with linnen Cloathes, and all this while the Tenant had the keys of the doors in her pocket, and found the doors in the morning fast lock'd as she left them over night: so, also, her Cheeses and meat were often carried out of one Room into another, whilst the doors were fast lock'd, and sometimes convey'd into the Orchard.

'Then the Tenant having set Cabbidg-Plants in her Garden, in the night the Plants were pull'd up, and laid in several formes, as Crosses, Flower-de-Luces, and the like. She caus'd them to be set again, and the Ground finely raked about, to the end they might see if any footsteps might be discovered in the morning, when the Plants were found pull'd up as before, and no track or footstep to be found or perceived; the Plants were set a third time, and then they continued unmoved.

'She had in her Cheese-chamber many Cheeses upon Shelves, and a Bag of Hops in the same Room. One night, the Cheeses were all laid on the floor in several formes, and the Hops all strewed about the Room, and the Chamber door found fast lock'd in the morning.

'Another night in the Buttery there were several dishes of cold Meat left upon a hanging Shelf; in the morning, the Table Cloath was found orderly laid on the Floor, and the Dishes set on it, and most of the Meat eaten, onely a manners bit left in every Dish; yet there were silver Spoons, which lay by the Dishes, and none of them diminished.

'At another time she had left half a rosted Pig, which was design'd for breakfast next day, when the Pig was call'd for, there was not one bit of either Skin or Flesh left, but the Bones of the Pig, lay orderly in the Dish, and not one of them unjoynted or misplac'd.

'Whilst these, and many other such pleasant tricks were play'd in the Rooms that were lock'd to make a discovery of any deceipt, if possible, the entrance of the doors were all strew'd with sifted ashes, and no footstep or track of anything was found in the morning, when such pranks were play'd in the Room.

'One night the Tenant having bought a quart of Vinegar in a Bottel, she set it in her Dairy-house, where there were six Cows Milk. In the Morning she found her Bottle empty, and her milk all turned, and made into a perfect Posset, with the Vinegar.

'And the Cheeses were sometimes convey'd by night out of the Cheese Chamber, and put into the Trines of Milk in the Dairy-house.

'The Tenant had, likewise, divers of her Cattel that dyed in a strange manner, among others, a Sow that leap'd and danc'd in several unusual postures, and, at last fell down dead.

'The Hagg, having thus for above a moneth together, almost every night acted the part of Hocus pocus Minor, lay quiet for some moneths, and then began to act the Major, and do greater mischiefs; and to this purpose, One night, as the Tenant and her Maid were going to bed, and passing by the Hall, which was dressed with green boughs tyed on the Posts, after the Country fashion, they were all of a flame, and no fire had been made in that Room of a fortnight before, nor any Candle that night; but the fire was soon quenched by throwing water on it, yet an outcry being made, the neighbours came in, and watched the House all night.

'Not long after, a Loft of Hay, dry, and well Inned, was set on fire in the daytime, and was, most of it, burnt, with the house it lay in; and no way could be found how it should come to pass, but by the same black hand. 'And, after some time, a Mow of pulse and pease was likewise fired in the daytime, and all the grayn either burnt or spoiled, and in the middle of the bottom of the Mow were found dead burnt Coales, which in all the Spectators Judgements, could not be conveyed thither but by Witchcraft.

'After these dreadful fires, which did endanger the whole Village had they not been at length quench'd by a numerous Company of the Neighbours, who came in to the Tenant's Assistance, the poor Tenant dirst stay no longer in the House, but quitted it, with all her losses, when one John Jones a valiant Welchman of the neighbourhood, would needs give a signal proof of his Brittish Valour, and to that purpose undertook to lye in the House, and to incounter the Hagg, to which end he carried with him a large Basket hilted Sword, a Mastive Dog, and a Lanthorn and Candle to burn by him; he had not long lain on the Bed, with his Dog, and Sword ready drawn by him, but he heard a great Knocking at the Door, and many Cats, as he conceived, came into his Chamber, broke the Windows, and made a hideous noise, at which the Mastive howll'd and quak'd, and crept close to his Master; the Candle went out, and the Welchman fell into a cold sweat, left his Sword unused, and with much adoe found the door, and ran half a Mile without ever looking behind him; protesting, next day, he would not lye another night in the House, for a hundred pounds.'

The next in point of time is the following:

'STRANGE AND WONDERFUL NEWS FROM YOWEL[11] IN SURREY.'[12]

'On Thursday, the 5th of October, one Mr. Tuers, a Gentleman, living at Yowell in the County of Surry, together with his wife, went forth upon occasion, leaving their Servant Maid, Elizabeth Burgiss, at home, to officiate in their absence, as she found occasion. In the meantime, or interim, one Joan Butts, a person that hath been for a long time suspected to be a Witch, came to the house of the aforesaid Mr. Tuers, and, framing some discourse to the Maid before named, she, at last, askt her for a pair of old Gloves; the Maid knowing her to be a person of ill repute, and being willing to be rid of her company, gave her a very short and sharp answer, telling her that she had no Gloves for her, or, if shee had, she could not spare time to look them out; whereupon this Joan Butts went away, but in a little time returned, asking the aforesaid Maid for a Pin to pin her Neckcloath, which she furnished her with, and so this Joan Butts departed, leaving the Maid without any dread or fear of any harm.

'But, about fourteen days after, there happened strange and miraculous wonders, amazing and frightening all the Spectators; for stones flew about the Yard at such a strange rate, as if it had rained down showers of them, and many of them were as big as a man's fist, and afterwards flew as thick about the House as before they did about the Yard, notwithstanding the doors were close shut, yet for all (that) they flew so thick about, they hit nobody but the Maid, to the great astonishment of her Master, Mistris and others; but more to be admired, the next day this maid was suddenly attacqued with intolerable pain in her back, and such unsufferable pricking of Pins, that she was not able to endure, or without lamentable complaining. The groans and skreeches she sometimes parted with, would have moved a stony heart to pitty her distress, and Mr. Tuers, her Master, commiserating her condition, asked if he should put his hand down her back, and feel what might be the cause of her pain or Torment, which she willingly agreed to, and, to the amazement of all persons present, pulled out a great piece of Clay as full of Pins as it could well be, and throwing them into the fire, she was for that present at great ease. But, after that, a second Torment did seize this Maid, which caused her to complain more grievously and lamentably than before; whereupon one Mr. Waters put his hand down her back, and pulled out a piece of Clay as thick of Thorns, as the other of Pins, so, throwing them into the fire, she was again at ease for that time.

'The next day, as she was going a Milking, she saw, in Nonsuch Park, this wretched old Caitiff sitting amongst the Thorns and Bushes, bedaggled up to the Knees in Dew, and looking like one that had lately had converse with some Infernal Fiend; and, wondring to see her there so early, in that pickle (being, as it were, doubtful of her wickedness); and supposing her to be the cause of her (before mentioned) pain and misery, returned home to her Master's house, telling him how she saw this Joan Butts in the place before named, adding in what strange garb and posture she sat in; which added to the suspicion of the (before doubtful) Master.

'But the same night the Maid going into the chamber where she lay, to fetch a Trunk which was intended to be sent to London, all on a sudden cryed out, Master, Master, here is the old Woman: the master running hastily to see whether it were so or no, could see no old woman, but the Andirons thrown after the maid, and all her own Linnen thrown about at such a rate, as it is hard to believe, but that it will, upon occasion, be attested by unquestionable Evidence; and likewise a Wooden Bar which belonged to the street door, was strangely removed and conveyed up stairs, and came tumbling down after the maid, in the sight of her master.

'About three days after, they were surprized with new wonders, for there was to be seen such sights as they never saw before, viz., the Bellows flew about the house, and Candlesticks and other things thrown after the Girl as she passed to and fro in her master's house; and, going to her Mother's house, which was at Astead, about three miles distant from Yowel, such numberless numbers of stones were thrown at her, that she found it hazardous to Travel, but had she returned, it might have been the same; and so she continued till she came to her mother's house, where, on Sunday the 9th of October, they were possest with admiration, as well as those of her Master's Family, for her Grandfather's Britches were strangely found to be on the top of the house, as near as can be imagined, over his Bed; and, besides, such great quantities of Nuts and Acorns flew about, that the Spectators never beheld the like before. The pewter danced about the house in a strange manner, and hits a Gentleman such a blow on the back, that I suppose he will have but little stomach hereafter, to go to see the Devil dance.

'But the same day happened another Wonder, no less strange than what is before recited, for there was a Fiddle close laid up in a Chest, which was strangely, and unknown to any of the house, hung up in the room, and, after, was removed to the top of the Bed-Tester, and, the third time, carried quite away, and hath no more been seen since.

'But, on Thursday, the 18th of this present October, there being a Fair kept at Yowel, the mother of this afflicted maid came thither, and, meeting with this old suspected Witch (whom she had great reason to imagine so to be,) fell foul upon her, and so evilly Treated her, that she fetcht out some of her Hellish Blood, but the effects and event thereof, I must get time to acquaint you with.'

The Rev. Joseph Glanvill was a great collector of these stories, and after his death many were published, as being found among his papers. One is a story of a Mr. Jermin, minister of Bigner in Sussex, who had noises in his house like guns going off whilst it seemed that people ran swiftly down stairs, into his chamber, and there seemed to wrestle, whilst one day, when a physician was dining with him 'there came a Man on Horseback into the Yard, in Mourning. His Servant went to know what was his Busness, and found him sitting very Melancholy, nor could he get any Answer from him. The Master of the House and the Physician went to see who it was; upon which, the Man clapt spurs to his Horse, and rode into the House, up Stairs into a long Gallery, whither the Physician followed him, and saw him vanish in a Fire at the upper end of the Gallery. But though none of the Family received hurt at any time, yet Mr. Jermin fell into a Fever with the Disturbance he experienced, that endangered his Life.'

Then we have the story of an extremely uncomfortable house 'at Welton, within a mile of Daventry,' where the younger daughter, ten years of age, took to vomiting three gallons of water in less than three days, and afterwards stones and coals, in number about five hundred. 'Some weighed a quarter of a Pound, and were so big, as they had enough to do to get them out of her mouth.... This Vomiting lasted about a Fortnight, and hath Witnesses good store.' Things got rather lively in the house, and were thrown about; the Bible, being laid upon a bed, was hid in another bed; the things from the parlour were turned out into the hall; their milk was spilt, their beer mixed with sand, and their salt with bran. The man of the house, one Moses Cowley, seems to have had an especially bad time of it. 'A knife rose up in the Window, and flew at him, hitting him with the Haft;' and, to make the place more uncomfortable, 'Every day abundance of Stones were thrown about the House, which broke the windows, and hit the people.' Probably the Devil was disappointed, inasmuch as 'they were the less troubled because, all this while no hurt was done to their Persons,' and after a while the persecution ceased, with the exception of 'great Knockings, and cruel Noise.'

Then there is 'The Relation of James Sherring, taken concerning the matter at old Gast's House of Little Burton.

'The first Night I was there with Hugh Mellmore and Edward Smith, they heard, as it were, the Washing in Water over their Heads. Then, taking a Candle, and going up Stairs, there was a wet Cloth thrown at them, but it fell on the Stairs. They going up farther, there was another thrown as before. And, when they were come up into the Chamber, there stood a Bowl of Water, some of it sprinkled over, and the Water looked white, as if there had been Soap used in it. The Bowl, just before, was in the Kitchin, and could not be carried up but through the Room where they were. The next thing that they heard, the same Night, was a terrible noise, as if it had been a clap of Thunder, and, shortly after, they heard great scratching about the Bed stead, and, after that, great Knocking with a Hammer against the Beds-head, so that the two Maids that were in the Bed cryed out for Help. Then they ran up the stairs, and there lay the Hammer on the bed, and on the Beds-head there were near a Thousand Prints of the Hammer, which the violent Strokes had made. The maids said they were scratcht and pincht with a Hand that was put into the Bed, which had exceeding long Nails. They said the Hammer was lockt up fast in the Cup board when they went to Bed.

'The second Night that James Sherring, and Tho. Hillary were there, James Sherring sat down in the Chimney to fill a pipe of Tobacco, he made use of the Fire-tongs to take up a Coal to light his Pipe, and by and by the Tongs were drawn up the Stairs, and after they were up in the Chamber, they were play'd withal (as many times Men do) and then thrown down upon the Bed. Although the Tongs were so near him, he never perceived the going of them away. The same Night one of the Maids left her Shoes by the Fire, and they were carried up into the Chamber, and the old Man's brought down, and set in their places. The same Night there was a Knife carried up into the Chamber, and it did scratch and scrape the Bed's head all the Night; but, when they went up into the Chamber, the Knife was thrown into the Loft. As they were going up the Stairs, there were things thrown at them, which were, just before in the low Room, and when they went down the Stairs, the old Mans Breeches were thrown down after them. These were the most remarkable things done that Night, only there was continual knocking and pinching the Maids, which was usually done every Night.'

There is a great deal more of this case, which reads like the senseless phenomena of a spiritual séance, but we will pass on to

CHAPTER VI

A Demon in Gilbert Campbell's Family--Case of Sir William York--Case of Ian Smagge--Disturbances at Stockwell.

'A REMARKABLE STORY TOUCHING THE STIRS MADE BY A DÆMON IN THE FAMILY OF ONE GILBERT CAMPBELL, BY PROFESSION A WEAVER, IN THE OLD PARISH OF GLENLUCE, IN GALLOWAY, IN SCOTLAND.

'It happened in October 1654, that after one Alexander Agnew, a bold and sturdy Beggar, who, afterwards, was hang'd at Dumfries, for Blasphemy, had threatened hurt to Gilbert Campel's family, because he had not gotten such an Alms as he required; the said Gilbert was oftentimes hindred in the exercise of his Calling, all his working Instruments being, some of them broken, some of them cut, and yet could not know by what means this hurt was done. Which piece of trouble did continue till about the middle of November; at which time the Devil came with new and extraordinary Assaults, by throwing of Stones in at Doors and Windows, and down through the Chimney head, which were of great quantity, and thrown with great force, yet by God's good Providence, there was not one Person of the family hurt, or suffer'd damage thereby. This piece of new and sore Trouble did necessitate Mr. Campel to reveal that to the Minister of the Parish, and to some other Neighbours and Friends, which, hitherto, he had endured secretly. Yet notwithstanding this, his Trouble was inlarged; for, not long after, he found oftentimes his Warp and Threads cut as with a pair of Sizzars, and the Reed broken; and not only this, but their Apparel cut after the same manner, even while they were wearing them, their Coats, Bonnets, Hose, Shoes, but could not discern how, or by what means. Only, it pleased God to preserve their Persons, that the least harm was not done. Yet in the Night-time they wanted liberty to Sleep, something coming and pulling their Bed-clothes and Linnens off them, and leaving their Bodies naked.

'Next, their Chests and Trunks were opened, and all things in them strewed here and there: Likewise the parts of the working Instruments that had escaped, were carried away, and hid in holes and bores of the House, where hardly they could be found again: Nay, whatever piece of Cloth or Household stuff was in any part of the House, it was carried away, and so cut and abused, that the Good-man was necessitated, with all haste and speed to remove, and to transport the rest to a Neighbour's House, and he himself compell'd to quit the Exercise of his Calling, whereby only he maintained his Family. Yet he resolv'd to remain in the House for a season. During which time some Persons thereabout, not very judicious, counselled him to send his Children out of the Family, here and there, (to try whom the Trouble did most follow, assuring him that this Trouble was not against all the Family, but against some one Person or other in it) whom he too willingly obeyed. Yet for the space of 4 or 5 Days after, there were no remarkable assaults, as before.'

After the Devil had twice set this poor man's house on fire, and 'the persons within the family suffering many losses, as the Cutting of their Coats, the throwing of Peits, the pulling down of Turf and Feal from the Roof and Walls of the House, and the stealing of their Apparel, and the pricking of their Flesh and Skin with pins, the Presbytery set apart a day for a solemn humiliation, which seems to have had some effect upon Satan, for soon after he found a voice.

'Upon Monday the 12th of February, the rest of the Family began to hear a Voice speak to them, but could not well know from whence it came. Yet, from Evening to Midnight, much vain Discourse was kept up with the Devil, and many idle and impertinent Questions proposed without that due Fear of God that should have been upon their Spirits, under so rare and extraordinary a Trial. The Minister hearing of this, went to the House upon the Tuesday, being accompanied with some Gentlemen, who, after Prayer was ended, heard a Voice speaking out of the Ground, from under a Bed, in the proper Country Dialect, saying, Would you know the Witches of Glenluce? I will call them, and so related four or five Persons Names, that went under an evil report. The said Gilbert informed the Company that one of them was dead long ago. The Devil answered, It is true, she is dead long ago, yet her Spirit is living with us in the World. The Minister reply'd, saying: The Lord rebuke thee, Satan, and put thee to silence, we are not to receive any Information from thee, whatsoever Fame any Persons go under; thou art but seeking to seduce this Family, for Satan's kingdom is not divided against itself.'

Then the Devil and the minister had a most unseemly wrangle, both battering each other with texts of Scripture; and the holy man's visit did no good, for all their annoyances returned, until poor Campbell again appealed to the Presbytery; which body ordered that a solemn humiliation should be kept through all the bounds of the Synod. This was in February, and Campbell's persecutions gradually decreased till April, when they altogether ceased, and so continued till August.

'About which time the Devil began with new Assaults, and taking the ready Meat that was in the House, did sometimes hide it in holes by the Door-posts, and at other times did hide it under the Beds, and sometimes among the Bed cloaths, and under the Linnens, and at last did carry it quite away, till nothing was left there save Bread and Water to live by. After this he exercised his Malice and Cruelty against all the Persons of the Family, in wearying them in the Night time, with stirring and moving through the House, so that they had no rest for noise, which continued all the month of August after this manner. After which time the Devil grew yet worse, and began with terrible Roarings and terrifying Voices, so that no Person could sleep in the House in the Night-time, and sometimes did vex them with casting of Stones, striking them with Staves on their Beds, in the Night time, and upon the 11th of September, about Midnight, he cryed out with a loud voice: I shall burn the House: and, about 3 or 4 nights after, he set one of the Beds on Fire, which was soon extinguished without any prejudice, except the Bed itself, and so he continued to haunt them.'

Here this thrilling narrative ends, and the minister and Presbytery seem to have given up the job of quelling the Devil. A much milder case is:

'A true and faithful Narrative of the disturbance which was in the House of Sir William York, in the Parish of Lessingham in Lincolnshire.'

It began in May, 1679, with the latch of the outer door being lifted very quickly, which was done for between two or three hours. In July the doors banged to, and the chairs all held a conversazione in the hall, after which they returned to their several rooms. In August the persecution took the form of knocking at the doors; in September the noise was of a man walking on stilts.

'Afterwards the said Noise began to be more dreadful and greater yet, and in more places, which mightily disordered Sir William's ancient Father; and his Lady and Children very much. Upon which they were thinking upon leaving the House. Sir William was willing that they should, but unwilling to leave it himself, and thereupon they all continued. At this time Sir William had a Plummer putting up Lead about the House, to convey the Rain which fell into a Cistern, and this knocking was often against the Lead, and often against the Iron that bore it, in imitation of the Plummers knocking in the Day-time. He likewise had Carpenters at the same time, and sometimes the Noise was like their Chopping at the Wood in the Yard, insomuch that the head Carpenter said, That if he had not known his Servants to be in the House, he would have thought they had been chopping. Sometimes it was like the Servants Chopping of Coals in the Coal Yard; sometimes knocking at the Doors of Out-houses, at the Wash-house, Brew-house, and Stable-doors; and, as they followed it from place to place, it was still immediately, and in one instant removed. These were the usual Noises that were every Night when it came, which was 3 or 4 times a Week.'

It got worse until October, when Sir William had to go to London, to Parliament, when it entirely ceased. As years went on, these manifestations appear to have been of a much milder type. The belief in witchcraft and the personal power of the Devil was much shaken in Queen Anne's reign, but the Ghost began to be introduced. In the following the two are well mixed, but, as we have nothing to do with such silly things as ghosts, this narrative will not take up much time.

'AN EXACT NARRATIVE OF MANY SURPRIZING MATTERS OF FACT UNCONTESTABLY WROUGHT BY AN EVIL SPIRIT, OR SPIRITS, IN THE HOUSE OF MASTER IAN SMAGGE, FARMER IN CANVY ISLAND NEAR LEIGH, IN ESSEX, UPON THE 10TH, 13TH, 14TH, 15TH, AND 16TH OF SEPTEMBER LAST, IN THE DAYTIME.' LONDON, 1709.

'This now Dwelling-House of Ian Smagge, standing in Canvy Island, in the County of Essex, is said to have been Built, and for a great while Inhabited by a certain Person deceased; who, with his Wife, were lookt upon in their Life-time, jointly to have scrap'd together in the said House, by Fraudulent and Oppressive means, a considerable lump of Pelf. Having for a long time carried on this groveling Employ, the Wife being in a declining Condition, went to London to be advis'd for her Health; but Sickness increasing, and she conceiving she should die, desir'd the Man with whom she lodg'd, that happened to be the same Person that now lives in the said disturb'd House, to acquaint her Husband, She would be Buried in a Place call'd Benfleet, near Canvy-Island, where her deceased Children lay: To which he answered, 'Twas all one where the Body was dispos'd, so the Soul was Happy.

'This discourse passed about Six a Clock in the Evening in the Summer time. Immediately on which, Ian Smagge affirms, He received a hard Stroke or Stroking on the Arm, from the Wrist upwards to his Shoulder; and then felt the Chair, that he sat in, to shake in an extraordinary manner. He lookt under the Chair, and about him, to see what caus'd the Motion, but discern'd nothing. His Wife and the sick Person were in the Room, but both distant from him.

***

'In two or three Days the said Person died, and her Husband was sent for, and acquainted with her Mind; but he, probably to save Charges, buried her in Town. The Funeral being over, he return'd to his Habitation in Canvy Island, and in a few Years made his Exit also, which the old Inhabitants compute to be upward of 20 Years since. Presently, upon his death, unaccountable Noises were frequently heard in the House, to the great trouble of those that succeeded him in it. Such as forcibly opening and Shutting the Doors at Noon-day, no one being near them, or the least Wind or Breeze of Air stirring to do it. Nay, whilst the people have had the Doors in their Hands, they have been violently snach'd from them, and shut to and fro, with exceeding quickness, for many times together.'

There were all sorts of noises and silly tricks, such as spirits seem to delight in--breaking windows, throwing stones, etc., and a ghost or two thrown in. The local minister did all he could to quiet matters, and 'throughout this sore Visitation discharged his sacred Function in a ready and constant attendance, in advising Mrs. Smagge to a Fast, and Prayers in the Family'; and no doubt his remedies were effectual, for the disturbances ceased.

Cases of this kind became scarce, possibly because the Devil got weary of such puerilities, and I shall only record one more case in which he, certainly, made a house very lively:

'AN AUTHENTIC, CANDID, AND CIRCUMSTANTIAL NARRATIVE, OF THE ASTONISHING TRANSACTIONS AT STOCKWELL IN THE COUNTY OF SURRY, ON MONDAY AND TUESDAY THE 6TH AND 7TH DAYS OF JANUARY 1772.

'On Monday, January the 6th 1772, about ten o'clock in the forenoon, as Mrs. Golding was in her parlour, she heard the china and glasses in the back kitchen tumble down and break; her maid came to her and told her the stone plates were falling from the shelves; Mrs. Golding went into the kitchen, and saw them broke. Presently after, a row of plates from the next shelf fell down likewise, while she was there, and nobody near them; this astonished her much, and while she was thinking about it, other things in different places began to tumble about, some of them breaking, attended with violent noises all over the house; a clock tumbled down, and the case broke; a lanthorn that hung on the staircase was thrown down and the glass broke to pieces; an earthen pan of salted beef broke to pieces, and the beef fell about.'

A carpenter gave it as his opinion that the house was going to tumble down, so Mrs. Golding removed to Mrs. Gresham's, her next door neighbour, and her effects were also removed as quickly as possible; but the demon followed with them.

'Among the things that were removed to Mrs. Gresham's, was a tray full of china, &c. a japan bread basket, some mahogany waiters, with some bottles of liquors, jars of pickles &c., and a pier glass, which was taken down by Mr. Saville, (a neighbour of Mrs. Golding's): he gave it to one Robert Hames, who laid it on the grass-plat at Mrs. Gresham's; but, before he could put it out of his hands, some parts of the frame on each side flew off. It raining at the time, Mrs. Golding desired it might be brought into the parlour, where it was put under a side-board, and a dressing glass along with it; it had not been there long, before the glasses and china which stood on the side board, began to tumble about and fall down, and broke both the glasses to pieces. Mr. Saville and others, being asked to drink a glass of wine or rum, both the bottles broke in pieces before they were uncorked.'

This made the poor lady very nervous indeed, and she could no longer stop in a house where there were such doings, so moved to that of a niece, Mrs. Pain, but while they were picking up some of her things to store away, 'a jar of pickles that stood upon a table, turned upside down, then a jar of rasburry jam broke to pieces; next two mahogany waiters and a quadrille-box likewise broke to pieces.'

Mrs. Golding doubtless thought that her troubles were ended, for everything was quiet in her new abode till about eight o'clock in the evening, when there was 'the Devil to pay.'

'The first thing that happened, was, a whole row of pewter dishes, except one, fell from off a shelf to the middle of the floor, rolled about a little while, then settled, and what is almost beyond belief, as soon as they were quiet, turned upside down; they were then put on the dresser, and went through the same a second time; next fell a whole row of pewter plates from off the second shelf over the dresser to the ground, and being taken up, and put on the dresser one in another, they were thrown down again.'

'The next thing was two eggs that were upon one of the pewter shelves, one of them flew off, crossed the kitchen, struck a cat on the head, and then broke to pieces.

'Next Mary Martin, Mrs. Pain's servant, went to stir the kitchen fire, she got to the right hand side of it, being a large chimney, as is usual in farm houses, a pestle and mortar that stood nearer the left hand end of the chimney shelf, jumped about six feet on the floor. Then went candlesticks and other brasses; scarce anything remaining in its place. After this, the glasses and china were put down on the floor for fear of undergoing the same fate, they presently began to dance and tumble about, and then broke to pieces. A tea-pot that was among them, flew to Mrs. Golding's maid's foot, and struck it.

'A glass tumbler that was put on the floor jumped about two feet, and then broke. Another that stood by it, jumped about at the same time, but did not break for some hours after, when it jumped again, and then broke. A china bowl that stood in the parlour jumped from the floor, to behind a table that stood there. This was most astonishing, as the distance from where it stood was between seven and eight feet, but was not broke. It was put back by Richard Fowler, to its place, where it remained some time, and then flew to pieces.

'The next thing that followed was a mustard pot, that jumped out of a Closet, and was broke, A single cup that stood upon the table, (almost the only thing remaining) jumped up, flew across the kitchen, ringing like a bell, and then was dashed to pieces against the dresser. A candle stick, that stood on the Chimney shelf, flew cross the kitchen to the parlour door, at about fifteen feet distance. A tea-kettle, under the dresser, was thrown out about two feet, another kettle that stood at one end of the range, was thrown against the iron that is fixed to prevent children falling into the fire. A tumbler with rum and water in it, that stood upon a waiter upon a table in the parlour, jumped about ten feet, and was broke. The table then fell down, and along with it a silver tankard belonging to Mrs. Golding, the waiter in which had stood the tumbler and a candle stick. A case bottle then flew in pieces.'

The food took to flying about, and it must have been heartbreaking for the ladies to witness the destruction of their property, which must have been aggravated by the conduct of Mrs. Golding's servant. 'At all the times of action, she was walking backwards and forwards, either in the kitchen or parlour, or wherever some of the family happened to be. Nor could they get her to sit down five minutes together, except at one time for about half an hour towards the morning, when the family were at prayers in the parlour; then all was quiet; but in the midst of the greatest confusion, she was as much composed as at any other time, and, with uncommon coolness of temper, advised her mistress not to be alarmed or uneasy, as she said these things could not be helped. Thus she argued, as if they were common occurrences which must happen in every family.'

Nowadays, perhaps, she would have been termed a very powerful 'medium,' but as the property still continued in an abnormal condition, and its destruction was proceeding at a very rapid rate, it was thought better to discharge her, 'and no disturbances have happened since.'

CHAPTER VII

Possession by, and casting out, Devils--The Church and Exorcisms--Earlier Exorcists--'The Strange and Grievous Vexation by the Devil of 7 Persons in Lancashire.'

The New Testament, especially the Gospels, decidedly and authoritatively teach that the Devil, or Devils, had power to enter into and possess men, and Jesus not only cast them out, but gave His disciples power to do the same; and, in order that this possession by the Devil should not be ascribed to disease, it is expressly classified apart, Matt. iv. 24: 'And they brought unto Him all sick people that were taken with divers diseases and torments, and those which were possessed with devils, and those which were lunatick, and those that had the palsy, and He healed them.' And even the Revised Version does not materially alter the text: 'And they brought unto Him all that were sick, holden with divers diseases and torments, possessed with aevils (or, demoniacs) and epileptic and palsied; and He healed them.'

The early Christian Church fully believed in its powers of casting out devils, and holy-water, accompanied with the sign of the cross, was very efficacious in this matter. Now, in these latter days, it seems to be of no effect of itself. In Addis and Arnold's 'Catholic Dictionary,' a work which has received the imprimatur of Cardinal Manning, we read, under the heading 'Holy-water': 'Water and salt are exorcised by the priest, and so withdrawn from the power of Satan, who, since the fall, has corrupted and abused even inanimate things; prayers are said that the water and salt may promote the spiritual and temporal health of those to whom they are applied, and may drive away the Devil with his rebel angels; and, finally, the water and salt are mingled in the name of the Trinity. The water thus blessed becomes a means of grace.... The reader will observe that we do not attribute to holy-water any virtue of its own. It is efficacious simply because the Church's prayers take effect at the time it is used.'

But this was not the belief of the Roman Catholic Church of the sixteenth and seventeenth centuries, as we may read in Boguet[13]: 'But it was a frightful thing to hear the Demon cry and yell when the priest had pronounced the holy name of Jesus, and when he invoked the assistance of the holy Virgin Mary, or when he approached the Demoniac with the Cross, or when he sprinkled him with holy-water, or made him drink some. For he said sometimes that they were burning him, and at others, that they had given him enough holy-water, and that if they persisted in throwing any more over him, he would not go out, and would torment Roland's body still further.'

But, before the Church took up this good work, it would seem that there were more or less effective agents for the purpose in existence, for Reginald Scot tells us, in 'A Discourse upon Diuels and Spirits,' chap. xv.: 'But when Saule was releeued with the sound of the harpe, they say that the departure of the diuell was by meanes of the signe of the Crosse imprinted in Dauid's veines. Whereby we maie see how absurd the imaginations and deuises of men are, when they speake according to their own fansies, without warrant of the word of God. But methinks it is verie absurd that Josephus affirmeth: to wit, that the diuell should be thrust out of anie man by virtue of a root. And as vaine it is that Ælianus writeth of the magicall herbe Cynospastus, otherwise called Aglaphotis; which is all one with Salomon's root, named Baaros, as hauing force to driue out anie diuell from a man possessed.'

Nowadays we put some of those possessed with devils into prison, and we endeavour to purify them by work, diet, good counsel, and the absence of temptations--a course which is sometimes, but not always, effective; but, then, the character of devils has certainly changed during the last four or five centuries.

The reading of cases of possession is somewhat dreary work, and some are evidently catch-pennies, extremely goody-goody, consisting of long-winded theological discussions between the possessed and the Devil, in which the former invariably gets the best of the argument, so that I shall not tarry long on this branch of my subject, giving only three or four cases in illustration.

'A TRUE NARRATION OF THE STRANGE AND GRIEVOUS VEXATION BY THE DEVIL OF 7 PERSONS IN LANCASHIRE, BY JOHN DARRELL, MINISTER OF THE WORD OF GOD. 1600.'

'At Cleworth in Lancashire, within the parish of Leigh, there dweleth one Nicholas Starchie, gentleman, who, having only two children, it went thus with them, in the beginning of februari, 1594: first, Anne, his daughter, being 9 Yeares olde, was taken with a dumpish and heauie countenaunce, and with a certaine fearefull starting and pulling together of her body; about a weeke after, Iohn Starchie, his sonne, of the age of 10 yeares, as he was going to the schoole, was compelled to shout, neither was able to staie himself. After, they waxed worse and worse, falling often into extreame fits, M. Starchie seeking for remedy, after 9 or 10 weekes, heard of one, Edmund Hartlay, a coniurer, to whom he repaired, made knowne his greife, and with large profers craued his helpe. Hartlay comes, and, after he had used certaine popish charmes and hearbs, by degrees the children were at quiet, and so continued, seeming to be well almost a yeare and halfe, all which time Hartlay came often to visit them. At length, he fained as though he would have gone into another country, but wether, M. Starchie might not know. When he begane to goe his way, Iohn fell of bleedinge; then, presently, he was sent for again, who affirmed that if he had bene 40 rodes off, no man could have stanched him, and thus it fell out at other times.

'M. Starchie hereupon fearing lest his children would be troubled in his absence, and he uncertaine where to find him, offered to giue him his table to tarie with them, and so he did for a certain space; but, after couenaunted with him to giue him an annuel pension of 40s. for his assistance in time of neede; which pension was assured him in writing, and began at Michael's day 1598; wherewith Hartlay not being satisfied, desiered more, an house and ground: whereunto, because M. Starchie would not accord, he threatned in a fume (M. Starchie being absent, but in the hearing of diuers), that, if he would not fulfil his minde, he would make such a shout as never was at Cleworth; and so ther was indeed, not only upon the day, and at the instant of their dispossession, but also the day before: when 7 of them, both in the afternoone and in the evening, sent forth such a strange, supernaturall, and fearfull noyse, or loud whupping,[14] as the like, undoubtedly, was neuer hard at Cleworth, nor it, I think, in England. This he said in September 1596, and on the 17 day of Nouember folowing, they both began to be troubled againe after so long rest.

'On a certaine time Hartlay went with M. Starchie to his father's house in Whally parishe, where he was tormented sore all night. The next day, beinge recouered, he went into a little wood, not farr from the house, where he maide a circle about a yarde and halfe wyde, deviding it into 4 partes, making a crosse at euery Diuision; and when he had finished his worke, he came to M. Starchie, and desiered him to go and tread out the circle, saying I may not treade it out my selfe; and further, I will meete with them that went about my death. When M. Starchie saw this wreched dealing of his, and his children still molested, he waxed wearie of him, howbeit he sought other helpe for his children.

'Then he tooke his sonnes water to a phisitian in Manchester, who sawe no signe of sicknes; after, he went to Doctor Dee, the warden of Manchester, whose helpe he requested, but he utterly refused, sayinge he would not meddle, and aduised him that, setting aside all other helpe, he should call for some godlye preachers, with whom he should consult concerning a Publicke or Privat fast. He also procured Hartlay to come before him, whom he so sharply reproved, and straitly examined, that the children had more ease for 3 weekes space after; and this was upon the 8 of December.

'About Newyeare's Day, the children (being in good case, as it seemed) went to Manchester, invited to a kinsman's house, whom Hartlay accompanied as their overseer, and in their returne homewardes, they were desirous to see Doctor Dee, according to their promise, and his request. But Hartlay withstood them, and, because they went to his house, notwithstanding his prohibition, he told them, with an angri loke, that it had bene better for them not to haue chaunged an old frend for a new, with other menacinge speaches, and so went before them in a rage, and neuer came neare them all the way home.

'Upon the Tuseday after newyeares day Ianuarie 4. Iohn Starchie was readinge, somethinge gave him such a blowe on the necke, that he was soddenlye stricken downe with an horrible scryke,[15] saying that Satan had broken his necke and laye tormented pitifully for the space of two howres. The same day, at night, being in bed, he lept out on the sudden, with a terrible outcry, that amased all the familye. Then was he tossed and tumbled a long tyme, was very feirce like a mad-man, or a mad dogge, snacted at and bite euery one that he layde hold on, with his teethe, not spareing his mother, smiting the next, and hurling Bed-staues, Pillowes, or whatsoeuer at them, and into the fire. From this day forwarde he had no great ease until the day of his deliuerance.

'His sister Anne likewise began againe to be troubled, and 3 other yong children in the house, of whom M. Starchie had the education and tuition, with there portiones committed unto him by ther parentes. The first was Margaret Hardman, of the age of 14 yeares, the 2. Elizabeth her sister of 10 yeares age, and the 3. Ellinor Holland of 12 yeares. The same day, at night, Hartlay himself, was also tormented, and the next day in like manner, where many held him, among whom one Margaret Byrom of Salford, by Manchester 33 yeares olde, a poore kinswoman of Mistris Starchies, was one; who beinge come thither to make merrie, was requested to sit downe behind Hartlay to hold him, and did so; but, when he was out of his fit, she endeoured to arise, was so benumb and giddi, that shee could not stand, yet, being lifted up shee stroue to goe, but being unable, fell downe, and was sencelesse, and very unruly.

'Which, Hartlay seeinge, saide, I feare I haue done her harme. Then she nicknamed and taunted all that were present, though she wyste not what she saide, nor knewe or sawe Hartlay onlye, whome she both knewe and saide she sawe, albeit her eyes were shut close, that she could see nothing: at him she rayled, and angerly smote. After her fit, Hartlay came to comforte her, for hee pretended to bere a louinge affection towards her: and it was thought he had kissed her. Nowe they iudged in the house that whomsoeuer he kissed, on them he breathed the diuell. He often kissed Iohn for loue, (as he saide) he kissed the little wenches in iest, he promised Margaret Hardman a thrane[16] of kisses. He wrastled with one Iohan Smyth, a maide seruaunte in the house to kisse her, but he fayled of his purpose; whereupon Elinor in a fitt saide, if hee had kissed her, 3 men coulde not haue helde her. When he cam to comfort Margaret, she could not abide his companye. He demaunded of her, why? She said for that she thought he had bewitched her. He asked the reason why she thought so? Shee answered, for thou art euer in myne eyes, absent and present.

'But let us returne to the other 5, who were first possessed, of whome we will say very little, seeing we have much to say of Margaret Byrom: and it is sufficient to heare at large of one of them, and were too much to discourse fully of euery of them, considering the number.

'The 2. of February, in the night, Iohn Starchie had verie shorte fittes, and thick; and at the recouery of euery one, gaue 3 Knockes with his hand on the seeling, and said that he must haue 20 such fits. The next day he left knocking, and fell to washing his hands after euery short fitt, and when so euer he washed, he would have newe water; if it were the same wherewith he washed before (for he could tell) he refused it. About the 14 of Ianuarie, these 5 beinge in theire fits, one of them began to barke and howle (according to theire custom); after that 2. then 3, lastly they were all in, like a ring of 5 bells for order and tune, and so continued almost a quarter of an houre. After theer howling, they fell to a tumbling, and after that became speachlesse, sencelesse, and as dead.

'On the 1. of February, 4. of them fell a daucing; Elizabeth Hardman singing and playinge the minstrell, whome Anne Starchie (the 5 being well) followed, laughing at their toyes; but, after a while, she fel down as dead. All the time of their daucing, they wist not what they did. If others called to them, they heard them not, answered not, and yet talked one to another.

'The 1. or 2. weeke of Lent, Mistres Starchie required them all 5. to tell her how they were handled, that certaine knowledge might be had thereof to the preachers: they all answered that an angell like a doue was come from god, and that they must follow him to heauen, which way soeuer he would lead them, though it were through neuer so little a hole, for he toulde them he could drawe them through, and soe they ran under the beds. And Elizabeth Hardman was under a bedde making a hole, and beinge asked what she did, she said that she must goe through the wall, for she on the one side, and her lad on the other, would soone make a hole.

'About a fortnight or three weekes before their delivery, Elinor Holland and Elizabeth Hardman foretould how many fits they shoulde haue before they slept, and, tomorrowe, quoth Elinor Holland in the forenoon I must haue a fit of 3 howers long. When the tyme came shee bad them set the hower glasse: they set it behind her, out of her sight; her eyes also was closed. She was sencelesse and speachlesse, saue the noting of the time, which she truly noted, saying, there is a quarter, the halfe hower, and, as the glasse was runne out, she sayde, turne the glasse; and thus did she 3 tymes, or 3 howers. After comming to herselfe, she said Iesus, blesse mee, which all of them usually said at the end of their fites. In like manner did Elizabeth Hardman, for 2 howers, who beinge demaunded how she knewe this, answered that a white Doue told them so.

'About the 19 of March, the 4 youngest went on ther knees all morning until afternoone, and they fleed from all the familye and neighbours, into other chambers, calling them deuils with hornes, creeping under the bed, when they had the use of their feete; their tongues were taken from them.

'When Maister Hopwood, a Justice of peace, came of purpose to take their testimony against Edmund Hartlay to Lancaster Assises, and had them before him to that end, they were speachlesse, and that daye, he gott no answer of them. Being called out of one chamber into another, they sank down by the way speachlesse. When they spake, they complayned that Edmund would not suffer them to speake against him.

'At the same time Iane Ashton, a maid seruant in the house (the 7th possessed person, of the age of 30 yeares) began to bark and houle when she should haue gon to bear witnes against Edmund Hartlay, wheruopon one of them in her fit said, Ah Edmund, dost thou trouble her now when she shold testify against thee? This was the second time she was troubled. Almost a yeare before, it first tooke her in her throat, as if she had a pyn sticking there, whereupon she strayned herselfe so sore that she got up bloud, and for two dayes was very sicke.

'About the 21 of March. Ellinor Holland and Elizabeth Hardman for 3 dayes and 3 nights together could nether eate, nor drinke, nor speake to any except it were one to another, and to ther lads, saue that their lads gaue them leaue (as they said) the one to eate a toast and drink, the other a sower milk posset. And, notwithstanding that permission, thei said he was angry that thei had eaten, and told them that thei should not be quiet, until they had cast it up againe. So thei vomited, saying, take it to thee, here it is agayne, for thou gauest us lisence to eate it, and nowe thou art angry. And if thei went about to swallow a little drink, thei were so taken by the throat, that thei pict it up againe. The 3 night, about 8 a cloke, Elinor Holland being asked when she would or could slepe, answered that ther were 4 howers yet to come before she could slepe. About an houre and halfe of that time she tooke a distafe and spane both faster and finer than at any tym before. When she had done spinning, she said unto them, now shall I worke you all, and thenceforth was so extreamly handled, that two could scarcely rule and hold her. At length reuerting, she said I haue bene sleeping 3 daies and 3 nights, and now I faint with hunger.

'About a weeke before there deliverance some of the youngest used these kind of speaches: thou naughtie lad, thou makest us sicke, for thou knowest the preachers will come shortly.

'This generally was observed in the 5 youngest, that when they gaue themselves to any sporte, they had rest and were pleasaunt though the time was longe. Their parents report beyng at a playe in a neighbour gentleman's house many houres together, they were quyet all the tyme (Hartlay boested that he had kept them so longe quyet); but on the contrary, as soon as they went about any godly exercise, they were trobled. And thus much brifly touching those 6 at Cleworth, and the strange accedents which fell out there, as also how in all probabilitie it came to be vexed, in like sort, by the appoyntment of God and by the same mediant hand, the devil, and Hartlay the coniurer.

'The 10 of Ianuary (beyng the 4 day after her trouble began), as Margaret Byrom sate by the kitchyne fyre, shee was throwne towardes the fire, lyinge hard by the chimneye barres, as though shee should haue bene rosted. Thence she drewe her, and hauinge continued a longe tyme in the fitte, and recouerynge, about halfe an houer after, as shee satte in a Chaire, she was throwne headlonge under the boarde[17] but had no harme, and thus was she suddenly and violently cast sundrie times after.

'She, being desired to tel how her fits held her, said that she thought something rouled in her belly like a calfe, and laye euer on her left side, and when it rose up from her belly towardes her hart, she thought that the head and nose thereof had bene full of nayles, wherwith being pricked, she was compelled to scrike aloud with veri paine and feare. When her belly was swollen, it lift her up, and so bounded, that it would picke off the hand of him that held her downe, and sometyme the parti himself, that held her, farr off. When her belly slaked, there went out of hir mouth a could breath (that made her mouth very coulde), which caused her to barke and houle; then plumpte it down into her body like a colde longe whetstone, on her left side, when her belly was smale, wherewith shee so quaked, that her teeth chattered in her head, and, if she went to warme her, she was presently pickt backward.

'About the end of Ianuary, from M. Starchie's, she went home to Salford, a towne adioyning to Manchester, accompanyed with Hartlay and one other. The next morninge as Hartlay prayed ouer her in a fite, came one M. Palmer, a preacher of Manchester, who asked him what he was doinge: he answeared, Praying. Thou pray, thou cans't not pray, quoth he, what prayer cans't thou say? None, saide he, but the Lorde's prayer. Say it, quoth he; the which, as I remember, he coulde not say. He then, as a privat man, examined him, and, after, had him before two Iustices of peace; from whom he brought him by ther appointment, to Margaret Byrom, to heare what she could say against him; but, as soone as she saw him shee straightwaye became speachlesse, and was cast downe backwardes, and so did she the 2 tyme; and 5 tymes was dumbe when Hartlay came in her sight.

'This morning as she came to the fier, she sawe a great blacke dogge, with a monstrous taile, and a long chaine, Open mouth, comming apace towardes her, and, running by her left side, cast her on her face hard by the fier, houlding her tounge for halfe an hower, but leauinge at libertie her eyes and handes. A little after, a bigge blacke catt, staringe fearfully at her, came runinge by her left side, and threwe her backward, taking from her the use both of her eyes and handes, which with yesking[18] were euer losed. About halfe hower after that fit, it came like a bige mouse, and lept upon her left knee, cast her backward, took away her tongue, eyes, and sences, that she lay as dead, and when she came to any feeling, it put up her bellye as before. These visions and fites ordinarily troubled her for 6 weeks every day, on the daytime, as is said; and commonly everi night (as she thought) it sat on her head, very heavi, laying (as it seemed to her) 4 great fingers on her browes, that she was not able to open her eies. Often times she cried to her mother that she should sit from off her Head, asking who it was that held her soe straight, and, though she could not ster her head, hir kerchefe was pulled off her head commonly, she, notwithstanding, lying still as a stocke from 9 to 3 in the morning, about which time it departed. In departing, it somtimes gaue her a great thumpe, on the hinder parte of her head, that it was verye sore for 2 dayes after.

'Sixe times within those 6 weekes, the sperit would not suffer her to eate or drincke; it tooke awaye, also, her stomake. If she offered to drincke (at the earnest motion of others) it cast her and the drincke downe together. At other tymes shee did eate greedily, slossinge up her meate like a greedy dogge, or hogge, that her mother and her friendes were ashamed of her. Styll shee was hungrye and cryed for more, saying shee had nothing, though she spared no kinde of meate: all was fish that cam to nett. After abundance of meate her belly semed neuer the fuller, that she marueiled which waye it went.

'The 10 of februari, it pulled her, as she thought, in an hundred peeces. Ther came out of her mouth such a stincking smoke and breath, that shee could not endure it her selfe. Her voyce and crying were quite altered, and so continued till night. But her breath stank soe yll a day and a nyght after, that her neighboures could not endure to come neare her.

'Often, her sences were taken away, and she made as styfe as iron, and oft as dead, euen breathlesse: somtymes it made a loud noyse in her bellye, like that in the bellye of a great troting horse.

'The two next nights before the day of her examination concerning Hartlay, appeared the deuill in the likenesse of Hartlay, requesting her to take heed what she sayd, and to speake the truth, for the time was come: promising her siluer and gould. She answered (thinking it to be Hartlay) that the truth she had spoken already, and that she would not favour him, neither for siluer nor gold. The 2 night he departed, saying, doe as thou wilt. The day before Hartlay, his execution, was a sore day unto her, after which, euery day, she went to morning prayer, and was never troubled in the Church, saue the 1 day, whereon it took her about the middest of the sermon, in heauing up her shoulders, depriuing her of her sences. After the recouery of her sences, it tooke away the use of her leggs, and thus it molested her in the Church, to the admyration of the people, about an hower and halfe.

'At the assises at Lancaster, was Hartlay condemned and hanged. The making of his circle was chiefly his ouerthrowe, which he denyed; but breaking the rope, he, after, confessed it.

'After this time, she had more ease in the day, than she was wont; but, in the night, she lay stif and stark, quaking and trembling, till the day she came to Cleworth.

'It going thus with the 6 at Cleworth and the 7 at Salford, M. Starchie according to the counsel before given him, procured first one preacher, then an other to see them, but they knew not well what to say to their affliction. After hauing intelligence, by D. Dee his butler, of the like greuous affliction of Thomas Darling, his uncle's son, and recouery upon the aduice given by myself, he requested D. Dee his letter unto me (though unacquainted) and obteyned it, wherwith he sent his owne also, which preuayled not with me.

'Thereuppon, he procured other letters, whereof one was from a Iustice of peace therby, and sent the second time unto me. Then I, crauinge first the aduice of many of my brethren in the ministery, met togither at an exercise, yealded to M. Starchie's request, and, about 3 weekes after, went thither.

'On the 16 of March '96 M. George More, pastor of Cawlke in Darbyshire, and myself, came to Cleworth. Whither when we were come, M. Starchie tould us, that his sonn had bene well about a fortnight, and his daughter 4 dayes: and, surely, to see to, they were, at that instant, as well and free from any possession by Sathan, as any other; which we suspected to procede from the subtilty of the diuel, and so it proved.

'Shortly after our comming, as we sat at dinner, came in Margaret Hardman and hir sister, and Elinor Holland, one after another, like players to bid us welcom. For as much as nobody sent for me, said one of them, I am come of my owne accord. And, hauing thus spoken, shee was throwen backward on a forme; and so all 3 were strangely and greuosly tormented. Their faces (as I remember) were disfigured, their bodyes (I am sure) greatly swelled, and such a sensible stiring and rumbling within their bodyes, as to one's sight and feling they had some quick thing within each of them; and not only so, but such a violent mouing there was also in their inward parts, (especially in M. Hardman) as was easily hearde of us that were present. I remember, also, among the manifold pleasant speaches they used, one or moe spake iocondly concerning Edmund Hartlay's hanging, who was then newly executed; and it was to this effect. Do they think they could hang the diuel? I wis no. They might hang Edmund, but they coulde not hang the diuel. No maruel though the rope broke; for there were two, Edmund and the diuel. By that which I heard of his fits (whereof we haue partly heard before) I, for my part, then thought, and doe so still, that in the end, he who had so sweetly (by kisses, forsooth,) sent the diuel into so many, had, by the iust iudgment of god, the diuell sent into him.

'Then hearde we Iane Ashton howling, and perceiueing it was supernaturall, and hearing also, other strange things concerning her, especiallye that which was new fallen out of the swelling of her belly, whereof you shal heare: we affirmed that we thought that she, also, was possessed, which neither the family, nor the mayd, herself, mistrusted or feared; and ther was cause, for besides her first taking with the hoke and the wordes Hartlay used thereupon, and kisses before, with promis of mariage (which all were, perhaps, forgotten), she was taken with barking, as the rest were, when M. Hopwoode cam to examine them. Againe, the children said no lesse in their fits, for, when she cam in their sight, they would say, come and help us, for thou art one of our company. And though they neither knew nor speake to any other, yet Iane they knewe, and speake to her onlye in these wordes, thou wilt shortlye come in amongst us. And shee, herself, acknowledged that sometimes, as she carrien up hot Ianoks,[19] she thought that she could haue eaten up a Ianoke, and often did eat much by stealth, being passing hungry like Margaret Byrom and the children, who, likewise, were sometymes exceedinglye greedye of meate. This day, also, an hower or two before we came, her belly began to swell greatly, so that she compared her bellye to a woman's great with child. When it abated a little, a breath came up her throat, which caused yelling: after, it fell downe into hir body like a cold stone, as it did with Margaret Byrom. And, as soone as tydings came that we were come, presently her belly was fallne, and as litle as in former time, and so contiuued.

'Not long after our comming, all 7 being had in a chamber, the one of us applyed his speach according to the present occasion: and then, behold, all of them, even Iane Ashton, and M. Starchie's children were presently greuiously tormented. Yea, Satan, in Iohn Starchie exceeded for crueltye.

'And thus they contynued all that afternoone. 3 or 4 of them gaue themselves to Scoffing and Blasphemy, calling the holy Bible, being brought up, bible bable, bible bable; and thus they did aloud and often. All, or most of them ioyned together in a strange and supernatural loud whupping, that the house and ground did sound therwith againe; by reason whereof we were dryven (as I maye say) out of the chamber, and keept out for that daye.

'This euening we did use some words of exhortation, for the sanctefying of ourselues and the family, against the next daye's seruice: immediately before which, they all sent forth as they had before, a supernaturall loud whupping and yellyng, such as would have amased one to haue gone into the roome wher they were, but, as one of us opened his mouth, they were presentely silent, and so continued.

'The next morning, all 7 being had into a faire larg parlor, and laid ther on couches, M. More, M. Dickens (a preacher, and their pastor) and myself, with about 30 more, assembled together, spent that day in prayer, with fasting, and hearing the word; all the parties afflicted remayninge in their fits the said whole day. Towards the end wherof, they, all of the sudden, began to be most extreamly tormented, beting up and downe with their bodies being held by others, crying also (6 of them) aloud, in strang and supernaturall manner; and, after, they lay as dead, where with they which were present were so affected, that, leuing that good order, which all the day had ben kept, confusedly, euery one with voice and hands lifted up, cryed unto god for mercy in their behalf, and the lord was pleased to heare us, so as 6 of them were shortly delyuered, wherein we, with them, reioyced, and praised god for the same.

'The first that was dispossessed, was Margaret Byrom, then all the residu (saue Iane Ashton) one shortly after another, between 5 and 6 at night. She began to be vexed by Sathan about 4 or 5 in the morning, and neuer had rest until her deliuerance. All that day she heard only a humming and a sound, but knewe nothing what was said: she could thus heare, but not see. Sometime she sawe, and then marueyled what the company did ther, and how she got thither: howbeit, she heard euery idle word that the children possessed had spoken: she was more extreamly handled that daye than any before, though she had had many sore daies. She was euer full of payne, and it semed to her, as though her hart would haue burst: she strayned up much fleamy and bloudy matter. Lastly, she lay as dead for the space of half an houre, taking no breath. Then start she up most ioyfully, magnifying god, with such a cherefull countenance and voyce, that we all reioyced with her, but were somwhat amazed at hir suddayn lauding of god, with such freedome and earnestnes in speach and gesture.

'Iohn Starchie, the next, was so miserably rent, that abundance of blod gushed out, both at his nose and mouth. As the day before, so that day, he gnashed fearfully with his teeth; he, also, lay as dead about the like time, soe that some sayd to us, he seemeth to be dead. Then start he up likwise on the suddain, and prayed god in most cherful and comfortable manner. And so did the rest, who also maide sundry tymes greate shewe of vomyting, and nowe and then vomyted indeede, somthing like fleam, thick spettle. These 4, especially 3 of them used much light behauiour and vayn gestures; sundry, also, filthy scurrilous speaches, but whispering them, for the most part, among themselves, so that they were no let to that holy exercise we then had in hand. Somtimes, also, they spake blasphemy, calling the word preached--bible bable; he will neuer haue done prating; prittle prattle. Margaret Hardman whylest M. More was preaching, used these wordes. I must goe, I must away; I cannot tarrie, whither shall I goe? I am hot, I am too hot, I will not dye; iterating them all: which wordes did greatly incourage us.

When these 6 were deliuered, some desired to know how they assured themselues thereof, and they answered as followeth. Margaret Byrom said that she felt it come up from her belly towardes her brest, thence to her throat; when it left her throate it gaue her a sore lug, and all this whyle a darke myst dazeled her eyes. Then she felt it to go out of her mouth, but it left behind it a sore throat and a filthy smel, that a weke after, her meate was unsauary. It went out in the likenes of a crowe's head, round, (as to her semed) and sate in the corner of the parlor, with darknes about it a whyle. Then went it with such a flash of fyer out of the windowe, that all the Parlor semed on fyer, to her onlye.

'Iohn Starchie said it went from him like a man with a bulch[20] on his backe, very yll fauored, and, presently, he returned to haue re-entered, but he withstood hym strong in faith. The same, in effect, said Margaret Hardman. Anne Starchie said, he went like a foule ugly man, with a white beard, and a great bulch on his brest as big as a man's head, and straightway returned to have re-entered, but she faithfully resisted. Euen so said Elinor Holland, the white beard excepted.

'Elizabeth Hardman said, it was like an urchin,[21] and went through a very little hole (as she thought) out of the parler, but, out of hand, returned againe in a very foule shape, promising her gold, and whatsoeuer shee would desier, if she would giue him leaue to enter againe, but she yealded not; then he threatened to cast her into a pit, saying, somtime thou wilt go alone. He said also, he would cast her into the fyre, and break her neck, but she, resisting, he departed like an urchine.

'And thus the first dayes work was happily ended. But behold the slight[22] of the wyly serpent, for when we were all at rest, the sperits sett upon the 5 little children, like so many wolues the seely Lambes. The poore children being newly recouered, and suddenly inuaded, were so frighted, that they clasped fast about their middles those that lay with them, and hid their faces with their bed clothes. M. Dickens was called down, who comming, saw them resisting, and encouraged them to stand fast, neuer to yeald, but to pray and resist with faith, and shortly they were well, and fell a slepe.

'The next day we inquired how they were assalted. Margaret Byrom said it cam to her like an ugly black man with shoulders higher than his head, promysing her enough if she would consent, and that he would lye still; when she utterly denyed him, and prayed against him, he threatened to cast her into a pitt as she went home. But, when she resisted, he cast her to the ground, and departed twise as byg and foule as hee came, with two flashes of fyer, one before and another after him, making a noyse like a great wynd among trees. She was not assaulted at midnight with the 5, but, after supper, before she went to bed.

'Iohn Starchie said he came in the former likenes, making many large proffers, baggs of gould &c. But, when he saw he nothing preuayled with sugred wordes, he used terrible menaces, saying he wold breake his necke &c. Anne Starchie said he came in the former likenes.

'Margaret Hardman said he came in the same forme he went out; proffering golde, but she refusing, he threatned to breake her necke, cast her into a pyt and drowne her, and so departed.

'Elizabeth Hardman said he came like a beare with fyer in his mouth, wherwyth she was so terrifyed that she lept quite out of her bed, and rann from him, she wist not whither, but one of the company stayed her. Then he desyred her to open her mouth, as he opened his, shewing her two bagges, one of siluer, an other of gold, promising her 9 times as much: but not preuayling, he ran away as a beare that breakes loose from the stake. When she was layd downe and prayed, he came agayn like an ape, promising her golde &c, at her pleasure. Then he menaced to cast her out of the windowe and into the fyer, if euer she stood neare it, and so departed very foule and with an horrible scryke.

'Ellinor Holland said he came like a great beare, with open mouth, upon her, and presently turned it selfe into the similytude of a white dove; but she resisted, and it departed.

'Thus we have heard of the dispossession of 6. and what thinges fell out therein, as also presently after the same. It resteth that we conuert our speach to Iane Ashton, the 7. Sathan, upon the aforesaid day, towardes euening, put her to extreame payne, and continued the same longe very near 2 houres after their deliuerance, intising her to say he was gon, and to make shew of welfare, promising that he would not molest her at all. She, to be at ease, consented, and pretended, in wordes, to be as well as the rest; but we thought otherwise, as the signes of dispossession were wanting. After she had herein yelded to the diuell (which she concealed untill after her deliuerance) she was as free from any vexation by him, as the rest, notwithstanding that we prayed, or shee prayed: whereas before for 3 houres togither, her fyt beinge ended, the shortest prayer that might be, being used, she wold be in an other most greuous to beholde.

'All night shee was very well, the next morning also, untill we 3, (who were to be the leaders that day, also, in that holy action we had in hand, having shut our doore,) had cast doune our selues before the throne of grace, to craue the direction and assistance of god's spirit, in the worke we were to enter upon. This (I say) we had no soner don, but, behold, the chamber wher we were, yea, the whol house did ring of her againe, whereby we were not a little comforted, and incouraged, to enter the second tym into the field, for thereby we were assured that we were not deceiued, and that satan was certainly in her. After we cam downe into the parlor, whither many more resorted that day, than the other, to the number of about 50, we being all exercised as the day aforesaid. This morning she was sore tormented. She often seemed to vomyt up all, and it got up only a litle fleame; and when she hanged down her head to vomyt, often the sperit would fall to shake her, as an angri mastife, a litle cur dogge, so that, after her delivery, she was very hoarce and weake. About one of the clocke, she being very extreamly tormented, fel a weping, that teares trickled downe, and after, lay as dead: a litle space reuerting, she said, he is gon, and gaue thanks for her deliuerance. It went out like a great breath, ugly like a toad, round like a ball, and within an houer after, it returned like a foule big blacke man, but she resisted, and it departed. When we saw clearly that she was dispossessed, we asked her why she dissembled the other night? She told us that the said euening it was com up from her belly to her brest, thence to her throat, wher it held her as at her first taking, thence to her head. Then, she said, it desired her to tell us that he was gon, and promised her not to moue or hurt her, and that she should lack nothing. Why, said we, would you harken to the deuill? Because, (said she) I was very sore, and he promysed me ease, but he hath deceaued me. Quoth M. Dickens, beleue the deuil againe, beware of lying, he teacheth to lye, and you are taught for lying.

'This day and 2 or 3 following, the uncleane spirits returned euer and anone in visible formes upon all 7, throwing some of them violently downe before us all, depriuing others for a litle space of the use of som member of their bodies, as arme or legg; seking also both by goodly promises, of siluer, gold, veluit, (which they thought verily, they saw,) and such like, and fearful threats, their consents to re-enter; without which, it would seem satan cannot re-enter, though he can first enter. But from giving such consent, and yealding unto satan, therein god, in mercy, keept 6 of them: who, since that tyme, (praysed be God therfore) were neuer more nor lesse, they nor any of them molested by satan until this day. Neyther the 7 Iane Ashton untill a good space after, when she, leauing M. Starchie's house, went and dwelt in a place of ignorance and among papists, and became popish herselfe, as I have heard. For which opertunitie and advantage, the deuill watching; and noe doubt compasing, he then recouered her, and now dwelleth there: whose last estat with Katherine Wrights and Will. Somers, shall be worse than their first.'

The learned (!) divine, John Darrell, then follows on with the case of Will Somers, which is too long and prosy for reproduction.

CHAPTER VIII

James I. on Possession--The Vexation of Alexander Nyndge--'Wonderful News from Buckinghamshire'--Sale of a Devil.

In King James I.'s 'Demonologie,' Philomathes asks Epistemon two questions. 'The first is, whereby shall these possessed folks be discerned fra them that are troubled with a naturall Phrensie, or Magic? The next is, how can it be, that they can be remedied by the Papists Church, whom we, counting as hereticks, it should appeare that one Diuell should not cast out another, for then would his kingdome be diuided in itselfe, as Christ said?'

Epistemon answers: 'As to your first question, there are diuers symptoms, whereby that heauie trouble may be discerned from a naturall sicknesse, and specially three, omitting the diuers vaine signes that the Papists attributes unto it: such as the raging at holy water, their fleeing a backe from the Crosse, their not abiding the hearing of God named, and innumerable such like vaine things that were alike fashious and feckles to recite. But to come to these three symptoms then, whereof I spake; I account the one of them to be the incredible strength of the possessed creature, which will farre exceed the strength of sixe of the wightest and wodest of any other men that are not so troubled. The next is the boldning up so far of the patients breast and bellie, with such an unnaturall sturring and vehement agitation within them: and such an ironie hardnesse of his sinewes so stiflely bended out, that it were not possible to pricke out, as it were, the skinne of any other person so far.... The last is the speaking of sundrie languages, which the patient is known by them that were acquaint with him, neuer to have learned, and that with an uncouth and hollow voice: and all the time of his speaking, a greater motion being in his breast than in his mouth.... It is easie, then, to be understood, that the casting out of Diuelles is by the virtue of fasting and praier, and in calling of the name of God, suppose many imperfections be in the person that is the instrument, as Christ himselfe teacheth us, of the power that false Prophets shall have to cast out Divels. It is no wonder, then, these respects of this action being considered, that it may be possible to the Papistes, though erring in sundry pointes of Religion, to accomplish this, if they use the right forme prescribed by Christ herein.'

A far more acute case of possession is the following:

'A TRVE AND FEAREFULL VEXATION OF ONE ALEXANDER NYNDGE: BEING MOST HORRIBLY TORMENTED WITH THE DEUILL, FROM THE 20 DAY OF IANUARY TO THE 23 OF IULY. AT LYERINGSWELL IN SUFFOCKE: WITH HIS PRAYER AFTER HIS DELIUERANCE.

'Written by his owne brother Edwn Nyndge, Master of Arts, with the names of the Witnesses that were at his vexation. London, 1615.

'... You shall understand therefore that the first fit, and vexation wherewith this Alexander Nyndge was so fearefully perplexed, began about seaven of the clocke at night. His father, mother, and brethren, with the residue of the household being at that time in presence. And it was in this manner. His chest and body fell a swelling, his eies a staring, and his backe bending inwards to his belly, which did strike the beholders into a strange wonder, and admiration at the first, yet, one of his brothers, then also present, named Edward Nyndge, a Master of Arts, being boulder than others were of the company, certainly perswading himselfe that it was some euill spirit that so molested him, gaue him comfortable words of mercy from the holy Scriptures, and also charged the spirit by the death and passion of Jesus Christ, that it should declare the cause of the torment. At which, the countenance of the same Alexander turned more strange, and full of amazement and feare than it was before, and so returned to his former state againe.

'This Alexander Nyndge having his speech then at liberty, said unto the same Edward, Brother, he is marvellous afraid of you, therefore I pray you, stand by me.

'With which words the same Edward was the more bold, and said to Alexander. If thou dost earnestly repent thee of thy sins, and pray to God for the forgivenesse of the same (my life for thine) the Diuell cannot hurt thee. No, rather than he should, I will goe to hell with thee. Then the Spirit, (for a small time) racked the said Alexander in a far more cruell manner, for he did use such strange and idle kinds of gestures in laughing, dancing, and such like light behavioure, that he was suspected to be mad: sundry times he refused all kinds of meat, for a long space together, insomuch as he seemed to pine away. Sometimes he shaked as if he had had an ague. There was heard, also, a strange noise or flapping from within his body. Hee would gather himselfe on a rounde heape under his bed cloathes, and, being so gathered, he would bounse up a good height from the bed, and beat his head and other parts of his body against the ground and bedstead, in such earnest manner, that the beholders did feare that he would thereby haue spoiled himselfe, if they had not, by strong hand, restrained him, and yet thereby he receiued no hurt at all.

'In most of his fits he did swell in his body, and, in some of them, did so greatly exceed therein, as he seemed to be twice so big as his natural body. He was often seene to haue a certaine swelling or variable lumpe, to a great bignesse, swiftly running up and downe betweene the flesh and the skin.

'Then would they carry the same Alexander downe the Chamber, willing him to call upon God for grace, and earnestly to repent him, and to put his trust only in Christ Iesus. And, setting him in a chaire, desired his Father to send for all his neighbours, to helpe to pray for him. And, on a suddaine, he would be strangely handled, for, (sitting in a chaire when the fit came) he would be cast headlong upon the ground, or fall downe, drawing then his lips away, gnashing with his teeth, wallowing and foming, and the Spirit would uexe him monstrously, and transforme his body, and alter the same by many violences. Then the said Edward, his brother, with one Thomas Wakefield, would lay hands on Alexander, and set him in the Chaire againe, and there hold him. All that were in the house praying earnestly.

'And the said Edward charging the Spirit with these words, Thou fowle Fiend, I coniure thee, in the name of Iesus our Sauiour, the Sonne of Almighty God, that thou speake unto us.

'Whereat the Spirit transformed him very ugly against his Chest, swelling upwards to his throat, plucking his belly iust to his backe, and so ceased for a time.

'The partie tormented, being somewhat restored, uttered these words, Sirs, He will speake with me, I pray you let him not speake with mee. Whereupon all that were present did pray earnestly, at which the Spirit began to vexe him very grieuously, and swelled sore in his Chest, and, in a base sounding, and hollow voyce, uttered these words, I will, I will, I will. Then replyed the said Edward, and said, Thou shalt not, and I charge thee in the Name of Iesus Christ that thou speak unto us, and not unto him. Then the Spirit, in a hollow voyce said, Why didst thou tell them? Then the said Edward did charge the Spirit, (as aforesaid) to tell them the cause of his comming, and why he did torment his brother? To the which the Spirit answered, I come for his Soule. Then the said Edward said unto the Spirit, Wee have a warrant in the Holy Scriptures, that such as doe earnestly repent them of their sins, and turn unto God, with the only hope of Saluation, through the merits of Iesus Christ, thou mayest not have them, for Christ is his Redeemer. The Spirit uttered (in a base, hollow sounding voyce) these words, Christ, that was my Redeemer. Then Edward said, Christ that is his Redeemer, not thy Redeemer but my brother Alexander, his Redeemer.

'Then the Spirit said in his hollow voyce, I will haue his Soule and body too, and so began to torment and racke the same Alexander, and disfigure him more horribly than before, forcing him to such strange and fearefull skriking, as cannot bee uttered by man's power, and was of such strength, as, sometimes, foure or fiue men, though they had much aduantage against him by binding him to a chaire, yet could they not rule him. And in shewing that strength, he was not perceiued to pant or blow, no more than he had not strained his strength, nor strugled at all. Sometimes he would cry extreamly, so as teares would come from him in great abundance. Presently, afterwards, hee would laugh aloude and shrill, his mouth being shut close. And sometimes, he was heaued up from the ground by force inuisible, the said Edward Nyndge, Thomas Nyndge, Thomas Wakefield, Thomas Goldsmith, William Miles and William Nyndge, Iunior hanging upon the said Alexander, unto the middest of the house, and the said Edward putting his mouth unto the eare of the said disfigured body of his brother Alexander, said, Brother, continue in your faith, and if you goe to hell, wee will goe with you. Then the force did somewhat faile, and the hangers on drew him to the Chaire againe. Then one of his younger brothers, named William Nyndge said, Wee will Keepe him from thee, thou foule Spirit, in despite of thy Nose.

'Whereat the transformed body looked very terribly against the said William, and turned his most ugly looks unto his brother Edward, standing on the other side, uttering these hollowe sounding words, Will you, Sir, will you, Sir. To which the said Edward answered; Not I, Sir, but the merits of Iesus Christ will, we earnestly pray, keepe him from thee. Then all that were present, to the number of 20 persons, and more, fell downe and said the Lord's Prayer, with other sentences, every one seuerally, and one of the Company uttered worde ioyning God and the blessed virgin Mary together, whereat there came a voyce much like Alexander's voyce, saying twice, There bee other good Prayers. Whereunto the said Edward made answere, and said, Thou lyest, for there is no other Name under Heauen whereby wee may challenge Saluation but the onely name of Christ Iesus. And then the Spirit roares with a fearefull voice, and stretched out his necke long to the Fyre; and then the saide Edward desired Peter

Bencham, Curate of the Towne, to coniure and charge him in the Name of Iesus the Sonne of the Almightie, that the Spirit should declare vnto them from whence hee came? And what was his Name? To which the Spirit made answere in this mumbling manner, I would come out, I would come out. Then Edward charged him (as before) that he should declare his name. And the Spirit said Aubon, Aubon. They charged him then (as is aforesaid) to make knowne vnto them whence hee came; and the Spirit made answere in a hollow uoyce; From Ireland, From Ireland. Then they laide the fourth Chapter of Saint Matthew against him, where Christ said, It is written Thou shalt worship the Lord thy God and him onely shalt thou serue. Which sentence, as it was pronounced, the hollow voyce sounded. My Master, My Master, I am his Disciple, I am his Disciple. Then they answered, Thy Master we graunt he is, but thou lyest, thou art none of his Disciple. Thou art onely an instrument and scourge to punish the wicked, so farre as pleaseth him. And then they layd unto him the eight Chapter of S. Luke, whereas Christ himselfe did cast out Deuils. And the Spirit answered hollowly, Baw-wawe, baw-wawe. And within a little space after, the body of the saide Alexander being as monstrously transformed as it was before, much like the picture of the Deuill in a play, with an horrible roaring voyce, sounding Hellhound, was most horribly tormented. And they that were present, fell to prayer, desiring God earnestly to take away the foule Spirit from him. The said Edward then desired to haue the window opened, for I trust in God, (said hee) the fowle Spirit is wearie of our company. The windowes being opened accordingly, within two Minuts after, the tormented body returned to the true shape againe, the said Alexander leaping up, and holding up his hands, and saying Hee is gone, hee is gone, Lord, I thanke thee. Whereat all the people that were there present, fell downe on their knees with due reuerence, and yeelded unto God exceeding praise and thanksgiuing. This fit ended about eleven of the clocke the same night, and so they went to Supper with great ioy and gladnesse.'

He seems to have had two or three fits afterwards, but they were of a very mild type, and the last we hear of the afflicted Alexander is: 'After this, they took the said Alexander, and all of them ioyfully accompany him to his brother Thomas Nyndge, his house, where, after his coming thither, hee was not knowne to be perplexed with the like terrible vexations.'

One more example of this branch of the devil's work in Britain must suffice. We find it in

'WONDERFUL NEWS FROM BUCKINGHAMSHIRE, OR A PERFECT RELATION HOW A YOUNG MAID HATH BEEN FOR TWELVE YEARS AND UPWARDS POSSEST WITH THE DEVIL, AND CONTINUES SO TO THIS VERY DAY IN A LAMENTABLE CONDITION. LONDON, 1677.

'This unhappy Maid, whose strange Afflictions this sheet undertakes to give a true and impartial account of, lives at Great Gadsdon in the County of Bucks. She is descended of honest Parents of good repute, and by them carefully educated in the Principles of Christianity; nor was there a young maid of more lovely innocent Beauty, sweet Carriage, or virtuous Disposition; or one that might have expected fairer preferment in Marriage than she: So that as there is no room for the Censures of the uncharitable, so neither, any place for the Surmises of the incredulous, it being impossible she or any of her Relations could imagine any advantage to themselves by counterfeiting or pretending a Possession; which on the Contrary brings them onely trouble, loss, vexation, and inconveniences, and that for a dozen years together. The beginning of her affliction was thus.

'In the year 1664, there happened to be some difference between this maid's Father and a certain woman who had an evil name, but whether Causelessly or not, I shall not here determine, nor assert any dubious opinions of any kind; onely relate the principal Circumstances that have occurred, being matter of Fact, to which, as well myself, as scores of other people, were Eye and Ear-witnesses; and so leave every one to judge as they shall see cause, touching the Maid's being Possest or not, and the evil Instruments that are suspected to have been accessory thereunto, when they have duely weighed the whole Discourse. This is certain, soon after the before mentioned Difference, this maid being then about Sixteen or Seventeen years of age, was taken with strange Fits, and something would rise in her throat like two great bunches, about the bigness of an Egg; and a strange voice was frequently heard within her, speaking Blasphemous words, not fit here to be repeated: And if the Hearers and Bystanders did reply to such voice, by asking any Questions that pleased him, he would answer and discourse with them; and that with a voice as different from hers as any two voices, I verily believe, in the world; she having a cleer, smooth, pleasant voice, and that being very rough, guttural, and coming, as it were from the Abdomen, or hollow of her belly, but yet intelligible: and, though I am not ignorant of a certain sort of Jugglers of old, called in Latine Ventriloqui, yet as no such Art nor designe could be imagined in this innocent creature, so the things he declared (impossible, many times, for her to know) wipes off all suspitions of that kind: So that those about her generally concluded she was really and exactly possessed with the Devil, and took occasion to ask him, How he came there? to which the Evil Spirit or voice answered, Here are two of us, and that they were sent thither by two women. The voice further said,

That they were sent first to the Maid's Father; but when they came, they found him at Prayer, and returned to those two women, and told them, they could have no permission to enter into him; whereupon they sent them to his Daughter, and that such a night, as she sat by the fire, they entred into her. Now, the Family did remember that that very night, she had, as she declared, a sudden pain that seized her, and, ever since, had continued in a bad condition, and, after a little time, the Swellings and Voice happen'd as aforesaid.

'By which the whole Neighbourhood and Country round about, were so alarmed at the strangeness of it, that multitudes of people went to See her, and returned full of wonder and amazement, at what they had seen and heard: The report whereof coming to my ears, I did not at first believe it, but hearing it still confirmed, did, at last, go to see her myself, resolving to make my observations as warily and curiously as I could. There were, I believe, at that time, Forty or Fifty Spectators present, and in strict observation two or three hours. I was, for my own part, fully satisfied that it was a Possession, it being, as I conceive utterly impossible that those things should be acted by her or any other person living, either by the force of Nature or power of the most afflicting Distemper.

'Her Father, being of the same opinion, and willing to use all lawful means for his only Child's recovery, having read that passage of our Saviour's--That kinde comes not out but by Prayer and Fasting; he resolves to use that means, and to that purpose, desired some Ministers to keep a day with him on that occasion. Having sent for them, the Devil told him, He expected five men to come, but there should only four come. This the Girl could not know of herself; yet so it happened: for one, by an unexpected accident, was prevented from coming. These four desired the assistance of several Godly Ministers and Christians in the Neighbourhood, who accordingly, met, and kept several days in Fasting and Prayer; and, according to the best judgment that could be made, one of the evil Spirits then departed, as was supposed from some accidents I shall relate by and by. I, myself, was present several of these days; First she had two great bunches rose up in her throat, and then a voice followed, uttering abominable Blasphemies; upon which, a godly Minister present, and since deceased, being stirred up with great Zeal and Indignation, going to Prayer, did earnestly beg of God, that he would plague and torment Satan for such of his Blasphemies; upon which the Spirit made a most dreadful crying, and bemoaning his condition, and said, I will do so no more: To which the Minister replied, Satan, that shall not serve thy turn: and, continuing his Prayer to God as before, the Devil again cried and roared most hideously, to the great amazement of all the people present; and, from that time, it was observed that there was but one bunch rose up in her throat, from whence it was conjectured that one of the Spirits was departed. However, one continued his possession still, and, after they had done Prayer, and were about to refresh themselves, he shewed strange tricks before them, tossing her up and down, and when she was going, took away the use of her legs, on a sudden. When she sate in a great Wicker chair, he would cause the Chair to fall down backwards, almost to the ground, and then lift it up again. One of the company bid her read in the Bible; the Devil said aloud, She shall not read: It was answered, She shall read, Satan, for all thee, and read thy Condemnation too. Whereupon, he plaid more tricks by tossing her about, and drawing her face to one side, as if it had been placed to look over her shoulder, and drawn in a very deformed manner; but, at last she read part of the 20 Chapter of the Revelations, though not without much opposition.

'When she got upon the Horse to go home, it was a great while before she was able to get upon him, and was flung sometimes backwards, other whiles turn'd with her face to the horse's tail, and handled very sadly; yet, 'tis observed, that he hath not much power to hurt her: for she often declares, that, being now accustomed to his tricks, and consequently not so much affrighted, the temptations he injects into her minde, are far worse than all the mischiefs he does her body.

'At another time I was with them, when in the time of Prayer, he barked like a Dog, bellowed like a Bull, and roar'd after a wonderful frightful manner, and, on a sudden, would fling her up a great height, yet without hurte; whereupon, she, being placed in a low Chair, a man sate upon the Table side, endeavouring to hold down her head, and myself and another stood on each side, pressing down her shoulders; and though it could not be imagined so weakly a creature could naturally have half the strength of any one of us, yet she was tossed up, do what we could, and, at length, the Spirit in a desperate rage cries out, If I come out, I will kill you all. I will throw down the house, and kill you all. I answered, Satan, come out and try. He continued raging till they concluded Prayer, and then was pretty quiet.

'There have since hapned many things considerable; I was once in her company at a house, where I was wholly unacquainted, and for aught I know, so was she; the people of the house gave us drink, and I drinking to her, she rising to make a Curtsey, he took away the use of her legs, and said, she should not drink. But when he found we were resolved to force the Cup of Beer on her, he said, There is a Well in the yard, go and drown thyself; when none of us that were strangers, knew there was such a Well.

'He will often talk to some of the Family, or those that come to see her, and many times utter blasphemous filthy words to their great trouble: sometimes tell strange Stories to move laughter;

sometimes be sullen and not speak a great while together; sometimes, he jumps her up and down, and draws her Body into a multitude of strange postures, too tedious here to be related.'

The pamphlet winds up with some pious and moral reflections, of no interest to the reader.

There is no doubt but that people verily believed that the Devil lived among them in a material shape, and we have throughout England divers of his punchbowls, dykes, quoits, and even the prehistoric flint arrow-heads were known as 'Devil's arrows.' But a most singular instance of this belief is to be found in Blount's 'Law Dictionary' (ed. 1717), under the word Conventio, an agreement or covenant. It is Latin, and is an extract from the Court Rolls of the Manor of Hatfield, near the isle of Axholme, in Yorkshire. It is also mentioned in the 'Antiquarian Repertory,' vol. ii., p. 395. The following is a translation:

'At a court held at Hatfield on the Wednesday next after the Festival--In the 11th Year of Edward III. (1337).

'Robert de Roderham appeared against John de Ithow, for that he had not kept the agreement made between them, and therefore complains that on a certain day and year, at Thorne, there was an agreement between the aforesaid Robert and John, whereby the said John sold to the said Robert, the Devil, bound in a certain bond, for three pence farthing, and thereupon, the said Robert delivered to the said John, one farthing, as earnest money, by which the property of the said Devil rested in the person of the said Robert, to have livery of the said Devil, on the fourth day next following: at which day the said Robert came to the forenamed John, and asked delivery of the said Devil according to the agreement between them made. But the said John refused to deliver the said Devil, nor has he yet done it, etc., to the great damage of the said Robert to the amount of 60 shillings, and he has therefore brought his suit, etc.

'The said John came, etc., and did not deny the said agreement; and because it appeared to the Court that such a suit ought not to subsist among Christians, the aforesaid parties are therefore adjourned to the infernal regions, there to hear their judgment, and both parties were amerced, etc., by William De Scargell, Seneschal.'

CHAPTER IX

The Witch of Endor--The 'Mulier Malefica' of Berkeley--Northern Witches.

Of all the extraordinary popular delusions that have existed, the wave of belief in witchcraft which flowed over this land in the sixteenth and seventeenth centuries is one of the most remarkable. The belief that some people have the power of exercising supernatural control over their fellow-creatures is not confined to any land, and dates from remote antiquity. But it is with the witches of Britain, and those of the Britons who emigrated from their country, that it is my province to deal.

The earliest English pictorial representation of a witch that I know of is in the Harleian MSS., 1776 (94, b), where the witch of Endor is represented as showing the ghost of Samuel to Saul. But she was a Pythoness, and did not at all come up to our idea of a witch. Nor can we exactly class in the same category the 'Mulier Malefica' of Berkeley, who is supposed to have been exhumed by the Devil about A.D. 852. She has been immortalized by William of Malmesbury, who says he had the story from an eye-witness, by Matthew of Westminster, by Schedel in the Nuremberg Chronicle, from whom this illustration is taken, and a short account of her is given by Olaus Magnus in his 'Historia de Gentibus Septentrionalibus' (lib. iii., c. 21), when he treats of the punishment of witches. Berkeley, however, in his hands becomes Bethelia. Southey also wrote about her.

THE OLD WOMAN OF BERKELEY.

A BALLAD, SHEWING HOW AN OLD WOMAN RODE DOUBLE, AND WHO RODE BEFORE HER.

William of Malmesbury thus gives the story: '(A.D. 1065) There resided at Berkeley, a woman addicted to Witchcraft, as it afterwards appeared, and skilled in ancient augury: she was excessively gluttonous, perfectly lascivious, and setting no bounds to her debaucheries, as she was not old, though fast declining in life. On a certain day, as she was regaling, a jackdaw, which was a very great favourite, chattered a little more loudly than usual. On hearing which, the woman's knife fell from her hand, her countenance grew pale, and, deeply groaning, "This day," said she, "my plough has completed its last furrow; to-day, I shall hear of, and suffer, some dreadful calamity."

'While yet speaking, the messenger of her misfortunes arrived: and, being asked why he approached with so distressed an air, "I bring news," said he, "of the death of your son, and of the whole family, by a sudden accident." At this intelligence the woman, sorely afflicted, immediately took to her bed, and, perceiving the disorder rapidly approaching her vitals, she summoned her surviving children, a monk and a nun, by hasty letters; and, when they arrived, with faltering voice, addressed them thus: "Formerly, my children, I constantly administered to my wretched circumstances by demoniacal arts: I have been the sink of every vice, the teacher of every allurement: yet, while practising these crimes, I was accustomed to soothe my hapless soul with the hope of your piety. Despairing of myself, I rested my expectations on you: I advanced you as my defenders against evil spirits, my safeguards against my strongest foes. Now, since I have approached the end of my life, and shall have those eager to punish, who lured me to sin, I entreat you, by your mother's breast, if you have any regard, any affection, at least to endeavour to alleviate my torments; and, although you cannot revoke the sentence already passed upon my soul, yet you may, perhaps, rescue my body by these means.

"'Sew up my Corpse in the skin of a stag; lay it on its back in a stone Coffin; fasten down the lid with lead and iron; on this lay a stone, bound round with three iron chains of enormous weight; let there be psalms sung for fifty nights, and masses said for an equal number of days, to allay the ferocious attacks of my adversaries. If I lie thus secure for three nights; on the fourth day, bury your mother in the ground; although, I fear, lest the earth, which has been so often burdened with my crimes, should refuse to receive and cherish me in her bosom."

'They did their utmost to comply with her injunctions: but, alas! vain were pious tears, vows, or entreaties; so great was the woman's guilt, so great the devil's violence. For, on the two first nights, while the choir of priests was singing psalms around the body, the devils, one by one, with the utmost ease bursting open the door of the Church, though closed with an immense bolt, broke asunder the two outer chains: the middle one, being more laboriously wrought, remained entire. On the third night, about cock-crow, the whole monastery seemed to be overthrown from its very foundation, by the clamour of the approaching enemy.

'One devil, more terrible in appearance than the rest, and of loftier stature, broke the gates to shivers by the violence of his attack. The priests grew motionless with fear, their hair stood on end, and they became speechless. He proceeded, as it appeared, with haughty steps, towards the Coffin; and, calling on the woman by name, commanded her to rise. She, replying that she could not, on account of the chains: "You shall be loosed," said he, "and to your cost;" and, directly, he broke the chain, which had mocked the ferocity of the others, with as little exertion as though it had been made of flax. He also beat down the cover of the Coffin with his foot; and, taking her by the hand, before them all, he dragged her out of the church.

'At the doors appeared a black horse, proudly neighing, with iron hooks projecting over his whole back; on which the wretched creature was placed, and, immediately, with the whole party vanished from the eyes of the beholders: her pitiable cries for assistance being heard for nearly the space of four miles.'

The Northern witches came nearer to our modern ones, and seem, if we can believe Olaus Magnus, to have been very powerful.[23]

'OF WOMAN WITCHES.

'I shall shew you by a few Examples, how cunning some Women were formerly amongst the Northern people in Magical Art. Hugbert, Daughter to Vagnostus the Giant, was wont to change her stature at pleasure; sometimes she was very great; sometimes less; sometimes exceeding small; sometimes wither'd faced; sometimes beautiful: sometimes she was as tall as the sky; sometimes so short as a Pygmy; and she was supposed to be able to pull down the Heavens, to lift up the Earth; to harden Fountains, to melt Mountains; to lift ships into the Ayr; to pull down the Gods; to extinguish the Stars, and to make Hell a light place.

'When Hadingus the King was at Supper, another Woman of the same Art, who carried pipes, was seen to lift up her head above the ground before the fire; and stretching out her bosome, she seemed to ask in what part of the World so new green Reeds grew; the King, that desired to know the matter, was carried by her under ground, wrapt in his own Cloak: and, having shewn unto him the Monsters of the Infernal Regions, she restored him back to the Earth again.

'Cvaca, a Woman of Norway, that desired to know the future fortune of her Son Rollerus, provided Water-gruel, and into this, she dropt the venemous moysture of three Land-Snakes, that were hung up above by a small Twig. But Ericus, son in law to Cvaca took to himself the Dish that was provided for her son Rollerus, and he, being refreshed with this happy meat, by the internal operation of it, arrived to the highest pitch of man's wisdome. For the force of this meat bred in him the Knowledge of all Sciences beyond belief; so that he could understand the meaning of the cryes of Birds and Wild Beasts. Besides, he was so eloquent and curious in his speech, that whatsoever he pleased to discourse of, he would constantly illustrate it with pleasant Proverbs. By his counsel King Frotho overcame the Army of the mighty Huns, that was assisted by 170 Kings. And, at length, Gestilblindus, King of the Goths, made this Ericus heir to himself, and to the Kingdome of Sweden; and that about the time of Christ's Nativity.

'But King Frotho, being lunged at by a Witch that turned into an Oxe, was slain by her upon a certain Sea-coast. Guthruna suddenly blinded the forces of King Larmericus, and made them fight one against another. An earthen pot useth to be the common Instrument of Witches, wherein they boyl their Myces, Herbs, Worms, and Entrals, and by that Witchery meat, they allure idle persons to them, and make ships, horses, and horsemen, to be as swift as a boyling pot.'

'OF THE CONJURERS AND WITCHES IN FINLAND.

'Also, I shall show very briefly what force Conjurers and Witches have in constraining the elements, enchanted by them or others, that they may exceed or fall short of their Natural Order: premising this, that the extream land of the North Finland and Lapland, was so taught Witchcraft formerly in the Heathenish times, as if they had learned this Cursed Art from Zoroastes the Persian; though other inhabitants by the Sea Coasts are reported to be bewitched with the same madness; and in this, and other such-like mischief, they commonly agree. The Finlanders[24] were wont formerly, amongst their other Errors of Gentil issue, to sell Winds to Merchants that were stopt on their Coasts by contrary weather; and, when they had their price, they knit three Magical Knots, not like to the Laws of Cassius, bound up with a Thong, and they gave them unto the Merchants; observing that rule, that when they unloosed the first, they should have a good gale of wind; when the second, a stronger wind; but, when they untied the third, they should have such cruel Tempests, that they should not be able to look out of the Forecastle, to avoid the Rocks, nor move a foot to pull down the Sails, nor stand at the helm to govern the ship: and they made an unhappy trial of the truth of it, who denied that there was any such power in those knots.'[25]

OF THE MAGICAL INSTRUMENTS OF BOTHNIA.

'They that desire to know the state of their Frends or Foes, at a very great distance from them, five hundred be it, or a thousand miles off, they enquire of a Laplander or Finlander, who is skilled in this matter, giving him a gift (namely, some Linnen Garment, or Girdle;) Whereupon he goes into his Conclave, content with one companion, or his wife, and he beats upon a frog of brass, or Serpent, with a hammer upon an anvil, so many strokes as are prescribed; and, by mumbling of charms he turns it up and down; and, presently falling, he is ravished into an extasie, and he lies a short time, as if he were dead. In the meanwhile he is safely guarded by his fore said Companion, lest any Living Creature, Gnat or Fly, or other Animal might touch him; for by the power of his Charms, his spirit, by the misleading of Devils, brings from far some token (namely, a Ring or a Knife), for a testimony of his Embassie or Commission fulfilled. And, presently, rising up, he declares the same signs to him that hired him, with the rest of the Circumstances.'

This illustration is from 'The History of Witches and Wizards' (1700 ?), and shows a Northern witch raising a storm by means of a pump, whilst a Laplander in his kayack rides in safety.

CHAPTER X

The Legal Witch--James I. on Witches--Reginald Scot on Witches--Addison on Witches.

The legal witch, as defined by our statute law (1 James I., cap. 12), is as follows:
'One that shall use, practise, or exercise any invocation, or conjuration of any evill or wicked spirit; or consult, covenant with, entertaine, or employ, feede, or reward any evill or wicked spirit, to or for any intent or purpose; or take up any dead man, woman or child, out of his, her, or their grave, or any other place, where the dead body resteth, or the skin, bone, or other part of any dead person, to be employed or used in any manner of Witchcraft, Sorcery, Charme, or Enchantment; or shall use, practise, or exercise any Witchcraft, Enchantment, Charme or Sorcery, whereby any person shall be killed, destroyed, wasted, consumed, pined, or lamed in his or her body, or any part thereof. Such offenders, duly and lawfully convicted and attainted, shall suffer death.
'If any person shall take upon him by Witchcraft, Inchantment, Charme or Sorcery, to tell or declare in what place any treasure of Gold or Silver, should or might be found, or had in the Earth, or other secret places, or where Goods, or things lost, or stolen, should be found, or become: Or to the intent to provoke any person to unlawfull love, or whereby any Cattell or Goods of any person shall be destroyed, wasted or impaired, or to destroy or hurt any person in his, or her body, though the same be not effected, &c, a yeares Imprisonment and Pillory, &c, and the second conviction, Death.'
Here, then, we have a clear definition of what a witch is, and as it does not state anything as to sex, we may imagine that it includes both male and female, both wizards and witches. But the softer sex undoubtedly predominated in the commission of this crime, wizards being very seldom brought to justice. And King James I.[26] gives us the reason:
'Philomathes. But before yee goe further, permit me, I pray you, to interrupt you one worde, which yee haue put mee in memory of, by speaking of Women. What can be the cause that there are twentie women giuen to that craft, where there is one man?
'Epistemon. The reason is easie, for, as that sexe is frailer than man is, so is it easier to be intrapped in these grosse snares of the Diuell, as was ouer well proued to be true, by the Serpent's deceiuing of Eua at the beginning, which makes him the homelier with that sex sensine.'
Reginald Scot, than whom there can be no better English authority, tells us[27] 'who they be that are called witches.'
'The sort of such as are said to bee witches, are women which be commonly old, lame, bleare-eied, pale, fowle, and full of wrinkles; poore, sullen, superstitious, and papists; or such as knowe no religion: in whose drousie minds the diuell hath gotten a fine seat; so as, what mischeefe, mischance, calamitie, or slaughter is brought to passe, they are easily persuaded the same is doone by themselues; imprinting in their minds an earnest and constant imagination thereof. They are leane and deformed, shewing melancholie in their faces, to the horror of all that see them. They are doting, scolds, mad, diuelish; and not much differing from them that are thought to be possessed with spirits: so firme and stedfast in their opinions, as whosoeuer shall onelie haue respect to the constancie of their words uttered, would easilie belieue they were true indeed.
'These miserable wretches are so odious unto all their neighbours, and so feared, as few dare offend them, or denie them anie thing they aske; whereby they take upon them; yea, and sometimes thinke, that they can doo such things as are beyond the abilitie of humane nature. These go from house to house, and from doore to doore for a pot full of milke, yest, drinke, pottage, or some such releefe; without the which they could hardlie liue: neither obtaining for their seruice and paines, nor by their art, nor yet at the diuel's hands (with whome they are said to make a perfect and visible bargaine) either beautie, monie, promotion, welth, worship, pleasure, honor, knowledge, learning, or anie other benefit whatsoeuer.
'It falleth out many times, that neither their necessities, nor their expectation is answered or serued, in those places where they beg or borrowe; but rather their lewdnesse is by their neighbors reproued. And further, in tract of time, the witch waxeth odious and tedious to her neighbors; and they, againe, are despised and despited of hir; so as sometimes she cursseth one, and sometimes another; and that from the maister of the house, his wife, children, cattell &c to the little pig that lieth in the stie.

Thus, in processe of time they have all displeased hir, and she hath wished euill lucke unto them all: perhaps with curses and imprecations made in forme. Doubtlesse (at length) some of hir neighbors die or fall sicke; or some of their children are visited with diseases that vex them strangelie; as apoplexies, epilepsies, conuulsions, hot feuers, wormes &c. Which by ignorant parents are supposed to be the vengeance of witches. Yea, and their opinions and conceits are confirmed and maintained by unskilful physicians: according to the common saieing; Inscitiæ pallium maleficio et incantatio. Witchcraft and inchantment is the cloke of ignorance: whereas, indeed, euill humors, and not strange words, witches or spirits are the Causes of such diseases. Also some of their cattell perish, either by disease or mischance. Then they, upon whom such aduersities fall, weighing the same that goeth upon this woman (hir words, displeasure and cursses meeting so iustlie with their misfortune) do not onelie conceiue, but, also, are resolued, that all their mishaps are brought to passe by hir onelie meanes.

'The witch, on the other side, expecting her neighbors' mischances, and seeing things sometimes come to passe according to her wishes, cursses and incantations (for Bodin himselfe confesseth that not aboue two in a hundred of their witchings or wishings take effect) being called before a Iustice, by due examination of the circumstances, is driuen to see hir imprecations and desires, and hir neighbors' harmes and losses, to concurre, and, as it were, to take effect; and so confesseth that she (as a goddes) hath brought such things to passe. Wherein, not onelie she, but the accuser, and also the Iustice, are fowlie deceiued and abused; as being, thorough hir confession and other circumstances, persuaded (to the iniurie of God's glory) that she hath done, or can doo that which is proper onelie to God himselfe.'

This is a good definition of a witch, and was published in 1584 when the witch mania was becoming a cult. Let us hear what Addison[28] writes of it in 1711, when it was decidedly on the wane:

'... It is with this Temper of Mind that I consider the Subject of Witchcraft. When I hear the Relations that are made from all parts of the World, not only from Norway and Lapland, from the East and West Indies, but from every particular Nation in Europe, I cannot forbear thinking that there is such an Intercourse and Commerce with Evil Spirits, as that which we express by the name of Witchcraft. But, when I consider that the ignorant and credulous Parts of the World abound most in these Relations, and that the Persons among us who are supposed to engage in such an Infernal Commerce, are People of a weak Understanding and crazed Imagination, and, at the same time, reflect on the many Impostures and Delusions of this Nature that have been detected in all Ages, I endeavour to suspend my Belief, till I have more certain Accounts than any which have yet come to my Knowledge. In short, when I consider the Question, Whether there are such Persons in the World as those we call Witches? My Mind is divided between the two opposite Opinions, or rather (to speak my Thoughts freely) I believe, in general, that there is, and has been such a thing as Witchcraft; but, at the same time, can give no Credit to any Particular Instance of it.

'I am engaged in this speculation, by some Occurrences that I met with Yesterday, which I shall give my Reader an Account of at large. As I was walking with my Friend Sir Roger, by the side of one of his Woods, an old Woman applied herself to me for my Charity. Her Dress and Figure put me in mind of a Description in Ottway, which I could not forbear repeating on this Occasion.

> "'In a close Lane as I pursu'd my Journey,
> I spy'd a wrinkled Hag, with Age grown double,
> Picking dry Sticks, and mumbling to her self.
> Her Eyes with Scalding Rheum were gall'd and red,
> Cold Palsy shook her Head; her Hands seem'd wither'd;
> And on her crooked Shoulders had she wrap'd
> The tatter'd Remnants of an old Striped Hanging,
> Which serv'd to keep her Carcass from the Cold:
> So there was nothing of a-piece about her.
> Her lower Weeds were all o'er coarsly patch'd
> With diff'rent colour'd Rags, black, white, red, yellow,
> And seem'd to speak Variety of Wretchedness."

'The Knight told me, upon hearing the Description, that this very old Woman had the Reputation of a Witch all over the Country, that her Lips were observed to be always in Motion, and that there was not a Switch about her House, which her Neighbours did not believe had carried her several hundreds of Miles. If she chanced to stumble, they always found Sticks or Straws that lay in the Figure of a Cross before her. If she made any Mistake at Church, and cryed Amen in a wrong place, they never failed to conclude that she was saying her Prayers backwards. There was not a Maid in the Parish that would take a Pinn of her, though she should offer a Bag of Mony with it. She goes by the Name of Moll White, and has made the Country ring with several imaginary Exploits that are palmed upon her. If the Dairy Maid does not make the Butter come so soon as she would have it, Moll White is at the bottom of the Churne.

If a Horse sweats in the Stable, Moll White has been upon his Back. If a Hare makes an unexpected Escape from the Hounds, the Huntsman curses Moll White. Nay, (says Sir Roger) I have known the Master of the Pack, upon such an Occasion, send one of his Servants to see if Moll White had been out that Morning.

'This Account raised my Curiosity so far, that I beg'd my Friend, Sir Roger, to go with me into her Hovel, that stood by it self under the Side of the Wood. Upon our first entering, Sir Roger winked to me, and pointed to something that stood behind the Door, which, upon looking that way, I found to be an old Broom-staff. At the same time he whispered me in the Ear, to take notice of a Tabby-Cat that sate in the Chimney-Corner, which, as the Knight told me, lay under as bad a Report as Moll White herself; for, besides that Moll is said often to accompany her in the same Shape, the Cat is reported to have spoken twice or thrice in her Life, and to have played several Pranks above the Capacity of an ordinary Cat.

'I was secretly concerned to see Human Nature in so much Wretchedness and Disgrace, but, at the same time, could not forbear smiling, to hear Sir Roger, who is a little puzzled about the old Woman, advising her, as a Justice of the Peace, to avoid all Communication with the Devil, and never to hurt any of her Neighbours' Cattle. We concluded our Visit with a Bounty, which was very acceptable.

'In our Return Home, he told me that old Moll had, often, been brought before him for making Children spit Pins, and giving Maids the Night-Mare; and that the Country People would be tossing her into a Pond, and trying Experiments with her every Day, if it was not for him and his Chaplain.

'I have since found, upon Enquiry, that Sir Roger was several times staggered with the Reports that had been brought him concerning this old Woman, and would, frequently, have bound her over to the County Sessions, had not his Chaplain, with much ado, persuaded him to the contrary.

'I have been the more particular in this Account, because I hear there is scarce a Village in England that has not a Moll White in it. When an old Woman begins to doat, and grow chargeable to a Parish, she is generally turned into a Witch, and fills the whole Country with extravagant Fancies, imaginary Distempers, and terrifying Dreams. In the mean time, the poor Wretch that is the innocent Occasion of so many Evils, begins to be frighted at herself, and, sometimes, confesses secret Commerces and Familiarities that her Imagination forms in a delirious old Age. This, frequently, cuts off Charity from the greatest Objects of Compassion, and inspires People with a Malevolence towards those poor decrepid Parts of our Species, in whom Human Nature is defaced by Infirmity and Dotage.'

CHAPTER XI

How a Witch was made--Her Compact with the Devil--Hell Broth--Homage and Feasting--The Witches' Sabbat.

But how did a woman become a witch, and attain to the full possession of her wicked powers? There is no doubt but that she must have been a mauvais sujet to start with, or else the Devil would not have thought of meeting her, and introducing himself to her. According to the witches' confessions, of which we shall have many, they generally first meet the Devil by chance, and their differing testimonies affirm that he was somewhat protean in shape, appearing to one as a great black man, to another in the form of some animal. Others, again, were regularly introduced to him by some perfected witch at one of their meetings, for it was part of their duty to beat up recruits for his Satanic majesty.

Their agreement with the Devil is forcibly described by Reginald Scot,[29] who quotes as his authorities such crushing names as the 'Malleus Maleficarum,' Bodin, Nider, Danæus, Psellus, Erastus, Hemingius, Cumanus, Aquinas, Bartholomæus Spineus, etc., so that doubtless he is correct.

'The order of their bargaine or profession is double; the one solemne and publike; the other secret and priuate. That which is solemne or publike, is where witches come togither at certaine assemblies, at the times prefixed, and doo not onelie see the diuell in visible forme; but confer and talke familiarlie with him. In which conference the diuell exhorteth them to obserue their fidelitie unto him promising them long life and prosperitie. Then the witches assembled, commend a new disciple (whom they call a nouice) unto him; and, if the diuell findeth that young witch apt and forward in renunciation of the christian faith, in despising anie of the seuen sacraments, in treading upon Crosses, in spitting at the time of the elevation, in breaking their fast on fasting daies, and fasting on sundaies, then the diuell giveth foorth his hand, and the nouice ioining hand in hand with him, promiseth to obserue and keepe all the diuel's commandements.

'This done the diuell beginneth to be more bold with hir, telling hir plainelie, that all this will not serue his turne; and therefore requireth homage at hir hands: yea, he also telleth hir, that she must grant him both hir bodie and soule to be tormented in everlasting fire, which she yeeldeth unto. Then he chargeth her, to procure as many men, women and children also, as she can, to enter into this societie. Then he teacheth them to make ointments of the bowels and members of children, whereby they ride in the aire, and accomplish all their desires. So as, if there be anie children unbaptised, or not garded with the signe of the crosse, or orisons; then the witches may and doo catch them from their mothers sides in the night, or out of their cradles, or otherwise kill them with their ceremonies; and, after buriall, steale them out of their graves, and seeth them in a caldron, untill their flesh be made potable. Of the thickest whereof they make ointments, whereby they ride in the aire; but the thinner potion they put into flaggons, whereof whosoever drinketh, observing certeine ceremonies, immediatlie becommeth a maister, or rather, a mistresse in that practise and facultie.'

But there were other hell broths used by witches, as we may see by the accompanying illustration from Molitor's 'Die Hexen' (1489?), in which a cock and serpent form part of the ingredients of the broth, which is being brewed during a violent hailstorm. In 'The Witch: a Tragi-comedie,' by Thomas Middleton, we have good notices of the component parts of these mixtures:

'HECCAT. Goe feed the vessell for the second houre.
STADLIN. Where be the magical herbes?
HEC. They're downe his throate.
His mouth cramb'd full; his eares, and nosthrills stufft.
I thrust in Eleoselinum--lately
Aconitum, frondes populus, and soote,
Then Sium, Acharum, Volgaro too,
Dentaphillon, the blood of a flitter-mouse,[30]
Solanum somnificum, et oleum.'

We all know the Witches scene in 'Macbeth,' but few are probably aware to what extent

Shakespeare was indebted to this play of Middleton's for its telling effect and language.

> 'HECCAT. Give me some lizard's braine: quickly, Firestone.
> Where's grannam Stadlin, and all the rest o' th' sisters?
> FIRESTONE. All at hand, forsooth.
> HEC. Give me Marmaritin; some Bear-Breech; when?
> FIRE. Heer's Bear-breech, and lizard's braine, forsooth.
> HEC. Into the vessell;
> And fetch three ounces of the red-haired girle
> I kill'd last midnight.
> FIRE. Whereabouts, sweet Mother?
> HEC. Hip; hip or flanck. Where is the Acopus?
> FIRE. You shall have Acopus, forsooth.
> HEC. Stir, stir about; whilst I begin to charme.

A CHARME SONG, ABOUT A VESSEL.

> Black spiritts, and white; Red spiritts and gray;
> Mingle, mingle, mingle, you that mingle may.
>   Titty, Tiffin, keepe it stiff in;
>   Fire-drake, Puckey, make it luckey;
>   Liard, Robin, you must bob in.
> Round, around, around, about, about.
> All ill come running in, all good keepe out!

> 1 WITCH. Heer's the blood of a bat.
> HEC. Put in that; oh put in that.
> 2 WITCH. Heer's libbard's bane.
> HEC. Put in againe.
> 1 WITCH. The juice of toad; the oile of adder.
> 2 WITCH. Those will make the yonker madder.
> HEC. Put in; there's all, and rid the stench.
> FIRE. Nay, heer's three ounces of the red-haired wench.
> ALL. Round, around, around, about, about.
> All ill come running in, all good keepe out!
> HEC. So, soe, enough: into the vessell with it.
> There, 't hath the true perfection: I am so light
> At any mischief; there's no villany
> But is a tune methinkes.
> FIRE. A Tune! 'tis to the tune of dampnation then, I warrant
> You that that song hath a villainous burthen.
> HEC. Come my sweet sisters; let the aire strike our tune,
> Whilst we show reverence to yond peeping moone.

> Here they daunce. The Witches daunce and Ex{t}.'

After this introduction to and instruction from the Devil, the novice has to do homage to her master. Still quoting Reginald Scot:

'Sometimes their homage, with their oth and bargaine is receiued for a certeine number of yeares; sometimes for euer. Sometimes it consisteth in the deniall of the whole faith, sometimes in part. The first is, when the soule is absolutelie yeelded to the Diuell and hell fier; the other is, when they have but bargained to obserue certeine ceremonies and statutes of the Church; as to conceale faults at shrift, to fast on sundaies, &c. And this is doone, either by oth, protestation of words, or by obligation in writing, sometimes sealed with wax, sometimes signed with bloud, sometimes by kissing the Diuell's bare buttocks; as did a Doctor called Edlin, who (as Bodin saith) was burned for witchcraft.

'You must also understand, that after they have delicatlie banketted with the Diuell and the ladie of the fairies; and have eaten up a fat oxe, and emptied a butt of malmesie, and a binne of bread, at some nobleman's house, in the dead of night, nothing is missed of all this in the morning. For the ladie Sibylla, Minerua, or Diana, with a golden rod striketh the vessell and the binne, and they are fullie replenished againe. Yea, she causeth the bullock's bones to be brought and laid togither upon the hide, and lappeth the foure ends thereof togither, laieing her golden rod thereon; and then riseth up the bullocke againe, in his former estate and condition: and yet, at their returne home, they are like to starve for hunger; as Spineus saith. And this must be an infallible rule, that euerie fortnight, or at the least, euerie moneth, each witch must kill one child, at the least, for hir part.

***

'And this is to be noted, that the inquisitors affirme, that during the whole time of the witch's excourse, the Diuell occupieth the roome and place of the witch, in so perfect a similitude, as hir husband in his bed, neither by feeling, speech, nor countenance can discerne hir from his wife. Yea, the wife departeth out of hir husbands armes insensiblie, and leaueth the Diuell in her roome visiblie.'

The novice is now a full-fledged witch, and according to the best authorities may, and must, commit certain crimes, of which the following are some:

'They denie God, and all religion.

'They cursse, blaspheme, and provoke God with all despite.

'They give their faith to the diuell, and they worship and offer sacrifice to him.

'They doo solemnelie vow and promise all their progenie unto the diuell.

'They sacrifice their owne children to the diuell before baptisme, holding them up in the aire unto him, and then thrust a needle into their braines.

'They burne their children when they have sacrificed them.

'They sweare to the diuell to bring as manie into that societie, as they can.

'They sweare by the name of the diuell.

'They boile infants (after they have murthered them unbaptized) until their flesh be made potable.

'They eate the flesh and drinke the bloud of men and children openlie.

'They kill men with poison.

'They kill men's Cattell.

'They bewitch men's corne, and bring hunger and barrennes into the countrie; they ride and flie in the aire, bring stormes, make tempests, &c.'

Scot, quoting Sprenger, gives yet a wider range to the wickedness of witches.[31] 'Although it be quite against the haire, and contrarie to the diuel's will, contrarie to the witch's oth, promise, and homage, and contrarie to all reason that witches should helpe anie thing that is bewitched; but rather set forward their Maister's businesse; yet we read In Malleo Maleficarum, of three sorts of witches; and the same is affirmed by all the writers hereupon, new and old. One sort, they say, can hurt and not helpe, the second can helpe and not hurt, the third can both helpe and hurt. And, among the hurtful witches, he saith there is one sort more beastlie than any kind of beasts, saving wooluees: for these usuallie deuoure and eate yong children and infants of their owne kind. These be they (saith he) that raise haile, tempests, and hurtfull weather; as lightening, thunder, &c. These be they that procure barrennesse in man, woman and beast. These can throwe children into waters, as they walke with their mothers, and not be seene. These can make horses kicke, till they cast their riders. These can so alter the mind of iudges, that they can haue no power to hurt them. These can procure to themselves and to others, taciturnitie and insensibilitie in their torments. These can bring trembling to the hands, and strike terror into the minds of them that apprehend them. These can manifest unto others, things hidden and lost, and foreshow things to come; and see them as though they were present. These can alter men's minds to inordinate love or hate. These can kill whom they list, with lightening and thunder. These can take awaie man's courage, and the power of generation. These can make a woman miscarrie in childbirth, and destroie the child in the mother's wombe, without any sensible meanes either inwardlie or outwardlie applied. These can, with their looks, kill either man or beast.'

CHAPTER XII

Familiar Spirits--Matthew Hopkins, the 'Witch-finder'--Prince Rupert's dog Boy--Unguents used for transporting Witches from Place to Place--Their Festivities at the Sabbat.

In order to enable the witch to carry out her benevolent intentions, the Devil supplied her with one or more familiar spirits, of which we shall hear much in the accounts of cases of witchcraft, and in this old English illustration we see the Devil presenting one to a young witch. They were of all kinds of shapes--perhaps the commonest was a cat or dog; but sometimes they took strange forms.

These familiars could talk and hold conversations with their mistresses, as witness the following story told by Giffard. A witch had confessed she had killed a man. 'And upon the ladder she seemed very penitent, desiring all the world to forgive her. She sayd she had a spirit in the likeness of a yellow dun Cat. This Cat came unto her, as she sayd, as she sat by her fire, when she was fallen out with a neighbour of hers, and wished that the vengeance of God might light upon him and his. The Cat bad her not be afraid, she would do her no harme, she had served a dame five yeares in Kent, that was now dead, and if she would, she would be her servant. And whereas, sayd the Cat, such a man hath misused thee, if thou wilt I will plague him in his cattell. She sent the Cat, she killed three hogs and one Cow. The man, suspecting, burnt a pig alive, and, as she sayd, her Cat would never go thither any more. Afterward, she fell out with that Man; she sent her Cat, who told her, that she had given him that, which he should never recover; and, indeed, the man died.'[32]

In 'The Lawes against Witches and Coniuration,' etc., the attention of justices of the peace is thus directed to these familiar spirits:

'1. These Witches have ordinarily a familiar, or spirit, which appeareth to them; sometimes in one shape, sometimes in another, as in the shape of a Man, Woman, Boy, Dogge, Cat, Foale, Fowle, Hare, Rat, Toad, etc. And to these their spirits they give names, and they meet together to christen them.

'2. Their said Familiar hath some big or little teat upon their body, where he sucketh them; and besides their sucking, the Devil leaveth other marks upon their bodies, sometimes like a Blew-spot, or Red-spot, like a flea-biting, sometimes the flesh sunk in and hollow, all which, for a time, may be covered, yea, taken away, but will come againe to their old forme; and these the Devil's markes be insensible, and being pricked will not bleed; and be often in their secret parts, and therefore require diligent and carefull search....

'So likewise, if the suspected be proved to have been heard to call upon their Spirit, or to talk to them, or of them, or have offered them to others.

'So, if they have been seen with their Spirits, or seen to feed something secretly, these are proofes that they have a familiar, &c.'

Matthew Hopkins (of whom more anon) was a past master in the matter of familiars, and thus relates his experience of some of them.[33] He is supposed to be asked where he had gained his experience.

'The Discoverer never travelled far for it, but in March 1644, he had some seven or eight of that horrible sect of Witches living in the Towne where he lived, a Towne in Essex called Maningtree, with divers other adjacent Witches of other towns, who every six weeks, in the night (being always on the Friday night) had their meeting close by his house, and had their severall solemne sacrifices there offered to the Devill, one of which this discoverer heard speaking to her Imps one night, and bid them goe to another Witch, who was thereupon apprehended, and searched by women, who for many yeares had knowne the Devill's marks, and found to have three teats about her, which honest women have not; so upon command from the Justice, they were to keep her from sleep, two or three nights, expecting in that time to see her familiars, which the fourth night she called in by their severall names, and told them what shapes, a quarter of an houre before they came in, there being ten of us in the roome; the first she called was:

'1. Holt, who came like a white kitling.

'2. Jarmara, who came in like a fat Spaniel, without any legs at all; she said she kept him fat, for she clapt her hand on her belly, and said he suckt good blood from her body.

'3. Vinegar Tom, who was like a long-legg'd Greyhound, with an head like an Oxe, with a long taile and broad eyes, who, when the discoverer spoke to, and bade him goe to the place provided for him and his Angels, immediately transformed himselfe into the shape of a child of foure yeeres old, without a head, and gave halfe a dozen turnes about the house, and vanished at the doore.

'4. Sack and Sugar, like a black Rabbet.

'5. Newes, like a Polcat. All these vanished away in a little time. Immediately after, this Witch confessed several other Witches, from whom she had her Imps, and named to divers women where their markes were, the number of their Marks, and Imps, and Imps' names, as Elemanzer, Pyewacket, Peck in the Crown, Grizzel Greedigut, &c., which no mortall could invent.'

Witches, however, were not the sole proprietors of familiar spirits, for the Roundheads declared that Prince Rupert had one, in the shape of a large white poodle dog, a present from Lord Arundel, whose name was Boy. Boy accompanied his master in many an engagement, but seemed to bear a charmed life, even having the credit given him of catching bullets and bringing them to his master. This evidently must be a dog of no common breed, and it was not thought so, as we read in one of the Commonwealth tracts, which was a reputed dialogue between Tobie's and Prince Rupert's dogs:

'TOBIE'S DOG. ... I heare you are Prince Rupert's White Boy.
P. RUP. DOG. I am none of his White Boy, my name is Puddle.
TOB. DOG. A dirty name, indeed, you are not pure enough for my company; besides, I hear on both sides of my eares that you are a Laplander, or Fin Land Dog, or, truly, no better than a Witch in the shape of a white Dogge.

***

P. RUP. DOG. No, Sirrah, I am of high Germain breed.
TOB. DOG. Thou art a Reprobate and a lying Curre; you were either whelpt in Lapland, or in Finland; where there is none but divells and Sorcerers live.'

Poor Boy met his fate at Marston Moor, by a silver bullet fired 'by a valiant Souldier, who had skill in Necromancy.' Judging by the hail of bullets by which he is surrounded, he must indeed have borne a charmed life, the loss of which an old witch deplores.

One of the duties of the familiar was to acquaint the witch with the next meeting between the witches and the Devil. This always (although authorities differ) took place on Fridays, after midnight, and was called the Sabbath or Sabbat. But Scot, quoting Danæus, says: 'The Divell oftentimes, in the likenes of a sumner, meeteth them at markets and Faires, and warneth them to appeare in their assemblies, at a certaine houre in the night, that he may understand whom they have slaine, and how they have profited.'

But these meetings might be many miles distant, and, consequently, the witches had to be provided with means of conveyance; which was effected with the aid of an unguent, as to the composition of which authorities vary. This was rubbed over the body, or upon a broomstick or dungfork, and hey, presto! they were in mid-air. But they must not make their exit by the door, only by such illegitimate ways as the chimney or the keyhole. Or, as we see, a wizard might mount his cat, or a witch a sheep; or, if a great favourite, the Devil himself would carry her, taking the form of a he-goat, in which shape he frequently presided at the Sabbat.

The broomstick was the orthodox old English style of aërial courses; but, as I have before said, an unguent was necessary. In 'The Witch,' before quoted, Heccat says:

'Here take this unbaptized brat:
Boile it well; preserve the fat;
You know 'tis pretious to transfer
Our 'noynted flesh into the ayre,
In moonelyght nights, on steeple topps,
Mountains, and pine trees, that like pricks or stopps,
Seeme to our height, high towres, and roofes of princes
Like wrinckles in the earth.'

Scot, on the authority of John Bapt. Neap, gives the following recipes for ointments, which are singularly like those in 'The Witch':

'R. The fat of yoong children, and seeth it with water in a brazen vessell, reseruing the thickest of that which remaineth boiled in the bottome, which they laie up and keepe, untill occasion serueth to use it. They put hereunto Eleoselinum, Aconitum, Frondes populeas, and Soote.'

Another receipt to the same purpose.

'R. Sium, acarum vulgare, pentaphyllon, the blood of a flitter mouse, solanum somniferum and oleum. They stampe all these togither, and then they rubbe all parts of their bodies exceedinglie, till they looke red, and be verie hot, so as the pores may be opened, and their flesh soluble and loose. They ioine herewithall either fat, or oil in steed thereof, that the force of the ointment maie the rather pearse inwardly, and so be more effectuall. By this means (saith he) in a moonlight night they seeme to be carried in the aire.'

Thus, then, their means of conveyance being assured, they all meet together, at some appointed place, it may be hundreds of miles away--in a social congress of a very mixed character, Continental writers giving a fuller and more detailed report of their transactions than do the English. One Henri Boguet, a French Grand Juge, in his 'Discours des Sorciers,' Lyons, 1608, is particularly lucid on this subject.

He says that at this assembly the first thing the witches do is to adore Satan, who appears in the form, either of a huge black man or as a he-goat, and by way of doing homage to him they offer him candles which burn with a blue flame, and kiss his back, some kissing his shoulders. Sometimes he holds a black image which the witches kiss, at the same time offering a candle or burning brand which they light at a candle, which the Devil carries between his horns. They next proceed to dance a curious circular dance, in which they are placed back to back, whilst the lame witches incite them to leap and dance. The music of the hautboy is not wanting, someone always being found who will thus oblige the company, besides which Satan himself sometimes plays the flute; but if no orchestra is forthcoming, the witches and devils sing each their own song, making a sort of 'Dutch medley.' Sometimes they dance two and two, at other times they perform pas seuls, but always in confusion, and they dance back to back, so that they may not be recognised; indeed, it is for that reason that they hold their assemblies at night.

After the dance they break into couples, and indescribable orgies take place.

The next part of the programme is a banquet, composed of different kinds of viands, according to the place of meeting and the quality of the guests; but, according to the illustrations, the pièce de résistance was a dead child. The table was covered with butter, cheese, and meat, and according to some authorities a large copper was provided, from which each witch could take her meat. They drank wine out of wooden goblets, but the chief drink was water. But at these feasts there was never any salt, because it is an emblem of immortality, which the Devil hates more than anything. Besides, it is put in holy-water, and the Apostles were called the 'salt of the earth'--sufficient reasons to disgust any Devil.

Before commencing the meal, and on finishing it, the witches say grace--not exactly as we do, but paraphrasing the benediction, filling it with blasphemies, and making Satan author and preserver of all things. And it is a curious thing that all authorities agree that the viands served at these feasts have no flavour or taste, and the meat is only horseflesh; also when the witches rise from table they are as hungry as when they sat down.

This highly unsatisfactory repast being finished, the witches tell Satan what they have done since their last meeting, and those are most welcome who have caused the greatest number of deaths among human beings and cattle, the most illness, or spoilt most corn; in short, those who have committed the most wickednesses and abominations. The others, who have behaved rather more humanely, are hissed at and mocked by all; they are set on one side, and are often beaten and ill-treated by their master.

They then renew their renunciation of God and the Sacraments of the Church, as also their oath never to speak of God, of the Virgin Mary, or the Saints, unless in mockery and derision; they give up all hope of heaven, and swear that they will always hold him to be their master, and be faithful to him. He then exhorts them to all evil deeds, such as harming their neighbours, making them ill, killing their cattle, and revenging themselves on their enemies, and even uses these words, Revenge yourselves, or you shall die. Moreover, he promises them to lay waste and spoil the fruits of the earth, and gives them powders and ointments for that purpose; at least, he makes them believe so. He also makes them swear solemnly that they should accuse each other, and never reveal anything which had passed between them.

The witches then cause a hailstorm, in order to spoil the crops and the fruit.

But they also celebrate a parody of the Mass, the celebrant being vested in a black chasuble, without a cross on it; and after having put water in the chalice, he turns his back on the altar, and then elevates a slice of black radish instead of the Host, and all the witches cry with a loud voice, 'Master, help us!' The Devil at the same time makes sham holy-water, with which he who celebrates the Mass sprinkles the congregation, using a black asperge.

Finally, the Devil, after having taken the form of a he-goat, is consumed by fire, and reduced to ashes, which the witches collect and hide, in order that they may assist them in their diabolical designs.

The Devil, in Britain and America

Of the English Sabbat we shall hear enough when we come to the various cases of witchcraft. Scot quotes Bodin, the great French exponent of witchcraft, 'who saith, at these magical assemblies the witches never fail to danse, and in their danse they sing these words: Har, har, diuell, diuell, danse here, danse here, plaie here, plaie here, Sabbath, Sabbath. And whiles they sing and danse, euerie one hath a broome in hir hand, and holdeth it up aloft. Item he saith that these night-walking, or rather, night-dancing witches, brought out of Italie into France that danse which is called La Volta.'

He also says that, according to Danæus, if the witches 'be lame, the diuell deliuereth them a staffe, to conueie them thither inuisiblie through the aire; and that then they fall a dansing and singing of foule songs, wherein he leadeth the danse himselfe; which danse, and other conferences being ended, he supplieth their wants of powders and roots to intoxicate withall; and giueth to euerie nouice a marke, either with his teeth, or with his clawes, and so they kisse the diuell's bare buttockes, and depart; not forgetting euery daie afterwards to offer to him, dogs, cats, hens, or bloud of their owne.'

In 'A Pleasant Treatise of Witches,' London, 1673, we have the following account of the Sabbat: 'They [witches] are likewise reported to have each of them a Spirit or Imp attending on, and assigned to them, which never leave those to whom they are subject, but assist and render them all the service they command. These give the witches notice to be ready on all solemn appointments and meetings, which are ordinarily on Tuesday or Wednesday night, and then they strive to separate themselves from the company of all other creatures, not to be seen by any; and, night being come, they strip themselves naked, and anoint themselves with their Oyntments. Then they are carried out of the house, either by the Window, Door, or Chimney, mounted on their Imps in the form of a Goat, Sheep, or Dragon, till they arrive at their meeting-place, whither all the other Wizards and Witches, each one upon his Imp, are also brought. Thus brought to the designed place, which is sometimes many hundred miles from their dwellings, they find a great number of others arrived there by the same means; who, before Lucifer takes his place on his Throne, as King, do make their accustomed homage, adoring and proclaiming him their Lord, and rendring him all Honour.

'This solemnity being finished they sit to Table, where no delicate meats are wanting to gratifie their appetites, all dainties being brought in the twinkling of an eye, by those spirits that attend the assembly. This done, at the sound of many pleasant instruments (for we must expect no Grace in the company of Devils,) the table is taken away, and the pleasing consort invites them to a Ball; but the dance is strange and wonderful, as well as diabolical, for, turning themselves back to back, they take one another by the arms and raise each other from the ground, then shake their heads to and fro like Anticks, and turn themselves as if they were mad. Then, at last, after this Banquet, Musick, and Ball, the lights were put out....

'At last, before Aurora brings back the day, each one mounts on his Spirit, and so returns to his respective dwelling place, with that lightness and quickness, that, in little space, they find themselves to be carryed many hundred miles; but are charged by their spirit on the way, not to call in any wise on the name of God, or to bless themselves with the sign of the Cross, upon pain of falling, with peril of their lives, and being grievously punished by their Demon.

'Sometimes, at their solemn assemblies, the Devil commands that each tell what wickedness he hath committed, and, according to the hainousness and detestableness of it he is honoured and respected with a general applause. Those, on the contrary, who have done no evil, are beaten and punished. At last, when the assembly is ready to break up, and the Devil to despatch them, he publisheth this law with a loud voice, Revenge yourselves, or else you shall dye: then each one, kissing the posteriors of the Devil, returns upon their aiery Vehicles to their habitations.'

CHAPTER XIII

Waxen Figures--Witches change into Animals--Witch Marks--Testimony against Witches--Tests for, and Examination of, Witches.

Among other things done at the Sabbat, the Devil instructed witches in the art of making waxen images, the use of which is to torment those against whom they have a spite. King James I. ('Demonologie,' lib. ii., cap. v.) says:

'To some others, at these times, he teacheth how to make pictures of waxe or clay: That by the roasting thereof, the persons that they beare the name of, may be continually melted or dried away by continuall sickenesse.... They can bewitch and take the life of men or women, by roasting of the pictures, which, likewise, is verie possible to their Maister to performe, for, although that instrument of waxe haue no vertue in that turne doing, yet may hee not very well, euen by the same measure that his coniured slaves melts that waxe at the fire, may hee not, I say, at these same times, subtily, as a spirite, so weaken and scatter the spirites of life of the patient, as may make him, on the one part, for faintnesse, to sweate out the humour of his bodie. And on the other part, for the not concurrence of these spirites which cause his digestion, so debilitate his stomache, that this humour radicall, continually sweating out on the one part, and no good sucke being put in the place thereof, for lacke of digestion, on the other, he, at last, shall vanish away, euen as his picture will doe at the fire? And that knauish and cunning workeman, by troubling him, onely at sometimes, makes a proportion, so neere betwixt the working of the one and the other, that both shall end, as it were, at one time.'

In 'The Witch' we find the following:

'HECCAT. Is the hart of Wax
Stuck full of magique needles?
    STADLIN. 'Tis done, Heccat.
    HEC. And is the Farmer's picture, and his wives,
Lay'd downe to th' fire yet?
    STAD. They are a roasting both too.
    HEC. Good:
Then their marrowes are a melting subtelly,
And three monethes sicknes sucks up life in 'em.
They denide me often floure, barme and milke,
Goose-greaze and tar, when I nere hurt their churnings,
Their brew-locks, nor their batches, nor fore spoake
Any of their breedings. Now I'll be meete with 'em.
Seauen of their yong piggs I have bewitch'd already,
Of the last litter; nine ducklyngs, thirteene goselings, and a hog,
Fell lame last Sunday after evensong too.
And mark how their sheepe prosper; or what soupe
Each milch-kine gives to th' paile: I'le send these snakes
Shall milke 'em all before hand; the dew'd skirted dayrie wenches
Shall stroak dry duggs for this, and goe home cursing:
I'll mar their sillabubs, and swathie feastings
Under cowes bellies with the parish-youthes.'

Some witches had the power of transforming themselves into divers animals, and Boguet gives a long list of witches who confessed to so doing, having become, for the nonce, wolves, pigs, asses, cats, horses, frogs or toads, and hares. Indeed, in France and Germany, the belief in loup-garou and währwolf has hardly yet died out. But not only could they change themselves into beasts, but others also, quite after the fashion of the enchantments in the 'Arabian Nights.' Reginald Scot tells a story (lib. v., cap. iii.) too good to be omitted:

'It happened in the citie of Salamin in the kingdome of Cyprus (wherein is a good hauen) that a ship loaden with merchandize staied there for a short space. In the meane time many of the souldiers and mariners went to shoare, to prouide fresh victuals. Among which number, a certaine English man, being a sturdie young fellowe, went to a woman's house, a little waie out of the citie, and not farre from the sea side, to see whether she had anie eggs to sell. Who, perceiuing him to be a lustie yoong fellowe, a stranger, and farre from his countrie, so as upon the losse of him there would be the lesse misse or inquirie, she considered with hirselfe how to destroie him; and willed him to staie there awhile, whilest she went to fetch a few eggs for him. But she tarried long, so as the yoong man called unto hir, desiring hir to make hast: for he told hir that the tide would be spent, and by that meanes his ship would be gone and leaue him behind. Howbeit, after some detracting of time, she brought him a few eggs, willing him to returne to hir, if his ship were gone when he came.

'The yoong fellowe returned towards his ship; but before he, went aboord, hee would needs eat an egg or twaine to satisfie his hunger, and, within short space, he became dumb and out of his wits, (as he afterwards said.) When he would haue entred into the ship, the marriners beat him backe with a cudgell, saieing: What a murren lacks the asse? Whither the Diuell will this asse? The asse, or yoong man, (I cannot tell by which name I should terme him,) being many times repelled, and understanding their words that called him asse, considering that he could speake neuer a word, and yet could understand euerie bodie; he thought that he was bewitched by the woman, at whose house he was. And, therefore, when by no means he could get into the boate, but was driuen to tarrie and see hir departure; being also beaten from place to place, as an asse; he remembered the witches words, and the words of his owne fellowes that called him asse, and returned to the witches house, in whose seruice he remained by the space of three yeares, dooing nothing with his hands all that while, but carried such burthens as she laied on his backe; haueing onely this comfort, that, although he were reputed an asse among strangers and beasts, yet that both this witch, and all other witches knew him to be a man.

'After three yeares were passed ouer, in a morning betimes he went to towne before his dame; who, upon some occasion, staied a little behind. In the meane time, being neere to a church, he heard a little saccaring bell ring to the eleuation of a morrowe masse, and, not daring to go into the churche, least he should haue beene beaten and driuen out with cudgells, in great deuotion he fell downe in the churchyard, upon the knees of his hinder legs, and did lift his forefeet ouer his head, as the preest doth hold the sacrament at the eleuation. Which prodigious sight, when certeine merchants of Genua espied, and with woonder beheld; anon commeth the witch with a cudgell in hir hand, beating foorth the asse. And bicause (as it hath beene said) such kinds of witchcrafts are verie usuall in those parts; the merchants aforesaid made such meanes, as both the asse and the witch were attached by the iudge. And she, being examined and set upon the racke, confessed the whole matter, and promised that, if she might have libertie to go home, she would restore him to his old shape: and, being dismissed, she did, accordinglie. So, as notwithstanding, they apprehended hir againe, and burned hir: and the yoong man returned into his countrie with a ioifull and merrie hart.'

Credulous as James I. was, yet he could not swallow lycanthropy:

'But to tell you simply my opinion in this, if any such thing hath beene, I take it to haue proceeded but of a naturall super-aboundance of Melancholie, which, as we reade, that it hath made some thinke themselues Pitchers, and some, horses, and some, one kinde of beast or other. So suppose I, that it hath so viciat the imagination and memory of some, as per lucida interualla, it hath so highly occupied them, that they haue thought themselues very Woolfes indeed, at these times: and so haue counterfeited their actiones in going on their hands and feete, preassing to deuoure women and barnes,[34] fighting and snatching with all the towne dogges, and in using such like other bruitish actiones, and so to become beastes by a strong apprehension as Nabucad-netzar was seuen yeares.'

But popular opinion still inclined to the belief in the ability of witches to change their form: and we will take only one instance, which occurs in the play of 'The Late Lancashire Witches,' by Heywood and Broome (London, 1634):

'MEG. Then list yee well, the hunters are
This day, by vow, to kill a hare,
Or else the sport they will forsweare;
And hang their dogs up.
    MAWD. Stay, but where
Must the long threatened hare be found?
    GIL. They'l search in yonder meadow ground.
    MEG. There will I be, and like a wily wat,
Untill they put me up, ile squat.'

And this belief has descended to quite modern times, for Mr. E. J. Wood, writing in Notes and Queries, October 25, 1862, says:

'In a certain hollow, or "bottom," not many miles from Sevenoaks, lived an old woman (now deceased) who had the local reputation of being a witch, and who could, according to the vulgar belief, convert herself into a hare at will. Her cottage had a drain-hole, or aperture, through which hole the so-called witch used to pass when she had metamorphosed herself into a "puss."'

To the outside world, a witch, be she young or old, looked like another woman, but to the cognoscenti there were certain marks about her which proclaimed her as a servant to the devil. All authorities agree that a witch had certain marks upon her which no one could mistake, and Scot sums it up very tersely:

'Item, if she haue anie priuie mark under hir arme pokes, under hir haire, under hir lip, or in hir buttocke, &c., it is a presumption for the iudge to proceed and giue sentence of death upon hir.'

But perhaps we find the fullest details of these marks in the abominable book 'The Discovery of Witches,' by the wretch Matthew Hopkins, the professional 'witch-finder.'

'Query 5. Many poore People are condemned for having a Pap or Teat about them, whereas many People, (especially antient People) are, and have been, a long time, troubled with naturall wretts[35] on severall parts of their bodies, and other natural excresscencies, and these shall be judged only by one man alone, and a woman, and so accused or acquitted?

'Answer. The parties so judging can justifie their skill to any, and shew good reasons why such markes are not meerly naturall, neither that they can happen by any such naturall cause as is before expressed, and for further answer for their private judgements alone, it is most false and untrue, for never was any man tryed by search of his body, but commonly a dozen of the ablest men in the parish or else where were present, and most commonly as many ancient skilfull matrons and midwives present when the women are tryed, which marks, not only he and his company attest to be very suspitious, but all beholders, the skilfulest of them, doe not approve of them, but likewise assent that such tokens cannot, in their judgements proceed from any of the above-mentioned Causes.

'Query 6. It is a thing impossible for any man or woman to judge rightly on such marks, they are so neare to naturall excresscencies, and they that finde them, durst not presently give Oath they were drawne by evill spirits, till they have used unlawfull courses of torture to make them say anything for ease and quiet, as who would not do? but I would know the reasons he speakes of, and whereby to discover the one from the other, and so be satisfied in that.

'Answer. The reasons, in breefe, are three, which, for the present, he judgeth to differ from naturall marks; which are

'1. He judgeth by the unusualnes of the place where he findeth the teats in or on their bodies, being farre distant from any usuall place, from whence such naturall markes proceed; as, if a witch plead the markes found are Emerods, if I finde them on the back bone, shall I assent with him? Knowing they are not neere that veine, and so, others, by child-bearing, when it may be, they are in the contrary part?

'2. They are most commonly insensible, and feele neither pin, needle, aule, &c, thrust through them.

'3. The often variations and mutations of these marks into severall formes, confirmes this matter; as, if a Witch hear a month or two before that the Witch-finder, (as they call him) is comming, they will, and have, put out their Imps to others to suckle them, even to their owne young and tender children; these upon search are found to have dry skinnes and filmes only, and be close to the flesh. Keepe her 24 houres with a diligent eye, that none of her Spirits come in any visible shape to suck her; the women have seen, the next day after, her Teats extended to their former filling strength, full of corruption, ready to burst; and, leaving her alone then one quarter of an houre, and let the women go up againe, and shee will have them drawn, by her Imps, close againe: Probatum est.'

This seems hard enough upon the poor friendless witch, but it is nothing to what Scot writes on the subject, giving his authorities, which, at the time he wrote, on behalf of the witch, was good law. As it is a very curious bit of history, and one, as far as I know, that has never been reproduced, I make a long extract bearing thereon:

'Excommunicat persons, partakers of the salt, infants, wicked servants, and runawaies are to be admitted to beare witness against their dames in the mater of witchcraft, bicause, (saith Bodin, the champion of witch mongers) none that be honest are able to detect them. Heretikes, also, and witches shall be received to accuse, but not to excuse a witch. And, finallie, the testimonie of all infamous persons in this case is good and allowed. Yea, one lewd person, (saith Bodin) may be received to accuse and condemne a thousand suspected witches. And although by lawe, a capitall enimie may be challenged; yet James Sprenger and Henry Justitor (from whom Bodin, and all the writers that euer I haue read, doo receiue their light, authorities and arguments) saie, (upon this point of lawe) that The poore frendlesse old woman must proue that hir capitall enemie would haue killed hir, and that hee hath both assalted and wounded hir; otherwise she pleadeth all in vaine. If the iudge aske hir, whether she haue anie capitall enemies; and she rehearse other, and forget her accuser, or else answer that he was hir capitall enemie, but now she hopeth that he is not so; such a one is neuertheles admitted for a witnes. And though by law, single witnesses are not admittable; yet, if one depose she hath witched hir cow, another hir sow; and the third hir butter; these saith, are no single Witnesses bicause they agree that she is a witch.

'Women suspected to be witches, after their apprehension may not be suffered to go home, or to other places, to seek suerties; for feare least at their returne home, they worke reuenge upon them. In which respect Bodin commendeth much the Scottish custome and order in this behalfe; where, (he saith) a hollowe piece of wood, or a chest is placed in the church, into the which anie bodie may freelie cast a little scroll of paper, wherein may be conteined the name of the witch, the time, place and fact &c. And the same chest being locked by three inquisitors or officers appointed for that purpose; which keepe three seuerall kaies. And then the accuser need not be knowne, nor shamed with the reproch of slander or malice to his poore neighbour.

'Item. there must be great persuasions used to all men, women and children, to accuse old women of witchcraft.

'Item. there may alwaies be promised impunitie and fauour to witches that confesse and detect others; and for the contrairie, there may be threatnings and violence practised and used.

'Item. the little children of witches, which will not confesse, must be attached; who (if they be craftilie handled saith Bodin) will confesse against their owne mothers.

'Item. witches must be examined as suddenlie, and as unawares as is possible; the which will so amaze them, that they will confesse anything, supposing the diuell hath forsaken them; whereas, if they should first be committed to prison, the diuell would tamper with them, and informe them what to doo.

'Item. the inquisitor, iudge, or examiner, must begin with small matters first.

'Item. they must be examined whether their parents were witches or no; for witches (as these Doctors suppose) came by propagation. And Bodin setteth downe this principle in witchcraft, to wit, Si saga sit mater, sic etiam est filia: howbeit the lawe forbiddeth it Ob sanguinis reuerentiam.

'Item. the examiner must looke stedfastlie upon their eies: for they cannot looke directlie upon a man's face, (as Bodin affirmeth in one place, although in another he saith, that they kill and destroie both men and beasts by their lookes).

'Item. she must be examined of all accusations, presumptions and faults, at one instant: least sathan should afterwards dissuade hir from confession.

'Item. a witch may not be put in prison alone, least the diuell dissuade her from confession, through promises of her indemnitie. For (saith Bodin) some that haue been in the gaole haue proued to flie awaie, as they were woont to doo when they met with Diana and Minerua &c, and so brake their owne necks against the stone walles.

'Item. if anie denie hir owne confession made without torture, she is neuerthelesse by that confession to be condemned, as in anie other crime.

'Item, the iudges must seeme to put on a pittifull countenance and to moue them; saieing that It was not they, but the diuell that committed the murther, and that he compelled them to doo it; and must make them beleeue that they think them to be innocents.

'Item. if they will not confesse nothing upon the racke or torture; their apparell must be changed, and euerie haire in their bodie must be shauen off with a sharpe razor.

'Item, if they have charmes for taciturnitie, so as they feele not the common tortures, and therefore confesse nothing; then some sharpe instrument must be thrust betwixt euerie naile of their fingers and toes; which (as Bodin saith) was King Childebert's devise, and is, to this daie, of all others the most effectuall. For by meanes of that extreme paine, they will (saith he) confesse anie thing.

'Item. Paulus Grillandus, being an old doer in these matters, wisheth that when witches sleepe, and feele no paine upon the torture, Domine labia mea aperies should be said, and so, (saith he) both the torment will be felt, and the truth will be uttered.

'Item. Bodin saith, that at the time of examination there should be a semblance of a great a doo, to the terrifieing of the witch; and that a number of instruments, gieues,[36] manacles, ropes, halters, fetters &c be prepared, brought foorth, and laid before the examinate; and, also, that some be procured to make a most horrible and lamentable crie, in the place of torture, as though he or she were upon the racke, or in the tormentor's hands: so as the examinate may heare it whiles she is examined, before she hir selfe be brought into the prison; and perhaps (saith he) she will by this meanes, confesse the matter.

'Item. there must be subborned some craftie spie, that may seeme to be a prisoner with hir in the like case; who, perhaps, may, in Conference, undermine hir, and so bewraie and discouer hir.

'Item. if she will not yet confesse, she must be told that she is detected, and accused by other of hir companions; although in truth there be no such matter; and so, perhaps, she will confesse, the rather to be reuenged upon hir aduersaries and accusers.

'If an old woman threaten or touch one, being in health, who dieth shortly after; or else is infected with the leprosie, apoplexie, or anie strange disease; it is (saith Bodin) a permanent fact, and such an euidence, as condemnation or death must insue, without further proofe; if anie bodie haue mistrusted hir, or said before that she was a witch.

'Item. if anie come in, or depart out, of the chamber or house, the doors being shut; it is an apparent and sufficient euidence to a Witches Condemnation, without further triall:

'Item, if a woman bewitch anie bodies eies, she is to be executed without further proofe.

'Item. if anie inchant or bewitch men's beasts, or come, or flie in the aire, or make a dog speake, or cut off anie man's members, and unite them againe to men or children's bodies; it is sufficient proofe to condemnation.

'Item. presumptions and coniectures are sufficient proofes against witches.

'Item. if three witnesses doo but saie, Such a woman is a witch: then it is a cleere case that she is to be executed with death. Which matter Bodin saith is not onelie certeine by the canon and civill lawes, but by the opinion of pope Innocent, the wisest pope, (as he saith) that ever was.

'Item. the complaint of anie one man of credit is sufficient to bring a poore woman to the racke or pullie.

'Item. a condemned or infamous person's testimonie is good and allowable in matters of witchcraft.

'Item a witch is not to be deliuered, though she endure all the tortures, and confesse nothing; as all other are in anie criminall cases.

'Item, though the depositions of manie women at one instant are disabled, as insufficient in lawe; bicause of the imbecillitie and frailtie of their nature or sex: yet, in this matter, one woman, though she be a partie, either accuser or accused, and be also infamous and impudent (for such are Bodin's words) yea, and alreadie condemned; she may, nevertheless serue to accuse and condemne a witch.

'Item, a witness uncited, and offering himselfe in this case, is to be heard, and in none other.

'Item, a Capitall enimie (if the enimitie be pretended to grow by meanes of witchcraft) may obiect against a witch; and none exception is to be had or made against him.

'Item, although the proofe of periurie may put back a witnesse in other causes; yet in this, a periured person is a good and a lawfull witnesse.

'Item, the proctors and advocates in this case are compelled to be witnesses against their clients, as in none other case they are to be constrained thereunto.

'Item, none can giue euidence against witches, touching their assemblies, but witches onelie; bicause, (as Bodin saith) none other can do it.'

Thus we see that the poor witch had everything against her, which will account in a great way for those marvellous confessions we read of, when the poor, weary, baited and tortured woman would confess to anything to get a few hours' respite from pain, well knowing that execution would follow, whether she confessed or no. In fact, no other hypothesis is possible, when we read of the extraordinary matters to which these poor women confessed.

CHAPTER XIV

Legislation against Witches--Punishment--Last Executions for Witchcraft--Inability to weep and sink--Modern Cases of Witchcraft.

There has not been much legislation against witches in England, the Acts simply keeping in force. It is said that Athelstane in 928 made witchcraft a capital crime, but our 'statutes at large' give 33 Henry VIII., cap. 8 (1541), as the first Act really touching witchcraft, as coming within the ken of this book. Next comes 5 Elizabeth, cap. 16 (1562), and then 1 James I., cap. 12 (1604), previously substantially quoted. This was the law of the land until it was abolished in 1736, 9 George II., cap. 5, which did away with capital punishment for witchcraft, and the present law on the subject dates from 1822, 3 George IV., where the word 'witchcraft' certainly disappears, and only 'All Persons pretending to be Gipsies: all Persons pretending to tell Fortunes, or using any subtle Craft, Means, or Device, by Palmistry, or other wise, to deceive or impose upon any of His Majestys subjects,' shall be adjudged 'Common Rogues and Vagabonds,' and sentenced as such.

Formerly the poor wretches were burned, a fearful fate, as Scot says, quoting Bodin. 'Item, if a woman confesse freelie herein, before question[37] be made; and yet afterward denie it; she is neuerthelesse to be burned.' Possibly the last case of burning for witchcraft is one I shall record later on, at Bury St. Edmunds, in 1644; but the same year one Alice Hudson was burned at York for receiving small sums of money from the Devil.[38]

The last case of burning in Scotland was in Sutherland, in 1722, and the last in Ireland at Glarus, a servant being burnt as a witch in 1786. Probably the last burning for witchcraft, in any so-called civilized country, is the following, taken from the Steamer Edition of the Panama Star and Herald of June 5, 1871: 'According to the Porvenir of Callao (Peru), 29th ult., a woman has been burnt in the public square of a town in the province of Guavina, about thirty-four leagues from the port of Iquique, for being a witch. This punishment, worthy of the flourishing days of the Spanish Inquisition, was ordered by the Lieutenant-Governor and Judge of the Province.'

Hutchinson, a very careful writer, whose 'Historical Essay concerning Witchcraft,' etc., was first published in 1718, and the second edition in 1720, says, referring to a case we shall hear of anon: 'Susan Edwards, Mary Trembles, and Temperance Lloyd, hanged at Exeter, confess'd themselves Witches, but died with good Prayers in their Mouths. I suppose these are the last Three that have been hanged in England. 1682.'

James I. was ruthless against witches, vide the following:

'PHILOMATHES. Then to make an ende of our conference, since I see it drawes late, what forme of punishment thinke yee merites these Magicians and Witches? For I see that yee account them to be al alike guiltie.

EPISTEMON. They ought to be put to death according to the Law of God, the civill and imperiall Law, and municipall Law of all Christian nations.

PHI. But what kinde of death, I pray you?

EPI. It is commonly used by fire, but that is an indifferent thing to be used in every countrey, according to the Law or custome thereof.

PHI. But ought no sexe, age, nor ranke to bee exempted?

EPI. None at al (being so used by the lawful magistrate) for it is the highest point of Idolatry, wherein no exception is admitted by the Law of God.

PHI. Then bairnes may not be spared?

EPI. Yea, not a haire the lesse of my conclusion. For they are not that capable of reason as to practise such things.'

Before quitting the subject of witches for cases of witchcraft, it occurs to me that I have omitted one or two peculiarities relating to them. First of all, one personal peculiarity they had, according to the infallible authority Bodin--an inability to weep, or, at all events, they could only screw out three tears. And this was a great test, so much so that a form of conjuration is given in the 'Malleus Maleficarum,' and translated by Scot, which bears strongly upon this point: 'I coniure thee by the amorous teares, which Jesus Christ our Saviour shed upon the crosse for the saluation of the world; and by the most earnest and burning teares of his mother the most glorious virgine Marie, sprinkled upon his wounds late in the euening; and by all the teares which euerie saint and elect vessel of God hath poured out heere in the world, and from whose eies he hath wiped away all teares; that, if thou be without fault, thou maist poure downe teares abundantlie; and, if thou be guiltie, that thou weepe in no wise: In the name of the father, of the sonne, and of the holie ghost: Amen. And note (saith he) that the more you coniure, the lesse she wepeth.'

But the same authority says: 'She must be well looked unto, otherwise she will put spettle priuilie upon hir cheeks, and seeme to weepe.' King James says, 'Not so much as their eies are able to shead teares, (threaten and torture them as yee please) ... albeit the women kinde especially, be able otherwaies to shead teares at every light occasion when they will, yea, although it were dissemblingly like the Crocodiles.'

He also says, with reference to their inability to sink in water: 'It appeares that God hath appointed (for a supernatural signe of the monstrous impiety of Witches) that the water shall refuse to receive them in her bosome, that have shaken off them the sacred Water of Baptisme, and wilfully refused the benefite thereof.'

This ordeal by water has been practised to a very late date, and 'swimming her for a witch' has been often heard in this century. The scientific and proper method of preparing the witch is by tying her right thumb to her left great toe, and vice versâ, and this ordeal had this simplicity: If the putative witch sank well, she was innocent; and if she swam, she could either be ducked and ill treated till she died, as too often was the case, or she was ipso facto a confessed witch.

Another ordeal was, to take a piece of the thatch from off the reputed witch's cottage, and set fire to it; if she came to the person so burning the thatch, her witchcraft was incontestable.

Another was, to weigh the witch against the church Bible, and this test, too, has come down to modern times. One instance will suffice. 'One Susana Hannokes, an elderly woman of Wingrove, near Aylesbury, was accused by a neighbour for bewitching her spinning wheel, so that she could not make it go round, and offered to make oath of it before a magistrate; on which, the husband, in order to justify his wife, insisted upon her being tried by the church Bible, and that the accuser should be present: accordingly, she was conducted to the parish church, where she was stript of all her cloathes to her shift and under-coat, and weighed against the Bible; when, to the no small mortification of her accuser, she out-weighed it, and was honourably acquitted of the charge.'[39]

But in this nineteenth century of ours, with all its boasted civilization, witchcraft is still believed in in England, as the following two or three instances will testify:

S. A. S., writing in Notes and Queries, June 25, 1853, says, 'A cottager, who does not live five minutes' walk from my house, found his pig seized with a strange and unaccountable disorder. He, being a sensible man, instead of asking the advice of a veterinary surgeon, immediately went to the white witch (a gentleman who drives a flourishing trade in this neighbourhood). He received his directions, and went home, and implicitly followed them. In perfect silence, he went to the pigsty; and, lancing each foot and both ears of the pig, he allowed the blood to run into a piece of common dowlas. Then, taking two large pins, he pierced the dowlas in opposite directions; and, still keeping silence, entered his cottage, locked the door, placed the bloody rag upon the fire, heaped up some turf over it, and, reading a few verses of the Bible, waited till the dowlas was burned. As soon as this was done, he returned to the pigsty; found his pig perfectly restored to health, and, mirabile dictu! as the white witch had predicted, the old woman, who it was supposed had bewitched the pig, came to inquire after the pig's health. The animal never suffered a day's illness afterwards. My informant was the owner of the pig himself.

'Perhaps, when I heard this story, there may have been a lurking expression of doubt upon my face, so that my friend thought it necessary to give me farther proof. Some time ago, a lane in this town began to be looked upon with a mysterious awe, for every evening a strange white rabbit would appear in it, and, running up and down, would mysteriously disappear. Dogs were frequently put on the scent, but all to no purpose, the white rabbit could not be caught; and rumours began to assert pretty confidently that the white rabbit was nothing more nor less than a witch. The man whose pig had been bewitched was all the more confident, as, every evening when the rabbit appeared, he had noticed the bedroom window of his old enemy's window open! At last, a large party of bold-hearted men, one evening, were successful enough to find the white rabbit in a garden, the only egress from which is through a narrow passage between two cottages, all the rest of the garden being securely surrounded by brick walls.

'They placed a strong guard in this entry, to let nothing pass, while the remainder advanced as skirmishers among the cabbages: one of these was successful, and caught the white rabbit by the ears, and, not without some trepidation, carried it towards the reserve in the entry. But, as he came nearer to his friends, his courage grew, and gradually, all the wrongs his poor pig had suffered took form and vigour in a powerful kick at the poor little rabbit. No sooner had he done this than, he cannot tell how, the rabbit was out of his grasp; the people in the entry saw it come, but could not stop it; through them all it went, and has never been seen again.

'But now to the proof of the witchcraft. The old woman, whom all suspected, was laid up in her bed for three days afterwards, unable to walk about, all the consequence of the kick she had received in the shape of a white rabbit!'

CHAPTER XV

Commencement of Witchcraft in England--Dame Eleanor Cobham--Jane Shore--Lord Huntingford--Cases from the Calendars of State Papers--Earliest Printed Case, that of John Walsh--Elizabeth Stile--Three Witches tried at Chelmsford--Witches of St. Osyth--Witches of Warboys--Witches of Northamptonshire.

At what date the higher cult of sorcery or magic became the drivel known as witchcraft is uncertain. I am almost inclined to place it (in England) at 1441; but then the charge was purely political, and I think that the Calendars of State Papers for nearly a century afterwards bear the statement out, that for some time afterwards they were so. The case of Dame Eleanor Cobham is very tersely told in 'Baker's Chronicle.'[40]

'Whilst these Alterations passed in France, a more unnatural (sic) passed in England; the Uncle riseth against the Nephew, the Nephew against the Uncle; the Duke of Gloucester brings Articles against the Cardinal, charging him with affecting Preheminence, to the Derogation of the King's Prerogative, and Contempt of his Laws; which Articles are delivered to the King, and by him to his Council, who, being most of the Clergy, durst not meddle in them, for fear of offending the Cardinal. On the other Side, the Cardinal, finding nothing whereof directly to accuse the Duke of Gloucester himself, accuseth his other self, the Lady Eleanor Cobham, the Duke's Wife, of Treason for attempting, by Sorcery and Witchcraft, the Death of the King, and Advancement of her Husband to the Crown: For which, tho' acquitted of the Treason, she is adjudged to open Penance, namely, to go with a Wax Taper in her hand, Hoodless (save through a Kerchief) through London, divers Days together, and after, to remain in perpetual imprisonment in the Isle of Man. The Crime objected against her was, procuring Thomas Southwel, John Hunne, Priests, Roger Bolingbroke, a supposed Necromancer, and Margery Jordan, called the Witch of Eye, in Suffolk, to devise a Picture of Wax in Proportion of the King, in such sort by Sorcery, that, as the Picture consumed, so the King's body should consume: For which they were all condemned. The Witch was burnt at Smithfield, Bolingbroke was hanged, constantly affirming upon his Death, That neither the Duchess, nor any other from her, did ever require more of him, than only to know, by his Art, how long the King should live. John Hunne had his Pardon, and Southwel died the Night before he should have been executed.'

Shakespeare takes up the common tale about the bewitchment of Richard III. (Act III., scene 4):

'GLOUCESTER. Then be your eyes the witness of their evil;
Look how I am bewitch'd; behold my arm
Is, like a blasted sapling, wither'd up:
And this is Edward's wife, that monstrous witch,
Consorted with that harlot-strumpet Shore,
That, by their witchcraft, thus have markèd me.'

Monarchs in the sixteenth century were especially jealous (for their own sakes) of this trafficking with the foul fiend. According to Hutchinson, in 1541, 'The Lord Hungerford beheaded for procuring certain Persons to conjure, that they might know how long Henry VIII. would live.' Another authority, however, states that 'Lord Hungerford was attainted and executed, for keeping an heretical chaplain.'

Queen Elizabeth in 1562 being suspicious of the Countess of Lenox, had her imprisoned on a trumped-up case of sorcery and witchcraft. But the Devil evidently had a spite against this Protestant Princess, for in the Calendar of State Papers for 1584 we read, 'The Names of the Confederates against Her Majesty, who have diverse and sundry times conspired her life, and do daily confederate against her.' Among others we find Lord Paget, Sir Geo. Hastings, Sir Thos. Hamner, 'Ould Birtles the great devel, Darnally the sorcerer, Maude Twogood enchantresse, the ould witch of Ramsbury, several other olde witches, Gregson the north tale teller, who was one of them 3 that stole awaye the Earle of Northumberlande's head frome one of the turrettes of York &c.'

We can scarcely wonder at the hatred of James I. of England to witches, seeing how he had been pestered with them in his realm of Scotland, two instances of which are recorded in the Calendars of

State Papers. '1591. 21 May. Witches have been discovered in Scotland, who practised the King's death, with the privity of Bothwell.' '1600 16/20 Ap. The Queen of Scotland is said to be a zealous Catholic, and the King inclined thereto, because an Agnus Dei given him by the Queen had miraculously saved him in a tempest at sea, stirred up by witches, as the Witches themselves confess.'

It is a curious fact, well worthy the thinking over, that England and Europe had a comparative immunity from the assaults of the Devil, until after the Reformation, when for a time he became rampagious, troubling even the arch-Reformer Luther himself.

The earliest English printed book on witchcraft, pure and simple, that I can find is 'The Examination of John Walsh,' London, 1566. He confessed to having trafficked with 'Feries' and learned much from them respecting stolen goods and bewitched people; but in replying to his eighth interrogatory, 'He being demaunded whether he had euer any Familiar or no; he sayth that he had one of his sayde mayster. Which Familiar (after his booke of Circles was taken from him by one Robert Baber of Crokehorne, then being Constable, in the yeare 1565) he could neuer do anything touching his Familiar, nor the use thereof, but hys Familiar dyd then depart from him, and wyll neuer come to him agayne, as he sayth. And further, he sayth upon his oth, that his familiar would sometyme come unto hym lyke a gray blackish Culuer,[41] and somtyme lyke a brended Dog, and sometimes lyke a man in all proportions, sauinge that he had clouen feete.

'Ninthly, he being demaunded howe long he had the use of the Familiar; he sayd one yeare by his sayd masters life, and iiii yeres after his death. And when he would call him for a horse stollen, or for any other matter wherein he would use him; he sayth hee must geue hym some lyuing thing, as a Chicken, a Cat, or a Dog. And further he sayth he must geue hym two lyuing thynges once a yeare. And at the first time when he had the Spirite, hys sayd maister did cause him to deliuer him one drop of his blud, whych bloud the Spirite did take away upon hys paw.

'Tenthly, he sayth that when the Familiar should doo anything at his commaundment, in going any arrant; he would not go, except fyrst two wax candels of Virgin Waxe should first haue bene layd a crosse upon the Circle, wyth a little Frankensence, and saynt John's woorte, and once lighted, and so put out agayne: which Frankensence must be layd then at euery end of the Candel, as he sayth a crosse, and also a litle Frankensence with saynt John's woort burned upon the grounde, or euen the Familiar would go the message, and returne agayne at the houre appoynted....

'... He being further demaunded to what end y{e} Spirits, in the likenes of Todes and the pictures of man or woman made in wax or clay, doo serue? He sayde, that Pictures made in wax wyll cause the partye (for whom it is made) to continue sycke twoo whole yeares ere the wax will be consumed. And, as for the Pictures of Claye, their confection is after this maner. They use to take the earth of a new made graue, the rib bone of a man or woman burned to ashes: if it be for a woman, they take the bone of a woman, if for a man, the bone of a man, and a blacke Spider, with an inner pith of an elder, tempered all in water, in which water the sayd Todes (? Images) must fyrst be washed. And after all ceremonies ended, they put a pricke, that is a pyn or a thorne in any member wher they wold haue the party greued. And if the sayde prycke be put to the harte, the party dieth within nine daies. Which Image they burne in the moste moystest place they can finde. And, as touching the using of the Todes, the which he sayth haue seueral names; soon they cal great Brownyng, or little Brownyng, or Boune, great Tom Twite, or litle Tom Twite, with other like names; Which Todes being called, the Witches strike with II withie sperres on both sydes of y{e} head, and saieth to the Spirit, their Pater noster backward, beginning at the ende of the Pater noster, but they wyll neucr say their Creede. And when he is stricken, they commaunde the Tode, to hurt such a man or woman as he would haue hurted. Whereto, if he swell, he will goo wher he is apointed, either to the deiry, brewhouse, or to the dry kill of malt, or to the Cattell in the field, to the stable, to the shepefold, or to any other like places, and so returne agayne to his place.

'The bodies of men or women bee hurt by the Images before named, and mens goods and cattels be hurt by the Todes, in commaunding and using them, as aforesaid as he sayth. And if the Tode Called forth, as afore said, do not swell, then will the Witch that useth them call forth an other to do the act, which, if he do not, then will they spy another tyme when they may cause the partye to be found lacking fayth, or els to bee more voide of grace, whereby he or they may be hurt. Furthermore he saith, that whoso doth, once a day saye the Lorde's prayer and his Creede in perfite charitie, the Witch shall haue no power on his body or goodes for that day.'

The witchcrafts of Elizabeth Stile[42] and her four companions were decidedly malicious according to her printed confession, but according to her own account they did not prosper, and her state before their trial and execution seems to have been most pitiable.

'Also this is not to be forgotten, that the said Mother Stile, beeyng at the tyme of her apprehension, so well in healthe of bodie and limmes, that she was able, and did goe on foote from Windsor unto Readyng unto the Gaile, which are twelue miles distant. Shortly after that she had made the aforesaid confession, the other Witches were apprehended, and were brought to the said Gaile, the said Mother Deuell did so bewitche her and others, (as she confessed unto the Iailer) with her

Enchantments, that the use of all her limmes and senses were taken quite from her, and her Toes did rotte offe her feete, and she was laied uppon a Barrowe, as a moste uglie creature to beholde, and so brought before the Iudges, at such tyme as she was arraigned.'

In the next little book of the same year 'A Detection of damnable driftes, practized by three Witches arraigned at Chelmissforde in Essex, at the late Assizes there holden, whiche were executed in Aprill 1579.' In reality there were four witches, but one was not convicted, as no manslaughter could be found about her. I propose to give one little anecdote of each, whereby we shall find out something of the Devil's appearance to witches, their families, and their extreme malice in petty things.

'Imprimis, the saied Elizabeth Fraunces confessed that about Lent last, (as she now remembreth) she came to one Poole's wife, her neighbour, and required some old yest of her, but beyng denied the same, she departed towards one good wife Osborne's house, a neighbour dwelling thereby, of whome she had yest; and, in her waie, going towards the saied good wife Osborne's house, she cursed Poole's wife, and badde a mischief to light uppon her, for that she would giue her no yest. Whereuppon, sodenly, in the waie, she heard a greate noise; and, presently there appered unto her a Spirite of a white colour, in seemyng like to a little rugged Dogge, standyng neere her uppon the grounde, who asked her whether she went? shee aunswered for such thinges as she wanted, and she tolde him therewith that she could gette no yeest of Poole's wife, and therefore wished the same Spirite to goe to her and plague her, whiche the Spirite promised to doe; but, first he bad her giue him somewhat; then, she, hauing in her hand a crust of white bread, did bite a peece thereof, and threwe it uppon the grounde, whiche she thinketh he tooke up, and so went his waie: but, before he departed from her, she willed hym to plague Poole's wife in the head, and since that she neuer sawe him, but she hath hearde by her neyghbours that the same Poole's wife was greuously pained in her head not longe after, and remayneth very sore payned still, for on saterdaie last past this Examinate Talked with her.'

In 'The euidence giuen against Elleine Smithe of Maldon' we find: 'Besides, the sonne of this Mother Smith confessed that his mother did keepe three Spirites, whereof the one called by her great Dicke, was enclosed in a Wicker Bottle; the seconde named little Dicke, was putte into a Leather Bottle; And the third, termed Willet, she kept in a Wollepacke. And thereupon the house was commaunded to be searched. The Bottles and packe were found, but the Spirites were vanished awaie.' Nevertheless this charming Master Smith had done his little utmost to hasten his mother's immortality.

Mother Staunton, of Wimbishe, was the one who was not convicted, but things must have looked rather black against her. 'Item, she came on a tyme to the house of one Richard Saunder of Brokewalden; and, beeyng denied Yeest, which she required of his wife, she went hir waie murmuryng, as offended with her answere, and, after her departure, the yonge child in the Cradle was taken vehemently sicke, in a merveilous strange maner, whereuppon the mother of the Childe tooke it up in her armes to comforte it, whiche beynge done, the Cradle rocked of it self, five or seuen tymes, in presence of one of the Earle of Surreis gentilmen; who, seying it, stabbed his dagger three or fower tymes into the Cradle ere it staied; merily jesting and saiyng, that he would kill the Deuill, if he would be rocked there.'

The worst I know about Mother Nokes, the last of this quatrain of witches, is as follows: 'A Certaine Seruant to Thomas Spycer of Lamberd Ende, in Essex, yoman, sporting and passing away the time in play with a great number of youth, chaunced to snatche a paire of Gloues out of the pockette of this Mother Nokes' Daughter, being a yong woman of the age of xxviij yeres, which he protesteth to haue done in iest. Her mother perceiuyng it, demaunded the Gloues of him, but he, geuing no greate eare to her wordes, departed towardes the feeldes to fetch home certeine Cattell. Immediately upon his departure, quoth the same Mother Nokes, to her Daughter, lette him alone, I will bounce him well enough; at which time he, being sodainely taken, and losing the use of his limmes, fell downe. There was a boye then in his Companie, by whome he sent the Gloues to Mother Nokes. Notwithstanding, his Maister was faine to cause him to be sent home in a Wheele Barrowe, and to bee laide into a bedde, wherewith his legges a crosse he lay bedred eight daies, and as yet hath not attayned to the right use of his lymmes.'

In 1582 were the witches of St. Osyth, in Essex,[43] but, as they are too many to particularize, a summary, which appears at the end of the book, may best be given:

'THE NAMES OF XIII WITCHES AND THOSE THAT HAUE BEEN BEWITCHED BY THEM.

'The Names of those persons that haue been bewitched and thereof haue dyed, and by whome, and of them that haue receiued bodyly harme &c. As appeareth upon sundrye Enformations, Examinations and Confessions, taken by the worshipfull Bryan Darcy, Esq{re}: And by him certified at large unto the Queene's Maiesties Justices of Assise of the Countie of Essex, the xxix of March, 1582.

'1. Ursley Kempe, alias Grey, bewitched to death Kempes Wife, Thorlowes Childe, Strattons

Wife.

'The said Ursley Kemp had foure spyrites, viz. their names, Tetty a hee, like a gray Cat; Jack, a hee, like a black Cat: Pygin, a she, like a black Toad, and Tyffyn, a she, like a white Lambe. The hees were to plague to death, and the shees to punish with bodily harme and to destroy cattell. Tyffyn, Ursley's white spirit did tell her alwayes (when she asked) what the other witches had done: And by her, the most part were appelled, which spirit telled her alwayes true. As is well approued by the other Witches Confession.

'2. Ales Newman and Ursley Kempe bewitched to death Letherdailes Childe and Strattons Wife.

'The sayd Ales Newman had the said Ursley Kemps spirits to use at her pleasure.

'The sayd Ales and Ursley Kempe bewitched Strattons Childe and Grace Thorlowe, whereof they did languish.

'3. Elizabeth Bennet bewitched to death William Byet and Joan his wife, and iii of his beasts. The Wife of William Willes and William Willingalle.

'Elizabeth Bennet bewitched William Bonners Wife, John Batler, Fortunes Childe, whereof they did languish.

'Elizabeth Bennet had two Spirits, viz. their name Suckyn, a hee, like a blacke Dog: and Lyard, red lyke a Lyon or Hare.

'Ales Newman bewitched to death John Johnson and his Wife, and her owne husband, as it is thought.

'4. Ales Hunt bewitched to death Rebecca Durrant and vi beasts of one Haywardes.

'Ales Hunt had two spirits lyke Coltes, the one blacke, the other white.

'5. Cysley Celles bewitched to death Thomas Deaths Child. And bewitched Rosses mayde, Mary Death, whereof they did languish.

'6. Cysley Celles and Ales Manfielde bewitched Richard Rosses horse and beasts, and caused their Impes to burne a barne with much corne.

'Cysley Celles had two Spirits by severall names, viz. Sothrons, Herculus, Jack, or Mercury.

'7. Ales Manfielde and Margaret Greuell bewitched to death Robert Cheston and Greuell Husband to Margaret.

'Ales Manfielde and Margaret Greuell bewitched the widdow Cheston and her husband's v beasts, and one bullocke, and seuerall brewinges of beere and batches of bread.

'Ales Manfield and Margaret Greuell had in common, by agreement, iiii spirits, viz. their names, Robin, Jack, Will, Puppet, alias Magnet, whereof two were hees, and two shees, lyke unto black Cats.

'8. Elizabeth Eustace bewitched to death Robert Stanneuette's Childe and Thomas Crosse. And bewitched Robert Stannevette's vii milch beasts, which gaue blood insteede of milke, and seuerall of his Swine dyed.

'Elizabeth Eustace had iii Impes or Spirits, of coulour white, grey and black.

'9. Annys Herde bewitched to death Richard Harrison's wife and two wives of William Dowsing, as it is supposed. And bewitched Cartwright two beasts. Wade, sheep and lambs, &c. West, swine and pigs. Osborne, a brewing of beere, and seuerall other losses of milke and creame.

'10. Annis Herd had vi Impes or spirites like auises and black byrdes, And vi other like Kine, of the bygnes of Rats, with short hornes: the Auises shee fed with wheat, barly, Otes and bread, the Kine with straw and hey.

'11. Margery Sammon had two spirits like Toads, their names Tom and Robyn.

'12. Annis Glascoke bewitched to death Mychell Steuens Childe, The base Childe at Pages, William Pages Childe.

'13. Annis Glascocke, Joan Pechey, Joan Robinson. These haue not confessed any thing touching the hauing of spirits.'

So we see that eleven out of fourteen women confessed not only all that was alleged against them; but many of them went out of their way to oblige Queen Elizabeth's judges, by confessing more. It seems incredible, nevertheless it is true.

Not half so interesting is 'The most strange and admirable discouerie of the three Witches of Worboys,' etc., London, 1593. And, besides, it is such a hackneyed case that it is not worth mentioning, save for the fact that three people were done to death for it, and that money was left for a sermon to be preached in Huntingdon, annually, in commemoration of the fact--a bequest that has now lapsed, the money, of course, disappearing into someone's pocket.

Far rarer is the story of 'The Witches of Northamptonshire, Agnes Browne, Joane Vaughan, Arthur Bill, Hellen Ienkenson, and Mary Barber, Witches, who were all executed at Northampton, the 22 of Iuly last, 1612.' Unfortunately, it is too long for reproduction here in its entirety, which is a pity, as the story is told by one who would have shone as a police-court reporter to a certain section of modern journals; but a portion of it I may give:

'This Agnes Browne led her life at Gilsborough in the county of Northampton, of poore parentage, and poorer education, one that, as shee was borne to no good, was, for want of grace neuer in the way to receiue any; euer noted to bee of an ill nature and wicked disposition, spightful and malitious, and many yeares before she died, both hated and feared among her neighbours: Being long suspected in the Towne where she dwelt, of that crime, which afterwards proued true. This Agnes Browne had a daughter whose name was Ioane Vaughan or Varnham, a maide (or at least unmarried) as gratious as the mother, and both of them as farre from grace as Heauen from Hell.

'This Ioane was so well brought up under her mother's elbow, that shee hangd with her for company under her mother's nose. But to the purpose. This Ioane one day happening into the company of one Mistris Belcher, a vertuous and godly Gentlewoman of the same towne of Gilsborough, this Ioane Vaughan, whether of purpose to giue occasion of anger to the said Mistris Belcher, or but continue her vile and ordinary custome of behauiour, committed something either in speech or gesture, so unfitting and unseeming the nature of womanhood, that it displeased the most that were there present: But especially it touched the modesty of this Gentlewoman, who was much mooued with her bold and impudent demeanor, that she could not contain herselfe, but sodainely rose up and strooke her; howbeit hurt her not, but forced her to auoid the Company: which this Chicken of the Damme's hatching, taking disdainfully, and beeing also enraged (as they that in this kind having power to harme, have neuer patience to beare) at her going out, told the Gentlewoman that shee would remember this iniury, and revenge it: To whom Mistris Belcher answered, that shee neither feared her, nor her mother; but bad her doe her worst.

'This trull holding herselfe much disgraced, hies home in all hast to her mother; and telles her the wrong which shee suggested Mistris Belcher had done unto her: Now was the fire and the tow all enflamed: Nothing but rage and destruction: Had they had an hundred Spirits at command, the worst and the most hurtfull had been called to this counsell, and imployed about this businesse. Howbeit upon advise (if such a sinne may take or giue aduise) they staied three or foure daies before they practised anything, to aduoid suspition, whether the mother aduised the daughter, or the daughter the mother, I know not, but I am sure the deuill neuer giues advise to any man or any woman in any act to be wary.

'The matter thus sleeping (but rage and reuenge doe neuer rest) within a while was awaked, which Mistris Belcher, to her intollerable paine too soone felt: For being alone in her house, she was sodainely taken with such a griping and gnawing in her body, that shee cried out, and could scarce bee held by such as came unto her. And being carried to her bed, her face was many times so disfigured by beeing drawn awrie, that it both bred feare, and astonishment to all the beholders; and euer as shee had breath she cried, Here comes Ioane Vaughan, away with Ioane Vaughan.

'This Gentlewoman being a long time thus strangely handled, to the great griefe of her friends, it happened that her brother, one Master Auery, hearing of his Sisters sicknesse and extremity, came to see her, and, being a sorrowfull beholder of that which before hee had heard, was much moued in his minde at his Sisters pitifull condition, and the rather, for that as hee knew not the nature of his disease, so hee was utterly ignorant of any direct way to minister cure or helpe to the same. Hee often heard her cry out against Ioane Vaughan alias Varnham, and her mother, and heard by report of the neighbours that which before had happened betwixt his Sister and the said Ioane. In so much as having confirmed his suspition that it was nothing else but Witch-craft, that tormented his Sister, following Rage rather than Reason, ran sodainly towards the house of the said Agnes Browne with purpose to draw both the mother and the daughter to his Sister for her to draw blood on; But, still as he came neere the house, hee was sodainely stopped, and could not enter, whether it was an astonishment thorough his feare, or that the Spirits had that power to stay him, I cannot iudge, but he reported at his comming backe that hee was forcibly stayed, and could not, for his life, goe any further forward; and they report, in the Country, that hee is a Gentleman of a stoute courage. Hee tried twice or thrice afterwards to goe to the house, but in the same place where he was staied at first, he was still staied: Belike, the Deuill stood there Centinell, kept his station well.

'Upon this Master Auery beeing sory and much agrieued, that he could not helpe his Sister in this tormenting distresse; and, finding also that no physicke could doe her any good or easement, tooke a sorrowfull leaue and heauily departed home to his owne house.

'The Impe of this Damme, and both Impes of the Deuill, being glad that they were both out of his reach, shewed presently that they had longer armes than he, for he felt, within a short time after his comming home, that hee was not out of their reach, beeing, by the deuilish practises of these two hel-houndes sodenly and grieuously tormented in the like kinde and with the like fits of his sister, which continued untill these two witches either by the procurement of Maister Auery and his friends (or for some other Deuilish practise they had committed in the Countrey) were apprehended and brought to Northampton Gaole by Sir William Saunders of Codesbrooke, Knight.

'To which place the Brother and the Sister were brought, still desirous to scratch the Witches. Which Act, whether it be but superstitiously obserued by some; or, that experience hath found any power for helpe in this kind of Action by others, I list not to enquire, onely this I understand that many haue attempted the practising thereof, how successfully, I know not. But this Gentleman and his Sister beeing brought to the gaole where these Witches were detained, hauing once gotten sight of them, in their fits the Witches being held, by scratching, they drew blood of them, and were sodainely deliuered of their paine. Howbeit, they were no sooner out of sight, but they felle againe into their old traunces, and were more violently tormented than before: for when Mischiefe is once a foote, she growes in short time so headstrong, that she is hardly curbed.

'Not long after, Maister Auery and his Sister hauing beene both in Northampton, and hauing drawne blood of the Witches, ryding both homewards in one Coach, there appeared to their view a man and a woman ryding both upon a blacke horse. M. Auery hauing spyed them a farre off, and noting many strange gestures from them, sodainely spake to them that were by, and (as it were Prophetically) cryed out in these words, That either they, or their Horses should presently miscarry. And, immediately, the horses fell downe dead. Whereupon Maister Auery rose up praysing y{e} grace and mercies of God, that he had so powerfully deliuered them, and had not suffered the foule spirits to worke the uttermost of their mischiefe upon men made after his image, but had turned their fury against Beasts. Upon this, they both hyed them home, still praysing God for their escape, and were neuer troubled after.

'I had almost forgotten to tell you before, that M. Auery was by the Judges themselves in y{e} Castle Yard of Northampton, seene in the middest of his fits, and that he strangely continued in them untill this Ioane Vaughan was brought to him.

'But now to draw neere unto their ends, this Agnes Browne and her daughter Ioane Vaughan, being brought to their Arraignment, were there indicted for that they had bewitched the bodies of Maister Auery and his sister Mistris Belcher in manner and forme aforesayd. Together with the body of a young Child to the death; (the true relation whereof came not to my hands). To all which they pleaded not guilty, and, putting themselues upon the countrey, were found guilty. And when they were asked what they could say for themselves, why y{e} sentence of death should not be pronounced against them, they stood stiffely upon their Innocence. Whereupon, Judgement beeing giuen, they were carried backe unto the Gaole, where they were neuer heard to pray, or to call uppon God, but with bitter Curses and execrations, spent that little time they had to liue, until the day of their Execution, when neuer asking pardon for their offences, either of God, or the world, in this their daungerous and desperate resolution, dyed.

'It was credibly reported that some fortnight before their apprehension, this Agnes Browne, one Katherine Gardiner, and one Ioane Lucas, all birdes of a winge, and all abyding in the Towne of Gilsborough did ride one night to a place (not aboue a mile off) called Rauenstrop all upon a Sowes back, to see one mother Rhoades, an old Witch that dwelt there; but, before they came to the house the old Witch died; and, in her last cast cried out, that there were three of her old friends comming to see her, but they came too late. Howbeit, shee would meete with them in another place within a month after.'

CHAPTER XVI

The Lancashire Witches--Janet Preston--Margaret and Philip Flower--Anne Baker, Joane Willimot, and Ellen Greene--Elizabeth Sawyer--Mary Smith--Joan Williford, Joan Cariden, and Jane Hott.

The foregoing sample must serve for the witches of Northamptonshire, nor will I touch on the Lancashire witches, whose story appears in nearly every modern work on witchcraft, and has been vulgarized by Harrison Ainsworth, except to give a portion of the evidence of one James Device, of the forest of Pendle, labourer, in the case of Janet or Jennet Preston, who was condemned as a witch, and executed at York in 1612.

'And he also further saith, That the said Prestons wife had a Spirit with her like unto a white Foale, with a blacke spot in the forehead. And further this Examinate saith, That since the said meeting, as aforesaid, that he hath been brought to the house of one Preston in Gisburne Parish aforesaid, by Henry Hargreiues of Goldshey, to see whether shee was the woman that came amongst the said Witches, on the said last Good Friday, to crave their aide and assistance for the killing of the said Master Lister; and hauing had full view of her, hee, this Examinate confesseth, That she was the selfe-same woman which came amongst the said Witches on the said last Good Friday for their aide for the killing of the said Master Lister; and that brought the Spirit with her, in the shape of a White Foale, as aforesaid.

'And this Examinate further saith, that all the said Witches went out of the said house in their owne shapes and likenesses, and they all, by that they were forth of the doores, were gotten on horse-backe like unto Foales, some of one colour, some of another, and Preston's wife was the last; and when she got on horse-backe, they all presently vanished out of this Examinate's sight; and before their said parting away, they all appointed to meete at the said Preston's wife's house that day twelve month; at which time the said Preston's wife promised to make them a great feast; and, if they had occasion to meet in the meane time, then should warning be giuen that they should all meet upon Romles Moore. And this Examinate further saith, That at the said feast at Malkin Tower, this Examinate heard them all giue their consents to put the said Master Thomas Lister of Westby to death; and after Master Lister should haue been made away by Witchcraft, then al the said Witches gaue their consents to ioyne altogether to hancke Master Leonard Lister, when he should come to liue at the Sowgill, and so put him to death.'

Then we have 'The Wonderful Discouerie of the Witchcrafts of Margaret and Philip Flower daughters of Ioan Flower, neere Beuer Castle: Executed at Lincoln March 11, 1618. Who were specially arraigned and condemned before Sir Henry Hobart, and Sir Edward Bromley, Iudges of Assise, for confessing themselues actors in the destruction of Henry, Lord Rosse, with their damnable practices against others the Children of the Right Honourable Francis Earle of Rutland. Together with the seuerall Examinations and Confessions of Anne Baker, Ioan Willimot, and Ellen Greene, Witches in Leicestershire.' London, 1611.

The first case is a very ordinary one. The Flowers were discharged servants, and the children, after their leaving, sickened and died. The only remarkable part about it is, that 'Ioane Flower, the Mother, before conviction (as they say) called for Bread and Butter, and wished it might neuer goe through her, if she were guilty of that, whereupon she was examined; so, mumbling it in her mouth, neuer spake more wordes after, but fell downe and died as she was carried to Lincolne Gaole, with a horrible excruciation of soule and body, and was buried at Ancaster.'

The portraits of the three witches do not prepossess us in their favour, and their confessions, on examination, fully bear out the feeling. Of the first: 'Further, she saith that shee saw a hand appeare unto her, and that shee heard a voyce in the ayre say unto her: Anne Baker, saue thyselfe, for to-morrow, thou and thy maister must be slaine; and the next day her maister and shee were in a Cart together; and suddainely shee saw a flash of fire, and said her prayers, and the fire went away; and shortly after, a Crow came and picked upon her cloathes, and she said her prayers againe, and bad the Crow go to whom he was sent, and the Crow went unto her Maister, and did beat him to death, and shee, with her prayers recouered him to life; but hee was sicke for a fortnight after, and saith, that if shee had not had more knowledge than her maister, both he and shee, and all the Cattell had been slaine.'

Joan Willimot tells the following extraordinary story: 'That shee hath a Spirit which shee calleth Pretty, which was given unto her by William Berry of Langholme, in Rutlandshire, whom she serued three yeares: and that her Master, when hee gaue it unto her, willed her to open her mouth, and hee would blow into her a Fairy which should do her good; and that shee opened her mouth, and hee did blow into her mouth; and that, presently, after his blowing, there came out of her mouth a Spirit, which stood upon the ground in the shape and forme of a Woman, which Spirit did aske of her her Soule, which shee then promised unto it, being willed thereunto by her Master.'

The third, Ellen Green, said 'that one Ioan Willimot of Goadby came about six yeares since to her in the Wowlds, and purswaded this Examinate to forsake God, and betake her to the diuel, and she would give her two spirits; to which she gave her consent, and thereupon, the said Ioan Willimot called two spirits, one in the likenesse of a Kitlin, and the other of a Moldiwarp:[44] the first the said Willimot called pusse, the other hisse, hisse, and they presently came to her, and she, departing, left them with this Examinate, and they leapt on her shoulder, and the Kitlin suckt under her right eare on her neck, and the Moldiwarp on the left side, in the like place. After they had suckt her, shee sent the Kitlin to a Baker of that Towne, whose name shee remembers not, who had called her Witch and stricken her; and bad her said spirit goe and bewitch him to death: The Moldiwarpe shee then bad go to Anne Dawse, of the same towne, and bewitch her to death, because she had called this examinate witch, jade, &c., and within one fortnight after, they both dyed.'

The case of Elizabeth Sawyer, known as the Witch of Edmonton, executed at Tyburn, April 19, 1621, is so extraordinary that I give a large portion of the tract in extenso:[45]

'A true relation of the confession of Elizabeth Sawyer, spinster, after her conviction of Witchery, taken on Tuesday the 17 day of Aprill, Anno 1621, in the Gaole of Newgate, where she was prisoner, then in the presence and hearing of diuers persons whose names to verifie the same are here subscribed to this ensuyng confession, made unto me, Henry Goodcole, Minister of the word of God, Ordinary and Visiter for the Gaole of Newgate. In dialogue manner are here expressed the persons that she murthered, and the Cattell that she destroyed by the helpe of the Diuell.

'In this manner was I inforced to speake unto her, because she might understand me, and giue unto me answere, according to my demands, for she was a very ignorant woman.

'Question. By what meanes came you to have acquaintance with the Diuell, and when was the first time that you saw him, and how did you know that it was the Diuell?

'Answere. The first time that the Diuell came unto me was when I was cursing, swearing, and blaspheming: he then rushed in upon me, and never before that time did I see him, or he me: and when he, namely the Diuell, came to me, the first words that he spake unto me were these: Oh! have I now found you cursing, swearing, and blaspheming? now you are mine.

***

'Question. What sayd you to the Diuell, when he came unto you and spake unto you, were you not afraide of him? If you did feare him, what sayd the Diuell then unto you?

'Answere. I was in a very greate feare when I saw the Diuell, but hee did bid me not to feare him at all, for hee would do me no hurt at all, but would do for mee whatsoeuer I would require of him; and as he promised unto me, he alwayes did such mischiefes as I did bid him to do, both on the bodies of Christians and beastes: if I did bid him vexe them to death, as oftentimes I did so bid him, it was presently by him done.

'Question. Whether would the Diuell bring unto you word or no, what he had done for you, at your command; and if he did bring you word, how long would it bee, before he would come unto you againe, to tell you?

'Answere. He would alwayes bring unto me word what he had done for me within the space of a weeke; he neuer failed me at that time; and would likewise do it to Creatures and beastes two manners of wayes, which was by scratching or pinching of them.

'Question. Of what Christians and Beastes, and how many were the number that you were the cause of their death, and what moued you to prosecute them to the death?

'Answere. I have been by the helpe of the Diuell the meanes of many Christians' and beasts' death; the cause that moued mee to do it was malice and enuy; for, if anybody had angred me in any manner, I would be so revenged of them, and of their Cattell. And do now further confesse that I was the cause of those two nurse children's death, for the which I was now indicted, and acquited by the Iury.

***

'Question. How long is it since the Diuell and you had acquaintance together, and how oftentimes in the weeke would hee come and see you, and you Company with him?

'Answere. It is eight yeares since our first acquaintance; and three times in the weeke the Diuell would come and see me, after such his acquaintance gotten of me; he would come sometimes in the morning, and sometimes in the evening.

'Question. In what shape would the Diuell come unto you?

'Answere. Alwayes in the shape of a dogge, and of two collors, sometimes of blacke, and sometimes of white.

'Question. What talke had the Diuel and you together, when that he appeared to you, and what did he aske of you--and what did you desire of him?

'Answere. He asked of me when he came unto me, how I did, and what he should doe for mee, and demanded of mee my soule and body; threatning then to tear me in pieces if I did not grant unto him my soule and my body, which he asked of me.

'Question. What did you after such the Diuel's asking of you, to have your Soule and Body, and after this his threatning of you, did you for feare grant unto the Diuell his desire?

'Answere. Yes; I granted for feare unto the Diuell his request of my soule and body; and, to seale this my promise made unto him, I then gave him leave to sucke of my bloud, the which hee asked of me.

'Question. In what place of your body did the Diuell sucke of your bloude and whether did hee himselfe chuse the place, or did you yourselfe appoint him the place?

'Answere. The place where the Diuell suckt my bloud was chosen by himselfe, and in that place, by continuall drawing, there is a thing in the forme of a Teate, at which the Diuell would sucke mee. And I asked the Diuell why he should sucke my bloud, and he sayd, it was to nourish him.

'Question. Whether did you pull up your Coates or no, when the Diuell came to sucke you?

'Answere. No. I did not, but the Diuell would put his head under my coates, and I did willingly suffer him to doe what he would.

'Question. How long would the time bee, that the Diuell would continue sucking of you, and whether did you endure any paine, the time that hee was sucking of you?

'Answere. He would be suckinge of me the continuance of a quarter of an houre, and when he suckt me I then felt no paine at all.

'Question. What was the meaning that the Diuell, when he came unto you, would sometimes speake, and sometimes barke?

'Answere. It is thus: when the Diuell spake to me, then hee was ready to doe for me what I bid him to doe; and when he came barking to mee, he then had done the mischiefe that I did bid him to doe for me. I did call the Diuell by the name of Tom.

**

'Question. Did you euer handle the Diuell when he came unto you?

'Answere. Yes, I did stroake him on the backe, and then he would becke unto me, and wagge his tayle as being therewith contented.

'Question. Would the Diuell come unto you all in one bignesse?

'Answere. No; when hee came unto mee in the blacke shape, he then was biggest, and in the white the least; and when that I was praying, hee then would come unto me in the white colour.'

In another narrative[46] we have a different description of the devil, and of his protean powers:

'Marie wife of Henrie Smith, Glouer, possessed with a wrathfull indignation against some of her neighbours, in regard that they made gaine of their buying and selling Cheese, which shee (using the same trade) could not doe, or they better, (at the least in her opinion than she did,) often times cursed them, and became incensed with unruly passions, armed with a setled resolution to effect some mischieuous proiects and designs against them. The diuell, who is skilfull, and reioyceth of such an occasion offered, and knoweth how to stirre up the euill affected humours of corrupt mindes, appeared unto her amiddes these discontentments, in the shape of a blacke man, and willed that she should continue in her malice, enuy, hatred, banning and cursing, and then he would be reuenged for her upon all those to whom she wished euill: and this promise was uttered in a lowe murmuring and hissing voyce: and, at that present, they entred tearmes of a compact, he requiring that she should forsake God, and depend upon him; to which she condescended in expresse tearmes, renouncing God, and betaking herselfe unto him.

'After this, hee presented himselfe againe at sundrie times, and in other formes, as of a mist, and of a ball of fire, with some dispersed spangles of blacke, and at the last in prison (after the doome of iudgement, and sentence of condemnation was passed against her) two seuerall times, in that figure as at the first: only at the last he seemed to haue a pair of horns upon his head.'

Mary Smith, if what is written about her be true, was a very powerful witch. Many instances of her bewitching are given; but I think her spells on one John Orkton, a sailor, were the worst. She cursed him, 'Whereupon, presently, hee grew weake, distempered in stomacke, and could digest no meate, nor other nourishment receiued, and this discrasie, or feeblenesse continued for the space of three quarters of a yeare; which time expired, the fore mentioned griefe fel downe from the stomacke into his hands and feete, so that his fingers did corrupt and were cut off; as also his toes putrified and consumed in a very strange and admirable manner. Neverthelesse, notwithstanding these calamities, so long as he was able, went still to Sea, in the goods and shippes of sundry Merchants (for it was his onely meanes of living) but neuer could make any prosperous voyage, eyther beneficiall to the Owners, or profitable to himselfe.

'Whereupon, not willing to bee hindrance to others, and procure no good for his owne maintenance by his labours, left that trade of life, and kept home, where his former griefe encreasing, sought to obtaine help and remedie by Chirurgerie; and, for this end, went to Yarmouth, hoping to be cured by one there, who was accompted very skilfull: but no medicines applyed by the Rules of Arte and Experience, wrought any expected or hoped for effect; for both his hands and feete, which seemed in some measure, euery euening, to be healing, in the morning were found to have gone backeward, and growne far worse than before. So that the Chirurgian, perceiuing his labour to bee wholly frustrate, gaue ouer the cure, and the diseased patient still continueth in a most miserable and distressed estate, unto the which hee was brought by the hellish practises of this malitious woman, who, long before, openly in the streetes, (when, as yet, the neighbours knew of no such thing,) reioycing at the Calamity, said, Orkton now lyeth a rotting.' She was executed January 12, 1616.

'The Examination, Confession, Triall and Execution of Joane Williford, Joan Cariden, and Jane Hott, who were executed at Faversham in Kent, for being Witches, on Munday, the 29 of September, 1645,' furnish us with other particulars, especially as they all confessed their crimes.

Joan Williford confessed 'That the divell, about seven yeeres ago, did appeare to her in the shape of a little dog, and bid her to forsake God, and leane to him; who replied that she was loath to forsake him. Shee confessed also that shee had a desire to be revenged upon Thomas Letherland and Mary Woodrufe, now his wife. She further said that the divell promised her that she should not lacke, and that she had money sometimes brought her, she knew not whence, sometimes one shilling, sometimes eightpence, never more at once: shee called her Divell by the name of Bunne. She further saith, that her retainer Bunne carried Thomas Gardler out of a window, who fell into a back side. She further saith, that neere twenty years since, she promised her soule to the Divell. She further saith that she gave some of her blood to the Divell, who wrote the covenant betwixt them. She further saith that the Divell promised to be her servant about twenty yeeres, and that the time is now almost expired. She further saith that the Divell promised her that she should not sinke, being throwne into the water, and that the Divell sucked twice since she came into the prison; he came to her in the forme of a Muce.'

Joan Cariden's confession was commonplace, but Jane Hott said that 'a thing like a hedge hog had usually visited her, and came to her a great while agoe, about twenty yeares agoe, and that if it sucked her, it was in her sleep, and the paine thereof awaked her, and it came to her once or twice in the moneth, and sucked her, and when it lay upon her breast, she strucke it off with her hand, and that it was as soft as a Cat.

'At her first coming into the Gaole, she spake very much to the other that were apprehended before her, to confesse if they were guilty; and stood to it very perversely that she was cleare of any such thing, and that, if they put her into the Water to try her, she should certainly sinke. But when she was put into the Water it was apparent that she did flote upon the Water. Being taken forth, a Gentleman to whom, before, she had so confidently spake, and with whom she offered to lay twenty shillings to one that she could not swim, asked her how it was possible she could be so impudent as not to confesse herselfe? To whom she answered, That the Divell went with her all the way, and told her that she should sinke; but when she was in the Water, he sate upon a Crosse beame and laughed at her.'

CHAPTER XVII

Confessions of Witches executed in Essex--The Witches of Huntingdon--'Wonderfull News from the North'--Trial of Six Witches at Maidstone--Trial of Four Witches at Worcester--A Lancashire Witch tried at Worcester--A Tewkesbury Witch.

A sickening story is told in 'A true and exact Relation of the seuerall Informations, Examinations, and Confessions of the late Witches, arraigned and executed in the County of Essex. Who were arraigned and condemned at the late Sessions, holden at Chelmesford before the Right Honorable Robert Earle of Warwicke and severall of his Majesties Iustices of Peace, the 29 of July 1645,' etc., London, 1645. In this veritable 'bloody assize,' the rascally Matthew Hopkins appears, and it would almost seem as if the poor women confessed anything in order to have the luxury of dying. The charges against them were so frivolous, and the confessions so silly, that they must have either been imbecile or reckless. The following is a list of them:

Elizabeth Clarke	confessed	executed
Elizabeth Gooding	denied	do.
Anne Leech	confessed	do.
Helen Clark	confessed	executed
Rebecca West	do.	acquitted
Mary Greenleife	denied	fate unknown
Mary Johnson	do.	do.
Anne Cooper	confessed	executed
Elizabeth Hare	denied	condemned, but reprieved
Margaret Moon	do.	died on the way to execution
Marian Hocket	do.	executed
Sarah Hating	do.	do.
Rose Hallybread	-	died in gaol
Elizabeth Harvie	confessed	executed
Joyce Boanes	do.	do.
Susan Cock	do.	do.
Margaret Landishe	do.	do.
Rebecca Jones	do.	do.
Joan Cooper	do.	died in gaol
Anne Cate	do.	executed

The confession (!) of this latter will serve as an example of the puerility of them all.

'This Examinant saith, that she hath four Familiars, which shee had from her mother, about two and twenty yeeres since; and that the names of the said Imps are James, Pricke eare, Robyn, and Sparrow; and three of these Imps are like Mouses, and the fourth like a Sparrow. And this Examinant saith, that to whomsoever shee sent the said Imp called Sparrow, it killed them presently; and that, first of all, she sent one of her three Imps like Mouses, to nip the Knee of one Robert Freeman, of Little Clacton, in the County of Essex, aforesaid, whom the said Imp did so lame, that the said Robert dyed on that lamenesse within half a yeere after: And this Examinant saith, that she sent her said Imp, Prickeare to kill the daughter of John Rawlins of Much-Holland aforesaid, which died accordingly within a short time after; and that she sent her said Imp Prickeare to the house of one John Tillet; which did suddenly kill the said Tillet.

'And this Examinant saith that shee sent her said Imp Sparrow, to kill the childe of one George Parby of Much-Holland aforesaid, which child the said Imp did presently kill; and that the offence this Examinant took against the said George Parby to kill his said childe, was, because the wife of the said Parby denyed to give this Examinant a pint of Milke; and this Examinant further saith that shee sent her said Imp Sparrow to the house of Samuel Ray, which, in a very short time did kill the wife of the said

The Devil, in Britain and America

Samuel; and that the cause of this Examinant's malice against the said woman was, because shee refused to pay to this Examinant two pence which she challenged to be due to her; And that, afterwards, her said Imp Sparrow killed the said Childe of the said Samuel Ray: and this Examinant confesseth, that as soon as shee had received the said four Imps from her said mother, the said Imps spake to this Examinant, and told her, shee must deny God and Christ, which this Examinant did then assent unto.'

In 'The Witches of Huntingdon, their Examinations and Confessions,' etc., London, 1646, we have eight cases of witchcraft which were tried at different times early in 1646. Among these eight, two were men; but there is no record of the fate of any of them. They are the same old story, the one with the most originality being that of Jane Willis, of Keiston, in the county of Huntingdon.

'This Examinate saith, as she was making of her bedde in her Chamber, there appeared in the shape of a man in blacke cloaths, and blackish cloaths about six weeks past, and bid her good morrow, and shee asked what his name was, and he said his name was Blackeman, and asked her if she were poore, and she said I:[47] then he told her he would send one Grissell and Greedigut to her, that shall do anything for her: Shee looking upon him, saw hee had ugly feete, and then she was very fearfull of him, for that sometimes he would seem to be tall, and sometimes lesse, and suddenly vanished away.

'And being demanded whether he lay with her, shee said hee would have lain with her, but shee would not suffer him: and after Blackeman was departed from her, within three or 4 dayes, Grissell and Greedigut came to her, in the shape of dogges, with great brisles of hogges haire upon their backs, and said to her they were come from Blackeman to do what she would command them, and did aske her if shee did want any thing, and they would fetch it: and shee said she lacked nothing. Then they prayed her to give them some victuals, and she said she was poore and had none to give them; and so they departed: Yet she confessed that Blackeman, Grissel and Greedigut divers times came to her afterwards, and brought her two or three shillings at a time, and more saith not.'

Another type of witchcraft is to be found in 'Wonderfull News from the North; or, a true relation of the sad and grievous torments inflicted upon the Bodies of three Children of Mr. George Muschamp, late of the County of Northumberland, by Witchcraft,' etc. London, 1650. It begins thus:

'First in harvest, some two Months before Michaelmas, about four or five of the Clock in the afternoone, Mistris Margaret Muschamp suddainly fell into a great Trance; her Mother being frighted, called Company, and with much adoe recovered her; as soone as the childe look'd up, cryed out, deare Mother, weepe not for me; for I have seene a happy Sight, and heard a blessed sound, for the Lord hath loved my poore Soule, that he hath caused his blessed Trumpet to sound in my eares, and hath sent two blessed Angels to receive my sinfull soule. O weepe not for me, but rejoyce, that the Lord should have such respect to so sinfull a wretch as I am, as to send his heavenly Angels to receive my sinfull soule: with many other divine expressions.'

After this she continued pretty well till Candlemas Eve, when she was taken very bad indeed, losing the use of her limbs and speech, 'and such torments, that no eyes could looke on her without compassion.' For 16 weeks she refused all food, saying 'that God fed her with Angel's food: for truely all the 16 weekes fast she did not appeare to diminish her fatness or favour anything at all.

'On Whitsun Eve in the morning, she had eight hours bitter torment. In the afternoone, her mother being abroad, left her Husband's Brother's Daughter, Mrs. Elizabeth Muschamp with her, who made signes to her to carry her into the Garden, in her mother's absence; her Cozen, casting a mantle about her, gave her her desire, and sate in the Garden with her on her knee; who, in the bringing downe, had so little strength in her neck, that her head hung wagging downe; but was not set a quarter of an houre, till showing some signes to her Cozen, bolted off her knee, ran thrice about the Garden, expressing a shrill voyce, but did not speake presently: she that was brought down in this sad condition came up stairs on her owne legs.'

However, this improvement did not last long; she had more illnesses, and in one of them she made signs that she wished to write; so 'they layd paper on her brest, and put a pen with inke in her hand, and she, not moving her eyes, writ, Jo. Hu. Do. Swo. have been the death of one deare friend, consume another, and torment mee.' The wiseacres puzzled over this, and at last came to the conclusion that Mistress Dorothy Swinnow, then wife to Col. Swinnow, who subsequently died, had bewitched her. At another time this Margaret Muschamp wrote the same words with the addition, 'two drops of his or her bloud would save my life; if I have it not, I am undone; for seven yeares to be tormented before death come.'

On this they sent to one John Hutton, a reputed wizard, who told them that it was Mistress Swinnow who was the culprit, and he gave them two drops of his own blood, which he wiped off his arm, with the paper on which the girl had written. Returning home, they applied this remedy, in some way unstated, and 'On Munday night she fell into a heavenly rapture, rejoycing that ever she was borne, for these two drops of blood had saved her life.' The girl was afterwards very ill, and Dorothy Swinnow, now a widow, was arrested, and committed to prison, where the narrative leaves off, with the addition of the confession of one Margaret White, who 'Confesseth and saith, That she hath beene the

Divells servant these five yeares past, and that the Divell came to her in the likenes of a man in blew cloaths, in her owne house, and griped her fast by the hand, and told her she should never want, and gave her a nip on the shoulder, and another on her back; and confesseth her Familiar came to her in the likenesse of a black Gray-hound. She also Confesseth upon Oath that Mrs. Swinnow and her sister Jane, and herselfe were in the Divels company in her sister Jane's house, where they did eate and drinke together, and made merry.

'And Mrs. Swinnow, and her the sayd Margaret's sister, with her selfe, came purposely to the house of Mr. Edward Moore of Spittle, to take away the life of Margaret Muschamp and Mary, and they were the cause of the Children's tormenting, and that they were three several times to have taken away their lives, and especially upon St. John's day at night gone twelve moneths: and sayth that God was above the Divell, for they could not get their desires perfected; and saith that Mrs. Swinnow would have consumed the childe that Mrs. Moore had last in her wombe, but the Lord would not permit her; and that after the childe was borne, Mrs. Swinnow was the occasion of its death; and that she and her sister were also the occasion, and had a hand in the death of the sayd child; and further confesseth that she and her sayd sister were the death of Thomas Yong of Chatton (by reason) a kill full of Oates watched against her sister's minde; And further saith that the Divell called her sister Jane (Besse); She confesseth that her sister Jane had much troubled Richard Stanley of Chatton, and that she was the occasion of his sore leg.'

In 'A Prodigious and Tragicall History of the Arraignment, Tryall, Confession and Condemnation of six Witches at Maidstone in Kent, at the Assizes there held in July, Fryday 30, this present year 1652,' a new feature is introduced.

'The said Anne Ashby further confessed, that the Divell had given them a piece of flesh, which whensoever they should touch, they should thereby effect their desires.

'That this flesh lay hid amongst grasse, in a certain place which she named, where, upon search, it was found accordingly.

'The flesh was of a sinnewy substance, and scorched, and was seen and felt by this Observator, and reserved for publique view at the sign of the Swan in Maidstone.'

They were duly hanged, but 'Some there were that wished rather they might be burnt to Ashes; alledging, that it was a received opinion amongst many, that the body of a witch being burnt, her bloud is prevented thereby from becomming hereditary to her Progeny in the same evill, which by hanging is not.'

However, in the case of four witches tried at Worcester on March 4, 1647,[48] they 'received Sentance to be Burnt at the Stak all Four together.

'When being come to the Place of Execution, they made a strange and lamentable Yeling and Howling, after which they Confessed the Crimes for which they Suffered, and also declared how they had kill'd abundance of Cattle for several years past, and that it was extream Pride, Malice, and Revenge, that caused them to enter into such a curssed and Hellish League with the Devil, who told them to the last, that he would secure them from Public Punishment, but now, too late, they found him a Lyer, as he was from the beginning of the World. Cock and Landish seemed penitent, desiring all young Women to take Warning by their Devilish Lives, and Shameful Deaths, assuring the Spectators, that as Satan in the first Infancy of the World, prevail'd on the Woman to bring his Hellish attempts to pass, so he still strives with that Sex, as the weaker Vessels, to Work their Distructions; they both said the Lord's Prayer very distinctly, but Rebecca West and Rose Hallybread dyed very Stuburn and Refractory, without any remorss, or seeming Terror of Conscience for their abominable Witch-craft.'

'A RELATION OF A LANCASHIRE WITCH, TRYED AT WORCESTER, IN THE YEAR 1649.[49]

'At Droitwich in the County of Worcester, a poor Woman's Boy in the Month of May, looking for his Mother's Cow, espied some Bushes in a Brake to shake; and, supposing the Cow to be Brousing there, went to the Place, where he found no Cow, but an Old Woman, who, upon his approach, said Boh to him: whereupon he presently lost his speech, and could only make a Noise, but could not speak any thing articulately, so as could be understood. In this condition he came home to his Mother, made a great Noise, but no body could understand what ailed him, or what he meant. A while after, he ran out, and, at Sir Edward Barret's door, found, about One a Clock, amongst other poor People, the same old Woman supping up a Mess of hot Pottage, and ran furiously upon her, and threw her Pottage in her Face, and offered some other Violence to her. Whereupon the Neighbours wondering at the condition of the Boy, and his rage against the old Woman, and suspecting that she had done him some hurt, Apprehended her, and she was committed to the Prison, which they call the Checker. At Night the Boy's Mother Lodged him in a Garret over her own Lodging; and, in the Morning, hearing a great Bussle over her, ran up, and found the Boy gotten out of his Bed, with the Leg of a Form in his hand, striking furiously at something in the Window; but saw nothing there that he should strike at. The Boy presently put on his Cloaths, and ran downe into the Street towards the Prison; and, as he was going, endeavouring to speak, found his Speech restored.

'When he came to the Prison, he asked for the old Woman, and told the Gaoler how she had served him, and how his Speech came to him again in the Way. The Gaoler, in the mean time, suspecting that she had Bewitched the Boy, would not let her have either Meat or Drink, unless she would first say the Lord's Prayer, and bid God bless the Boy: which, at last, her Hunger forced her to do; and it appeared to be at the same instant, as near as can be guessed, that the Boy had his Speech restored to him. The Boy asked the Gaoler, why he did not keep her faster, but let her come out, and trouble him? The Gaoler answered, he had kept her very safe. The Boy replied No, he had not; for she came and sat in his Chamber Window, and grinned at him; and that, thereupon, he took up a Form Leg, and therewith gave her two good bangs upon the Back, as she would have scutled from him, before she could get away. Whereupon the Gaoler caused some Women to search her, who found the Marks of two such Strokes upon her, as the Boy said he had given her. All this was Sworn upon her Tryal by the Boy, his Mother, the Gaoler, and the Women. Upon Examination she was found to be a Lancashire Woman; who, upon the Scarcity in those Parts, after the Defeat of Duke Hamilton, wandred abroad to get Victuals.'

'ANOTHER RELATION OF A TEUKSBURY WITCH, TRYED AT GLOUCESTER ABOUT THE SAME TIME.

'At Teuksbury, about the same time, a Man, who had a Sow and Pigs, observing his Sow to have great store of Milk, and yet the Pigs to be almost Famished, and consulting with his Neighbours about it, they all concluded that she must needs be Sucked by something else, and so the Pigs be robbed of their milk. Whereupon he resolved to watch till he found out the Matter: and, having placed himself conveniently for that purpose, at last he saw a black Four footed Creature, like a Pole Cat, come and beat away the pigs, and having a pitchfork in his Hand, he ran the Prongs into the Thigh of it, and ran it to the ground. Yet it struggled so as to get off from him at last. There were some Neighbours not far off, but they saw no such creature, but saw a Wench go away, and that Blood fell from her as she went: whereupon they searched her, and found her so Wounded, as the Man said he had wounded the thing which he found Sucking: And, thereupon, she was Apprehended and Tryed at Gloucester Assizes, where this Matter was given in Evidence against her.'

CHAPTER XVIII

A Case of Vomiting Stones, etc., at Evesham--Anne Bodenham--Julian Cox--Elizabeth Styles--Rose Cullender and Amy Duny.

Baxter, in his 'Certainty of the Worlds of Spirits,' etc. (London, 1691), gives what he considers an indisputably authentic case of witchcraft, as follows:

'But the certaintest and fullest Instance of Witchcraft that ever I knew, I shall here give you in the words of others: Only adding that about twenty years ago, at the time it was doing, my worthy and dear Friend, Mr. George Hopkins, the then Faithful Minister of the Gospel at Evesham, told it me himself, and told me of their Care and Watchfulness, to see that there were no Fraud committed in it. And the Witch was hanged at Worcester, and the Woman herself is yet living in Evesham, and the thing never there doubted of: But, having occasion lately to instance the fact against some Unbelievers, I sent to Evesham, to a Godly, Credible Friend to send me word, whether any doubt had, in these years past, risen concerning it, and to send me some of the Flint Stones which were voided by the Girl; who sent me word, that there were no doubt of the thing, and procured the now Minister of the Place to write me the Narrative which I here subjoin. And he sent me One stone, about the breadth of a small Groat, and the thickness of a Half-crown, which, he said, was all that is there kept of them, taken by the Major's Wife her self, and kept by her, and, therefore, I must send it back again: Many had sent for the Stones, and so many troubled the House about them, that they threw away, or buried the rest: And Mr. Boyle told me that the Earl of South Hampton, Lord Treasurer, for his Satisfaction, had got a great number of them. I carried this about me, a quarter of a year, and then sent it home. But that which I chiefly inform the Reader of, is, that the thing was so long in doing, and so Famous, and so many Pious, Understanding Persons minded it, that suspition of Fraud was by their Diligence avoided.

'The Narrative as lately sent me from most Credible Persons in Evesham, is as followeth:

'About the Month of April 1652 Mary, the daughter of Edward Ellins, of the Burrough of Evesham, in the County of Worcester, Gardner, then about nine or ten years old, went in the fields on a Saturday, with some other Children, to gather Cowslips, and, finding in a Ditch by the way-side, at the said Town's end, one Catherine Huxley, a single Woman, aged then about forty years, the Children called her Witch, and took up stones to throw at her, the said Mary also called her Witch, and took up a stone, but was so affrighted that she could not throw it at her; then they all run away from her, and the said Mary being hindmost, this Huxley said to her (Ellins you Shall have enough stones in you.) Whereupon Mary fell that day very ill, and continued so weak and Languishing that her Friends feared she would not recover; but, about a Month after, she began to void stones by the urinary passages, and some little urine came away from her; also, when she voided any stone, the stone she voided was heard by those that were by her, to drop into the Pot or Basin; and she had most grievous pains in her Back and Reins, like the pricking of Pins. The number of the stones she voided was about eighty, some plain pebbles, some plain flints, some very small, and some about an ounce weight. This she did for some space, (a month or two, or there abouts) until, upon some strong suspitions of Witchcraft, the forenamed Huxley was Apprehended, Examined and Searched, (at whose Bed's Head there was found several Stones such as the said Mary Voided) and was sent to Worcester, where, at the Summer Assizes in the said year 1652 (then at hand) she was, at the Prosecution of the Friends of the said Mary, Condemned and Executed: upon whose Apprehension and Commitment, Mary ceased to void any more stones; but, for a while, voided much blackish and muddy Sand, and also, in short time, perfectly recovered, and is yet living in the Town, in good and honest Repute, and hath been many years Marryed, and hath had seven Children; but never voided any stones since, nor been troubled with the pain fore mentioned. Abundance of people yet living, know the Substance of this to be true, and her Mother in Law (since dead) kept the stones till she was tired with the frequent Resort of people to see them, and the said Mary, and to hear the Relation of the matter, and beg the stones; (for though many offered Money for them, yet she always refused it, nor did they ever take any, but it cost them much upon the Girl, and the Prosecution of the said Huxley) and then she buried them in her Garden. Edward Ellins, the Father of the said Mary, is also yet living, and a Man of honest Repute, and utterly free (as is also the said Mary, and all the rest of her Friends) from the least Suspition of any Fraud or Cheat in the whole business:

The Devil, in Britain and America

This was known to hundreds of People in the said Town, and parts Adjacent, and many of them, yet living, are ready to attest to the truth of it.'

In the case of Anne Bodenham,[50] which is too long and intricate to give even a résumé of, we have some entirely new features, partaking more of the magician than the witch. She lived at Fisherton-Auger, Wilts, was a married woman, and at the time of her malpractices kept a small elementary school. She was considered a 'cunning,' or 'wise,' woman, and was resorted to by the people round about, for consultation as to the recovery of lost or stolen property, and, according to this pamphlet, her doings were marvellous. The first case records a woman going to consult her as to the loss of some gold money.

'The Witch put on her Spectacles, and, demanding seven shillings of the Maid, which she received, she opened three Books, in which there seemed to be severall pictures, and amongst the rest, the picture of the Devill, to the Maid's appearance, with his Cloven feet and Claws; after the Witch had looked over the book, she brought a round green glass, which glass she layd down on one of the books, upon some picture therein, and rubbed the glass, and then took up the book with the glass upon it, and held it up against the Sun, and bid the Maid come and see who they were that she could shew in that glass, and the Maid, looking in the glass, saw the shape of many persons, and what they were doing of in her Master's house, in particular, shewed Mistriss Elizabeth Rosewel standing in her Mistriss Chamber, looking out of the Window with her hands in her sleeves, and another walking alone in her Master's Garden, one other standing in a room within the kitchen, one other standing in a matted room of her Masters, against the window, with her Apron in her hand, and shewed others drinking, with glasses of Beer in their hands. After the Witches shewing this to the Maid, she then bad her go home; which, when she came home, she asked the people (she so saw in the Witches glass) what they had been doing while she had been wanting, and by their answers to her, she found that they had been doing what she saw they were in the glass: and the Maid relating this to Elizabeth Rousewel, she replyed, that Mistriss Boddenham (meaning the said Witch) was either a Witch, or a woman of God.'

She was also able to raise devils, and had several at her command, Beelzebub, Tormentor, Satan, and Lucifer, and one scene with them is thus described: 'And, presently, the back Door of the house flying open, there came five spirits, as the Maid supposed, in the likeness of ragged Boys, some bigger than others, and ran about the house, where she had drawn the Staff, and the Witch threw down upon the ground Crumbs of Bread, which the Spirits picked up, and leapt over the Pan of Coals oftentimes, which she set in the middest of the circle, and a Dog and a Cat of the Witches danced with them; and, after some time, the Witch looked again in her book, and threw some great white seeds on the ground, which the said Spirits picked up, and so, in a short time, the wind was layd, and the Witch, going forth at her back Door, the Spirits vanished.'

But she also dabbled in poisoning: 'And in a short time after, Mistress Rosewel sent her again to the Witch, to know of her when the day should be, that Mistris Goddard should be poysoned; and delivered her eight shillings to give the Witch; so the Maid went again to the Witch accordingly, and gave her the eight shillings, and the Witch replyed she could not tell her then, but gave the Maid one shilling, and bid her go to an Apothecary, and buy some white Arsenick, and bring it to her to prevent it, which the Maid did, and carried it to the Witch, who said to her she would take it and burn it, to prevent the poysoning, but she burnt it not, as the Maid could see, at all....

'The next day following, the Maid was sent again to the Witch, to get some example shewen upon the Gentlewoman that should procure the poyson, upon which the Maid went again to the Witch, and told her for what she was sent. Then the Witch made a Circle, as formerly, and set her pan of Coles, as formerly, and burnt something that stank extremely, and took her book and Glass, as before is related, and said Beelzebub, Tormentor, Lucifer, and Satan, appear! And then appeared five Spirits as she conceived, in the shapes of little ragged Boyes, which the Witch commanded to appear, and go along with the Maid to a meadow at Wilton, which the Witch shewed in the Glass, and there to gather Vervine and Dill, and, forthwith, the ragged Boys ran away before the Maid, and she followed them to the said meadow; and, when they came thither the ragged Boys looked about for the Herbs, and removed the Snow in two or three places, before they could find any; and, at last, they found some, and brought it away with them, and then the Maid and the Boys returned back to the Witch, and found her in the Circle paring her Nayls, and then she took the said Herbs, and dryed the same, and made powder of some, and dried the leaves of other, and threw Bread to the Boys, and they eat and danced as formerly; and then the Witch, reading in a book, they vanished away. And the Witch gave the Maid in one paper the powder, in another the leaves, and in the third, the paring of the Nayls; all which the Maid was to give to her Mistress. The powder was to put in the young Gentlewomens Mistriss Sarah and Mistriss Ann Goddard's drink or broth, to rot their Guts in their Bellies; the leaves to rub about the rims of the Pot, to make their Teeth fall out of their Heads; and the parings of the Nayls to make them mad and drunk. And the Witch likewise told the Maid, that she must tell her Mistriss, and the rest, that, when they did give it to them, they must cross their Breasts, and then say, In the name of our Lord Jesu Christ, grant that this may be, and that they must say the Creed backward and forward.'

The death of this wicked woman was worthy of her life: 'Afterwards, she fell into a rage, and wished for a Knife: she said she would run it into her heart-blood. Being replyed unto by some, Oh M{ris} Boddenham, you would not offer to doe such wickednesse? would you? She swore by the Name of God, but she would, had she but a Knife. She then went forth to the place of her Execution, where a numerous company were spectators; and, as she went along towards the gallows, by every house she went by, she went with a small piece of silver in her hand, calling for Beer, and was very passionate when denyed. One of the men that guarded her on the way, told her that Mr. Sheriff would not let her be buryed under the gallows, upon which she railed at the man extremely that told her so, and said she would be buryed there. When she came to the place of execution, she went immediately to go up the Ladder, but she was pulled back again and restrained: I then pressed her to confesse what she promised me she would, now before she dyed, but she refused to say anything. Being asked whether she desired the prayers of any of the people, she answered, she had as many prayers already, as she intended or desired to have, but cursed those that detained her from her death, and was importunate to go up the Ladder, but was restrained for a while, to see whether she would confesse any thing, but she would not. They then let her go up the Ladder, and when the rope was about her neck, she went to turn herself off, but the Executioner stayed her, and desired her to forgive him: she replyed, Forgive thee? a pox on thee, turn me off: which were the last words she spake. She was never heard, all the while she was at the place of Execution, to pray one word, or desire any others to pray for her, but the contrary.'

'Julian Cox, aged 70 years, was indicted at Taunton in Somersetshire, about summer assizes, 1663, before Judge Archer, then judge of assize there, for witchcraft.[51]

'For the proof of the first particular. The first witness was a huntsman, who swore that he went out with a pack of hounds to hunt a hare, and not far off from Julian Cox's house, he, at last, started a hare. The Dogs hunted her very close, and the third ring hunted her in view, till, at last, the huntsman, perceiving the hare almost spent, and making towards a great bush, he ran on the other side of the bush to take her up, and preserve her from the dogs; but, as soon as he laid hands on her, it proved to be Julian Cox, who had her head grovelling on the ground. He, knowing her, was affrighted, so that the hair on his head stood on end, and he spake to her, and asked her what brought her there? But she was so far out of breath that she could not make him any answer: his dogs also came up, with full cry, to recover the game, and smelt at her, and so left off hunting any farther. And the huntsman, with the dogs, went home presently, sadly affrighted.

***

'Thirdly, Another swore that Julian passed by his yard while his beasts were in milking, and stooping down, scored upon the ground for some small time. During which time his cattle ran mad, and some ran their heads against trees, and some of them died speedily: Whereupon, concluding they were bewitched, he was, after, advised to this experiment, to find out the Witch, viz. to cut off the ears of the bewitched beasts, and burn them; and that the witch would be in misery, and could not rest till they were plucked out. Which he tried; and while they were burning, Julian Cox came into the house, raging and scolding, that they had abused her without a cause; but she went presently to the fire, and took the ears which were burning and then she was quiet.

***

'The prisoner was called for up to the next bar in the court, and demanded if she could say the Lord's Prayer? She said, she could, and went over the prayer readily till she came to that petition. Then she said And lead us into temptation, or, And lead us not into no temptation, but could not say, And lead us not into temptation, though she was directed to say it after one that repeated it to her, distinctly, but she could not repeat it otherwise than is expressed already; though tried to do it near half a score times in the open Court. After all which the Jury found her guilty, and, judgement having been given, within three or four days, she was executed without any confession of the fact.'

'Elizabeth Styles, her confession of her Witchcraft January 26 and 30 and Feb. 7, 1664. before Robert Hunt Esqre.[52] She then confessed, That the Devil, about ten years since, appeared to her in the shape of a handsome man, and after, of a black dog. That he promised her money, and that she should live gallantly, and have the pleasure of the world for 12 Years, if she would with her own blood, sign his paper, which was to give her soul to him, and observe his laws, and that he might suck her blood. This, after four solicitations, the examinant promised him to do. Upon which, he pricked the fourth finger of her right Hand, between the middle and upper joint (where the sign, at the Examination, remained) with a drop or two of blood, she signed the paper with an O. Upon this, the Devil gave her Sixpence, and vanished with the paper.

'That, since, he hath appeared to her in the shape of a man, and did so on Wednesday seven night past: but more usually, he appears in the likeness of a dog, or cat, or a Fly like a Miller; in which last (shape) he usually sucks her on the Poll, about four of the Clock in the morning; and did so Jan. 27, and that it usually is pain to her to be so sucked.

'That when she hath a desire to do harm, she calls the Spirit by the name of Robin; to whom, when he appeareth, she useth these words, O Satan, give me my purpose. She then tells him that he should so appear to her, was part of her contract with him.

'That about a Month ago, he appearing, she desired him to torment one Elizabeth Hill, and to thrust thorns unto her Flesh, which he promised to do, and the next Time he appeared, he told her he had done it.

'That a little above a month since, this Examinant, Alice Duke, Ann Bishop, and Mary Penny, met about nine of the clock, in the night, in the common near Trister Gate, where they met a man in black Cloaths, with a little band, to whom they did courtesie and due observance; and the examinant verily believes that this was the Devil. At that time Alice Duke brought a picture in Wax, which was for Elizabeth Hill: The man in black took it in his Arms, anointed it's Forehead, and said, I baptize thee with this oyl, and used some other words. He was God father, and the examinant and Anne Bishop, God mothers; they called it Elizabeth or Bess. Then the man in black, this examinant, Anne Bishop, and Alice Duke, stuck thorns into several places of the Neck, Hand wrist, Fingers, and other parts of the said picture. After which they had wine, cakes and roast meat, (all brought by the man in black,) which they did eat and drink; they danced and were merry, were bodily there, and their cloaths.

'... She saith, before they are carried to their meetings, they anoint their foreheads and hand wrists with Oyl the Spirit brings them, (which smells raw) and then they are carried in a very short time; using these words as they pass, Thout, tout a tout, tout, throughout and about; and when they go off from their meetings, they say, Rentum Tormentum.

'That, at their first meeting the man in black bids them welcome, and they all make low obeysance to him, and he delivers some wax candles, like little torches, which they give back again at parting. When they anoint themselves, they use a long form of words, and when they stick thorns in the picture of any they would torment, they say, A pox on thee, I'll spite thee.

'That, at every meeting, before the Spirit vanishes away, he appoints the next meeting, place and time; and at his departure there is a foul smell. At their meeting, they have usually Wine or good beer, cakes, meat or the like; they eat and drink really; when they meet in their bodies, dance also, and have musick. The man in black sits at the hither End, and Anne Bishop usually sat next to him: He useth some words before meat, and none after; his voice is audible, but very low.

'That they are sometimes carried in their bodies and their clothes, sometimes without, and, as the examinant thinks, only their spirits are present; yet they know one another.... The man in black sometimes plays on a pipe or cittern, and the company dances: at last the Devil vanisheth, and all are carried to their several homes, in a short space. At their parting, they say, Hey boy, merry meet, merry part.'

The story of the trial of Rose Cullender and Amy Duny at Bury St. Edmund's, before Sir Matthew Hale in 1664, has been often told, but in one particular it differs from other cases of witchcraft.

'Diana Bocking Sworn and Examined, Deposed. That she lived in the same Town of Leystoff, and that her said Daughter having been formerly Afflicted with swooning fits, recovered well of them, and so continued for a certain time; and, upon the First of February last, she was taken, also, with great pain in her Stomach, like pricking with Pins; and, afterwards, fell into swooning fitts, and so continued till the Deponents coming to the Assizes, having during the same time taken little or no food, but daily vomiting crooked Pins; and, upon Sunday last, raised Seven Pins. And, whilst her fits were upon her, she would spread both her Arms, with her hands open, and use postures as if she catched at something, and would instantly close her hands again; which being immediately forced open, they found several Pins diversely crooked, but could neither see nor perceive how, or in what manner they were conveyed thither. At another time, the same Jane being in another of her fitts, talked as if she were discoursing with some persons in the Room (though she would give no answer, nor seem to take notice of any person then present) and would in like manner cast abroad her Arms, saying, I will not have it, I will not have it; and at last, she said, Then I will have it, and so waving her Arm with her hand open, she would presently close the same; which, instantly forced open, they found in it a Lath-Nail.'

The two witches were executed, neither confessing.

CHAPTER XIX

The Case of Mary Hill of Beckington--The Confession of Alice Huson--Florence Newton of Youghal--Temperance Lloyd (or Floyd), Mary Trembles, and Susannah Edwards.

But this case of vomiting pins is as nothing compared with the following, which is taken from Baxter's 'Certainty of the World of Spirits,' etc.:

'Mr. John Humphreys brought Mr. May Hill to me, with a Bag of Irons, Nails and Brass, vomited by the Girl. I keep some of them to shew: Nails about three or four inches long, double crooked at the end, and pieces of old Brass doubled, about an Inch broad, and two or three Inches long, with crooked edges. I desired him to give me the Case in Writing, which he hath done as followeth. Any one that is incredulous, may now, at Beckington, receive Satisfaction from him, and from the Maid her self.

'In the Town of Beckington, by Froome in Somersetshire, liveth Mary Hill, a Maid of about Eighteen years of Age, who, having lived very much in the Neglect of her Duty to God, was some time before Michaelmas last past, was Twelve-Month, taken very ill, and, being seized with violent Fits, began to Vomit up about two hundred crooked Pins. This so Stupendous an Accident, drew a numerous Concourse of People to see her: To whom, when in her Fits, she did constantly affirm, that she saw against the Wall of the Room wherein she lay, an old Woman, named Elizabeth Currier, who, thereupon, being Apprehended by a Warrant from a Justice of Peace, and Convicted by the Oaths of two Persons, was committed to the County Goal.

'About a Fortnight after, she began to Vomit up Nails, Pieces of Nails, Pieces of Brass, Handles of Spoons, and so continued to do for the space of six Months and upwards. And, in her fits, she said there did appear to her an old Woman, Named Margaret Coombes, and one Ann Moore; who, also, by a Warrant from two Justices of the Peace, were Apprehended and brought to the Sessions, held at Brewton, for the County; and, by the Bench, committed to the County Gaol. The former of these dyed as soon as she came into Prison: the other two were tryed at Taunton Assizes, by my Lord Chief Justice Holt, and for want of Evidence, were acquitted by the Jury. The Persons bound over to give Evidence, were Susanna Belton, and Ann Holland, who, upon their Oaths, Deposed, that they hookt out of the Navel of the said Mary Hill, as she lay in a dead fit, crooked Pins, small Nails, and small pieces of Brass, which were produced in Court before the Judge; and, from him, handed to the Jury to look upon them. Whereupon Mr. Francis Jesse, and Mr. Christopher Brewer declared, that they had seen the said Mary Hill, to Vomit up, at several times, Crooked Pins, Nails, and Pieces of Brass, which they, also, produced in open Court; and to the end, they might be ascertained it was no Imposture, they declared they searched her Mouth with their Fingers before she did Vomit.

'Upon which, the Court thought fit to call for me, who am the Minister of the Parish, to testifie the knowledge of the Matter, which I did to this Effect, That I had seen her, at several times, after having given her a little small Beer, Vomit up Crooked Pins, Nails, and Pieces of Brass. That, to prevent the Supposition of a Cheat, I had caused her to be brought to a Window; and, having lookt into her Mouth, I searcht it with my Finger, as I did the Beer before she drank it. This I did, that I might not be wanting in Circumstantial Answers to what my Lord and Court might propose.

'I well remember a Gentleman, on a Saturday, came to my House (Incognito) to know of me the truth of the Country Report about this Maid, having seen some of the Nails &c she had Vomited up. I told him it was very true; and, if he would stay in Town till the Morning, he might see it himself, for his own Satisfaction. Which he did; and, early in the Morning, was called to see her. But, because Beer was not given her when she wanted it, she lay in a very Deplorable Condition, till past two in the Afternoon; when, with much Difficulty, she brought up a piece of Brass, which the said Gentleman took away with him. Though, before the said Piece of Brass came up, he told me he was satisfied of the Truth of the thing, because it was impossible for any Mortal to Counterfeit her miserable Condition. She, sometimes, lying in a dead Fit, with her Tongue swelled out of her Head, and then reviving, she would fall to Vomiting, but nothing came up till about two a Clock in the Afternoon.

'Nay, so curious was he to Anticipate any Cheat, that he searcht her Mouth himself, gave her the Beer, held her up in his hand, and likewise the Bason into which she Vomited, and continued with her all this time, without eating and drinking, which was about eight hours, that he might be an Eye-Witness of the Truth of it. Nay, further, he found the maid living only with a Brother, and three poor Sisters, all young Persons, and very honest, and the Maid kept at the Charge of the Parish, were sufficient testimonies that they were incapable of making a Cheat of it. The Gentleman I now mentioned, was (as I afterwards learnt) Esquire Player of Castle-Cary.

***

'After the Assizes afore mentioned was ended, and she was turned home, she grew worse than ever, by Vomiting of Nails, pieces of Glass, &c. And, falling, one day, into a Violent Fit, she was swelled to an extraordinary bigness; some Beer being given her, she throws up several Pieces of Bread and Butter, besmeared with a Poysonous matter, which I judged to be white Mercury. This so affrighted the Neighbours, that they would come no more near her, and Compassionating the Deplorableness of her Condition; I, at last, resolved to take her into my own House; where, in some short time, the Vomiting ceased; though, for some space, her Distorting Fits followed her. But, blessed be God, is now, and has been, for a considerable time last past, in very good health, and fit for Service.

'MAY HILL,
'Minister of Beckington in the county of Somerset.

'April 4, 1691.'

Here is one of those extraordinary confessions, for which, nowadays, no one can account, except upon the supposition that the poor woman was insane:

'THE CONFESSION OF ALICE HUSON, 28 OF APRIL 1664 TO MR. TIM. WELLSET, VICAR OF BURTON AGNES (IN HER OWN WORDS) AS IT WAS GIVEN IN TO THE JUDGES AT YORK ASSIZES.[53]

'Three Years I have had to do with, and for the Devil: He appeared to me like a Black Man on a Horse upon the Moor; He told me I should never want, if I would follow his ways: He bid me give myself to him, and forsake the Lord; and I promised him I would. He did, upon that, give me five Shillings; and another time he gave me seven Shillings: And for six several times he did so; and Thom. Ratle had 20s. of the Mony I had of him. He appeared like a Black Man upon a Black Horse, with Cloven Feet: and then I fell down, and did Worship upon my Knees, because I promised him I would do so. I have hurt Mrs. Faith Corbet by my Evil Spirit: I did, in my Apprehension, ride her: And, when I was Examined by Mr. Wellset, our Minister, the Devil stood by, and gave me my Answer. I was under the Window like a Cat, when Mrs. Corbet said I was; and Doll Bilby had a hand in this tormenting Mrs. Corbet. Doll Bilby said, Let us make an end of her; and I said it was pity to take away her Life, for we had done her overmuch hurt already. The Devil did appear to me and Doll Bilby both together: Doll Bilby had of the Devil on Thursday or Friday, some Mony: I had, about a Fortnight ago, ten shillings of the Devil at Ratle's door, about Twi-light, or Day-gate: and I gave two Shillings of this Mony for two Pecks of Barly, Pease and Wheat mix'd, to Will. Parkly. He told me, if I would kill Mrs. Alice Corbet, I should never Want: He twitches me at the Heart, as if it were drawn together with Pincers. I have, I confess, a Witch-pap, which is sucked by the Unclean Spirit: This Sucking lasteth from Supper time, till after Cock Crowing. The Devil did bid me deny to Mr. Wellset that he was sent by me. I had a purpose to practice Witchcraft when I begg'd a piece of Cloth and Black-hood. I confess that I did, by this Evil Spirit, kill Dick Warren; which was done by my wicked Heart, and wicked Eyes: If I had not employ'd this wicked Spirit, I had not hurt him. I lent Lancelot Harrison eight Shillings of the ten Shillings the Devil gave me. I did forsake God, because I promised the Devil to serve him.'

But most incredible of all were the doings of an Irish witch, one Florence Newton of Youghal, who was tried at the Cork Assizes, 1661. One extract, showing her power, must suffice:[54]

'John Pyne being likewise sworn and examin'd, said, That about January last, Mary Longdon, being his Servant, was much troubl'd with little Stones that were thrown at her, wherever she went, and that he hath seen them come, as if they were thrown at her, others, as if they dropp'd on her; and that he hath seen very great quantities of them, and that they would, after they had hit her, fall on the Ground, and then vanish, so that none of them could be found. And farther, That the Maid once caught one of them, and he himself another; and one of them, with a Hole in it, she ty'd to her Purse, but it vanish'd in a little time, but the Knot of the Leather that ty'd it, remain'd unalter'd. That, after the Stones had thus haunted her, she fell into most grievous Fits, wherein she was so violently distracted, that four Men would have very much to do to hold her; and that, in the greatest of her Extremities, she would cry out of Gammer Newton for hunting and tormenting of her. That sometimes the Maid would be reading in a

Bible, and on the sudden he hath seen the Bible struck out of her Hand into the Middle of the Room, and she, immediately, was cast into a violent Fit. That, in the Fits he hath seen two Bibles, laid on her Breasts, and in the Twinkling of an Eye, they would be cast between the two Beds the Maid lay upon; sometimes thrown into the middle of the Room; and that Nicholas Pyne held the Bible in the Maid's Hand so fast, that it being suddenly snatch'd away, two of the Leaves were torn. That in many other Fits, the Maid was remov'd strangely, in the Twinkling of an Eye, out of the Bed, sometimes into the Bottom of a Chest with Linnen, and the Linnen not at all disorder'd; sometimes betwixt the two Beds she lay on; sometimes under a Parcell of Wooll, sometimes betwixt his Bed and the Mat of it in another Room; and, once, she was laid on a small Deal Board which lay on the top of an House between two solar[55] Beams, where he was forc'd to rear up Ladders to have her fetch'd down. That, in her Fits she hath often vomited up Wooll, Pins, Horse nails, Stubs, Straw, Needles and Moss, with a kind of white Foam or Spittle, and hath had several Pins stuck into her Arms and Hands, that, sometimes, a Man must pull three or four times before he could pull one of them out, and some have stuck between the Flesh and the Skin, where they might be perfectly seen, but not taken out, nor any Place seen where they were put in.'

The confessions of Temperance Lloyd (or Floyd), Mary Trembles, and Susannah Edwards, who were executed at Exeter, August 25, 1682, are curious, as showing how it is possible for three persons to have similar hallucinations.

'Temperance Lloyd saith, That about the 30th day of September last past, she met with the Devil in the shape or likeness of a black Man, about the middle of the Afternoon of that day, in a certain Street or Lane in the Town of Biddiford aforesaid, called Higher Gunstone Lane: And then and there he did tempt and sollicite her to go with him to the house of the said Thomas Eastchurch to torment the Body of the said Grace Thomas; which this Examinant, at first, did refuse to do: But, afterwards, by the temptation and perswasion of the Devil in the likeness of a Black Man, as aforesaid, she did go to the house of the said Thomas Eastchurch, and that she went up the stairs after the said black Man; and confesseth that both of them went up into the Chamber where she the said Grace Thomas was, and that there they found one Anne Wakely, the wife of William Wakely of Biddiford, rubbing and stroaking one of the Arms of the said Grace Thomas.

'And the said Examinant doth further confess that she did then and there pinch with the Nails of her Fingers, the said Grace Thomas in the Shoulders, Arms, Thighs and Legs; and that, afterwards, they came down from the said Grace Thomas her Chamber, into the Street together; and that there this Examinant did see some thing in the form or shape of a Grey or Braget Cat; and saith that the said Cat went into the said Thomas Eastchurch's shop.

'The said Examinant, being further demanded whether she went any more unto the said Thomas Eastchurch's house, saith and confesseth that the day following she came again to the said Thomas Eastchurch's house, invisible, and was not seen by any person; but there this Examinant did meet with the Braget Cat as aforesaid, and the said Cat did retire and leap back into the said Thomas Eastchurch's Shop.

'The said Examinant, being further demanded when she was at the said Thomas Eastchurch's house, the last time, saith, that she was at the said Mr. Eastchurch's house upon Friday the 30th day of June last past; and that the Devil, in the shape of the said black Man was there with her: And that they went up again into the said Chamber, where she found the said Grace Thomas lying in her Bed in a very sad condition. Notwithstanding which, she, this Examinant and the said Black Man did torment her again: And saith and confesseth that she, this Examinant had almost drawn her out of her Bed, and that on purpose to put her, the said Grace out of her Life.

'And further saith, that the black Man (or rather the Devil) did promise this Examinant that no one should discover her.

'And further confesseth that the said black Man (or rather the Devil) as aforesaid, did suck her Teats, and that she did kneel down to him in the Street, as she was returning to her own house, and after that they had tormented the said Grace Thomas in manner as last above mentioned.

'Being demanded of what stature the said black Man was, saith, that he was about the length of her Arm: And that his Eyes were very big; and that he hopt or leapt in the way before her, and, afterwards, did suck her again as she was lying down; and that his sucking was with a great pain unto her, and, afterwards vanish'd clear away out of her sight.

'This Examinant doth further confess, That upon the first day of June last past, whilst the said Mr. Eastchurch and his Wife were absent, that the said Examinant did pinch and prick the said Grace Thomas (with the aid and help of the black Man) in her Belly, Stomach and Breast; and that they continued so tormenting of her, about the Space of two or three hours, with an intent to have killed her.'

She also confessed to have tortured several others to death.

Mary Trembles said that about three years since Susannah Edwards persuaded her to become a witch, and that the Devil appeared to her in the shape of a lion.

'Susannah Edwards being brought before us, and accused for practising of Witchcraft upon the Body of Grace Barnes, the wife of John Barnes of Biddiford, Yeoman, was demanded by us how long since she had Discourse or Familiarity with the Devil; saith, That about two years ago she did meet with a Gentleman in a Field called the Parsonage Close in the Town of Biddiford, and that his Apparel was all of black. Upon which she did hope to have a Piece of Money of him. Whereupon, the Gentleman drawing near unto this Examinant, she did make a Curchy, or Courtesie unto him, as she did use to do to Gentlemen.

'Being demanded what and who the Gentleman she spake of, was, the said Examinant answered and said, that it was the Devil.

'And confessed, that the Devil did ask of her whether she was a Poor woman? unto whom she answered that she was a Poor woman; and that, thereupon, the Devil, in the shape of the Gentleman, did say unto her, that if this Examinant would grant him one request, that she should neither want for Meat, Drink, nor Clothes: Whereupon this Examinant did say unto the said Gentleman, In the Name of God, what is it I shall have? Upon which the said Gentleman vanished clear away from her.

'And further confesseth, That, afterwards, there was something in the shape of a little Boy, which she thinks to be the Devil, came into her house, and did lie with her, and that he did suck at her breast. And confesseth that she did afterwards meet him in a place call'd Stambridge-lane in this Parish of Biddiford, leading towards Abbotisham, (which is the next Parish on the west of Biddiford aforesaid), where he did suck blood out of her breast.

'And further confesseth, That on Sunday, which was the 16th day of July instant, she, this Examinant, together with Mary Trembles, did go unto the house of John Barnes, and that nobody did see them: and that they were in the same room where Grace, the wife of the said John Barnes was, and that there they did prick and pinch the said Grace with their fingers, and put her to great pain and torment, insomuch that the said Grace Barnes was nearly dead.

'And confesseth that this present day, she did prick and torment the said Grace again, (intimating with her Fingers how she did it). And also confesseth that the Devil did intice her to make an end of the said Grace; and that he told her he would come again to her once more before she should go out of Town. And confesseth that she can go into any place invisible, and yet her Body shall be lying in her Bed. And further confesseth that the Devil hath appeared unto her in the shape of a Lyon, as she supposed.

'Being demanded whether she had done any bodily hurt unto any other person besides the said Grace Barnes, saith and Confesseth, that she did prick and torment one Dorcas Coleman, the wife of John Coleman of Biddiford Mariner. And saith that the said Mary Trembles was a Servant unto her, in like manner as she was a Servant unto the Devil.'

CHAPTER XX

Elizabeth Horner--Pardons for Witchcraft--A Witch taken in London--Sarah Mordike--An Impostor convicted--Case of Jane Wenham--The Last Witch hanged in England.

Hutchinson gives an account of a very curious case of witchcraft in 1696:

'Elizabeth Horner was tried before the Lord Chief Justice Holt at Exeter. Three Children of William Bovet were thought to have been bewitched by her, whereof one was dead. It was deposed that another had her Legs twisted, and yet from her Hands and Knees, she would spring five Foot high. The children vomited Pins, and were bitten (if the Depositions were true) and pricked, and pinched, the Marks appearing. The Children said Bess Horner's Head would come off from her Body, and go into their Bellies. The Mother of the Children deposed, that one of them walked up a smooth plaistered Wall, till her Feet were nine Foot high, her Head standing off from it. This, she said, she did five or six times, and laughed and said, Bess Horner held her up. This poor Woman had something like a Nipple on her Shoulder, which the Children said was sucked by a Toad. Many other odd things were deposed, but the Jury brought her in Not Guilty and no Inconvenience hath followed from her Acquittal.'

She was lucky, not only inasmuch as the belief in witchcraft was on the wane, as also to have been tried by so enlightened a judge as Sir John Holt, of whom the story is told (of which, however, I can find no authentication) that a witch was once brought before him, and a charm, written on parchment, was adduced against her. This charm, which consisted of a line or two of Greek verse, Sir John recognised as having been written by himself in his student days at Oxford to cure a poor woman's daughter of the ague.

But although the majority of so-called witches were executed after trial and sentence, all were not, for we find in the Calendars of State Papers several instances of pardons:

1597. 30 Ap. Pardon for Elizabeth Melton, late of Collingham, co. York, condemned for witchcraft.

1597. 3 May. Pardon to Alice Brerely of Castleton, co. Lanc., spinster, condemned for killing Jas. Kirshaw and Rob. Scolefield by witchcraft.

1604. 16 Ap. Grant to Christian, wife of Thomas Weech, co. Norfolk, of pardon for witchcraft.

She was one of the extremely fortunate, for she was again accused of this crime.

1610. 3 Ap. Grant to Christian Weech of pardon for the murder of Mary Freeston by witchcraft.
1608. 15 Feb. Grant to Simon Reade of pardon for conjuration and invocation of unclean spirits.
1611. 7 May. Grant of pardon to Wm. Bate, indicted twenty years since, for practising invocation of spirits for finding treasure, the evidence being found weak, etc.

With the beginning of the eighteenth century, the belief in witchcraft was dying out rapidly, and very few are the cases narrated. I give the following from a broadsheet; but to my mind it has not the true ring of former cases, and I doubt its authenticity; still, I give it as amongst the few reported cases in this century.

The Devil, in Britain and America

'A FULL AND TRUE RELATION OF THE DISCOVERING, APPREHENDING, AND TAKING OF A NOTORIOUS WITCH, WHO WAS CARRIED BEFORE JUSTICE BATEMAN IN WELL-CLOSE, ON SUNDAY JULY THE 23RD, TOGETHER WITH HER EXAMINATION AND COMMITMENT TO BRIDEWELL, CLERKENWELL.'

'Sarah Griffith who Lived in a Garret in Rosemary lane, was a long time suspected for a bad Woman, but nothing could be prov'd against her, that the Law might take hold of her: Tho' some of the Neighbors Children would be strangely affected with unknown Distempers, as Vomiting of Pins, there Bodies turn'd into strang Postures, and such like; many were frighted with strange Apperitions of Cats, which, of a sudden, would vanish away; these, and such like, made those who lived in the Neighbourhood, both suspicious and fearful of her: Till, at last, the Devil (who always betrays those that deal with him) thus brought the Truth to Light. One, Mr. John ---- at the Sugarloaf, had a good jolly fellow for his Apprentice: This Old Jade came into his shop to buy a quartern of Sope. The Young fellow happened to Laugh; and the Scales not hanging right, cryed out he thought that they were be-Witched; The Old Woman hearing him say so, fell into a great Passion, judging he said so to ridicule her, ran out of the Shop, and threatened revenge. In the Night was heard a lumbring noise in the Shop, and the Man, coming down to see, found a strang confusion; every thing turn'd topsy turvy; all the goods out of order. But, what was worse, the next day, the poor fellow was troubled with a strange Disease, but [by] the good prayers of some Neighboring Divines, the power of the Devil was restrain'd.

'Two or three days after, it happened that the Young Man, with two or three more, walking up to the New River Head, who should they see, but Mother Griffith walking that way. They consulted together to try her; and one of them said, Let us toss her into the River, for I have heard, that if she Swims, 'tis a certain sign of a Witch. In short, they put their design in execution; for, coming up to her, they tossed her in; but, like a Bladder when forc'd under Water, pops up again, so this Witch was no sooner in, but Swam like a Corke; they kept her in some time, and, at last, let her come out again. She was no sooner out, but she smote that Young man on the Arm, and told him he should pay dear for what he had done. Immediately, he found a strange pain in his Arm, and, looking on it, found the exact mark of her hand and Fingers as black as a Cole. He went home, where he lay much tormented, and wonderfully affrighted with the Old Woman coming to afflict him; and, at last, died with the pain, and [was] Buried in St. Pulchres Church Yard.

'Mr. John ---- fearing some further mischief, takes a Constable, and goes to her Lodging, where he finds the Old Woman, and charges the Constable with her. She made many attempts to escape, but the Devil, who owed her a shame, had now left her, and she was apprehended. As she was conducted towards the Justice's house, she tried to leap over the Wall, and had done it, had not the Constable knocked her down. In this manner she was carried before the Justice. There was Evidence that was With him in his Sickness could Witness that he had unaccountable Fits, Vomitted up Old Nails, Pins and such like, his body being turned into strange postures, and, all the while, nothing but crying out of Mother Griffith, that she was come to torment him. His Arm rotted almost off, Gangreen'd, and kill'd him. When she came before the Justice, she pleaded innocence, but the circumstances appeared so plainly, that she was committed to Bridewell, where she now remains.

'24 July, 1704.'

If we needed any evidence to show the decadence of witchcraft, it can be found in the case of Sarah Mordike, who was (luckily for her) tried by Lord Chief Justice Holt in 1701. Hutchinson gives the best report of this case that I can find.

'Richard Hathaway, Apprentice to Thomas Wellyn, a Blacksmith in Southwark, had either real Convulsions, or counterfeit Fits; at the time when he was bound first to his Master. When he had served about three Years, he was thought to be so ill, that he was put into the Hospital, and was judged to be a very miserable Spectacle, lying in strange Fits, and going double; and, after seven Weeks was turned out as incurable.

'In September 1690 (?1700) he said he was bewitched, and vomited great Numbers of Pins, and seemed to be dumb and blind, and was thought to live without Meat for ten Weeks together, tho' he was put with Keepers into an empty House a great part of the Time, and had a bed bought on purpose, and was watched Day and Night by Persons that were Strangers to him. One of his Watchers deposed, That a Lump of Hair, loose Pins, a Stump of a Nail, half a Nutshell, and two or three pieces of Stone came from him. A second Witness confirmed this, and added, That he stood over him at the Time, with a drawn Sword in his Hand. His Face would be drawn on one side, He foamed at the Mouth, and crooked Pins were found in the Foam. His Head was bent to the Reins of his Back, and he went, sometimes, almost upon his Ankles. He would lie as if he was dead; and, once, was brought to himself by Cupping Glasses. Screeking and other Noises were heard in the Bed, and about the House, and Charms were applied to him, and were said to do him good. It was also deposed, That he barked like a Dog, and in his Fits burnt like a Flame of Fire.

'The Person that he accused of the Witchcraft was one Sarah Morduck, of the same Parish. He intimated by Signs, that, if he might scratch her, he should be well. He did scratch her, and then he eat and drank, and had his Sight, and was well for six Weeks together.

'After that, he seemed to be ill again, and signified that she had bewitched him again, and he must scratch her again. Upon this, the said Sarah Morduck was assaulted in her own House, and grievously abused; her Hair and Face torn; she, was kicked, thrown to the Ground, stamped on, and threatened to be put into a Horse-Pond, to be tried by Swimming, and very hardly escaped with her Life. In hopes to avoid these Dangers, she removed out of Southwark, and lodged in London; but, still, she was not suffered to be in safety, but was followed in the Streets, and often thought herself in danger of being pulled in Pieces.

'About Easter, 1701, she was carried before Sir Thomas Lane, and was stript and searched by his Order, and Hathaway scratched her before him, and then he eat and drank, and was thought to be well. Sir Thomas committed her, and Hathaway continued free from his Fits. Near the Time of Tryal, the Prayers of several Churches were desired, and Money was gathered for him: between six and seven Pounds at one Collection; and other Sums at other Times, to bear his Charges to the Assizes.

'In the latter end of July, at Guildford Assizes, this Sarah Morduck was tried before the Right Honourable, the Lord Chief Justice Holt, and was acquitted, and Richard, himself, was committed as a Cheat and Impostor: But both Judge, and Jury, and Witnesses were slandered, as if they had not done fairly.

'For several Days after his Commitment to the Marshalsea, he eat, and drank, and slept: but, some time after, he was again as if under the Power of Witchcraft, dumb and fasting.

'That it might be certain whether he did really live without Meat or not, my Lord Chief Justice put him into the House of Mr. Kensy, a Surgeon, in November following, that he might make Tryal of him.

'March 25, 1702, this Hathaway was tried before Lord Chief Justice Holt, and Mr. Baron Hatfell, in Southwark, the Place in which the Fact was best known, and where any witnesses might appear without Charge.

'On Hathaway's side, these things were sworn that I have mentioned already.

'To convict him of Imposture, it was deposed, That on purpose for an Experiment, Dr. Martin, Minister of the Parish, had contrived that he scratch'd another Woman, when he thought he had scratch'd this Sarah Morduck; and upon that, he opened his Eyes; but, being told he had scratch'd the wrong Woman, he pretended to be blind and dumb again. And the manner of his doing it was such, as showed him a crafty fellow, taking care of himself; for he felt her Arm four times over, before he would scratch her.

'To prove that his vomiting Pins was by a Trick, it was deposed, That immediately after he had vomited great Numbers in appearance upon the Ground, and was going to vomit more, Care being taken that he should vomit into a Basin, and his Hands being kept down below it, there was not a Pin in the Basin, but a great many crooked ones in his Pockets, in readiness to have play'd his Tricks with.

'Some of the Noises that were said to be made in the Bed, were shewed to be made by his own Feet scratching the Bed Post.

'Besides what he got by Gifts and Collections, it was proved that he had tried to make a Gain, by printing a Narrative of his own Case.

'With respect to his Fasting, it was said by one of his own Witnesses, that there came from him five Times more than he took. After two Days fasting, and refusing to take any thing from Mr. Kensy, for fear he should really starve himself, rather than own his knavery, Mr. Kensy contrived to let him have Meat in a private Way, by this Device. He pretended to fall out with his Maid in Hathaway's hearing, and said she gave him Meat; and therefor he gave her Warning to be gone. She carried on the Design, and told him she was as ready to be gone as he was to have her go; and, after this feigned Quarrell, she spake kindly to Richard, and bad him take nothing from her Master; for, while she stay'd she would take Care of him. After this, he took Meat from her; but a Child being in the Room, he pointed that it might not see him. He eat and drank any Thing she gave him, Ale, Brandy, Fish, Pudding, Mutton, &c. Once he was drunk, and spew'd, and covered his Vomit with Ashes; But if either Mr. Kensy, or anyone else offered him any, he refused to take it; and, when he had eaten heartily, he would shew them his Belly clung up to his Back, as though there had been nothing in it. The Maid saw this openly, Mr. Kensy saw it through a private Hole; and, once, he had four Neighbours with him, that saw it as well as he. He eat in this manner for eleven Days together, and yet pretended to continue his Fast. If they asked him how many Weeks he had fasted before he came to Mr. Kensy's House? he counted Ten upon his Fingers. If they asked him how many Weeks he had fasted since his coming thither? he counted Two, tho' they had seen him eat eleven Days of the two Weeks.

'When they had Proof enough, Mr. Kensy told him he was discover'd, and said his Friends were in Custody, and had confess'd the whole Matter. Upon that he cried passionately and said he would tell the Lord Chief Justice the whole Truth, and asked, If his Mother was safe? But, my Lord not being at his Chamber, he, in about an Hour after, recanted, and said again that he was bewitched.

'These Things were deposed at large by many and substantial Witnesses; insomuch that the Jury, without going from the Bar, returned him Guilty.

'Some Months after, my Lord Chief Justice Holt past Sentence upon him, That he should suffer Imprisonment a Year, and stand in the Pillory three Times.'

The last case of witchcraft in England, where a so-called witch was tried and condemned by judge and jury (although she was not executed), was that of Jane Wenham in 1712. I am aware that another and later case is cited in 1716 of one Mrs. Hicks and her daughter, said to have been executed at Huntingdon, for 'selling their souls to the devil, making their neighbours vomit pins, and raising a storm by which a certain ship was almost lost'; but as no one yet has been able to find any record of this case, I beg leave to doubt its existence.

But Jane Wenham's was a cause célèbre. She lived at Walkern, a village in Hertfordshire, about four miles from Stevenage. The account of the proceedings at her trial is very long, so that I shall only give two or three of the informations laid against her:

'Matthew Gilston, of the Parish of Walkerne, says upon Oath, that, on New Years Day last past, he carrying Straw upon a Fork from Mr. Gardiner's Barn, met Jane Wenham, who asked him for some Straw, which he refused to give her; then she said she would take some, and accordingly took some away from this Informant.

'And farther, this Informant saith, that on the 29th of Jan. last, when this Informant was threshing in the Barn of his Master, John Chapman, an Old Woman in a Riding-hood, or Cloak, he knows not which, came to the Barn Door, and asked him for a Penyworth of Straw; he told her he could give her none, and she went away, Muttering.

'And this Informant saith, that after the Woman was gone, he was not able to work, but ran out of the Barn, as far as a place called Munders-Hill, (which is about Three Miles from Walkerne) and asked at a House there for a Penyworth of Straw, and they, refusing to give him any, he went farther, to some Dung-heaps, and took some Straw from thence, and pull'd off his Shirt, and brought it Home in his Shirt; he knows not what mov'd him to this, but says he was forc'd to it, he knows not how.

'Susan Aylott, the Wife of William Aylott, of the Parish of Walkerne, saith upon Oath, that about 12 Years ago last Christmas, she, this Informant, was sent for to the Wife of Richard Harvey, lying very Ill in a strange Condition; and, as soon as she came thither, Jane Wenham followed her, and she, this Informant, wonder'd that Jane Wenham followed her, since Richard Harvey's Wife had told her that she, the said Jane Wenham had bewitched her: Then Jane Wenham went under the Window where the sick Woman lay, and said, Why do they let this Creature lye there? Why don't they take her and hang her out of the way? At which she, this Informant, had some Words with Jane Wenham, saying, Take you, and hang you out of the Way: and then Jane Wenham answer'd, Hold you your Tongue, I don't meddle with you, and that Night, the sick Woman, aforesaid, died.

'And this Informant farther saith, That, soon after, Jane Wenham came to this Informant's House, and look'd upon a Child which was in her Lap, and stroaked it; and said, Susan, you have a curious Child; you and I had some Words, but I hope we are Friends; and asked this Informant to lend her a Glass to carry some Vinegar in from the Shop; then this Informant sent Jane Wenham a Glass, who went away. And this Informant was afraid of her Child, remembering she was thought to have bewitched Richard Harvey's Wife.

'This Informant further saith, That on Sunday following, she was at her brother Jeremy Harvey's House, with her Child, and that her Child was taken in a grievous Condition, stark Distracted, and so died on the Thursday following; and this Informant saith, she thinks Jane Wenham bewitched her Child; and saith also, that Jane Wenham has had the Reputation of a Witch for several Years before.

'Thomas Adams, Junior, of Walkerne, maketh Oath, that about Three Weeks, or a month before Christmas last, he met Jane Wenham in his Turnip Field, with a few of his Turnips, which she was carrying away; and upon his Threatning her, she threw them down; he, this Informant, told her she might keep them, for she should pay dear for them; then she was very submissive, and begg'd Pardon, saying, she had no Victuals all that day, and had no money to buy any; afterwards, they parted, and he saw her not after; But, on Christmas-Day Morning, One of his best Sheep died without any Signs of Illness found upon the Body after it was open'd, and Nine or Ten Days after, died another Sheep, in an unaccountable Manner; and, shortly after, Two more Sheep died also, some of them having no Marks of Disease upon 'em, but being sound in all their Parts, as his Shepherd informs him. He also saith that his Shepherd tells him that one other Sheep was taken strangely, skipping and standing upon its Head, but in half an Hour was well, and continues so; and another Sheep was likewise Ill, Two or Three Days, but it is now well again: And Jane Wenham having the Common Fame of a Witch, he does believe that if they were bewitch'd, she did bewitch them.'

All these charges convinced the jury that she was indeed a witch, and the judge had no option but to sentence her; but he got her a reprieve, and she was let out of prison, when she was kindly befriended by Colonel Plummer, of Gilston, who gave her a cottage in which she harmlessly lived the remainder of her days.

But although this was the last capital conviction in England, the belief in witchcraft was far from dead; nay, it is still living in some remote districts, but cannot long exist, as education makes its way.

CHAPTER XXI

Scotch Witches--Bessie Dunlop--Alesoun Peirson--Dr. John Fian--The Devil a Preacher--Examination of Agnes Sampson--Confession of Issobel Gowdie.

But Scotland was the real home of the witch. Comparatively speaking, the English hardly knew what a witch was, and the reports of trials are so numerous that space prohibits my making more than a selection of them. Witches were important personnages--at least, in the sixteenth century--for we read in the trial of Bessie Dunlop, 1576, how many noble ladies consulted her. 'And demandit,--To quhom sche applyit the powder in drink? Declarit,--That the Lady Johnstoune the elder, send to hir ane servand of the said ladies, &c ... Interrogat--Quhair sche gaif the gentile woman the drink? Answerit--In hir awin sisteris hous, the young Ladye Blakhallis.... Demandit--Gif ony uther personnes had bene at hir for the lyke caus? Declarit--That the Lady Kilbowye elder, send for hir &c.... Demandit--Quhat personnes thar wer? Answerit--The Ladye Thridpairt in the barronye of Renfrew, send to hir, and sperit at her, Quha was it that had stollin from hir twa hornis of gold, and are croune of the sone, out of hir pyrse?... The Ladye Blaire sundrie times had spokin with hir, about sum claise that was stollin fra hir.'

Again, in the trial of Alesoun Peirson, May 28, 1588: 'And in speciall, scho said, that he tauld hir that the Bischop of Sanct Androus[56] had mony seiknessis, as the trimbling fewer,[57] the palp,[58] the rippilis,[59] and the flexus;[60] and baid hir mak ane faw,[61] and rub it on his cheikis, his craig, his breist, stommak and sydis.'

A favourite place of meeting, where they held their Sabbat, was at North Berwick-Kirk. In the trial of Johnne Feane, alias Cwninghame, December 26, 1590, we find: 'Item. Fylit, ffor being in cumpany with Satan in the Kirk of North Berwick, quhair he apperit to him in the forme of ane blak maun within the pulpett thairof; and efter his out-cuminge of the Kirk, poyntit the graues and stwid aboue thame; quhilkis wer opnit in thre sindrie pairtis, twa within and ane without; quhilk the wemen demembrit the deid corps and bodeis being thairin, with thair galleis;[62] and in contment wes transportit, without wordis.... Item. Fylit. for being in North Berwick Kirk, at ane conventioune with Sathan and utheris witches; quhair Sathan maid ane dewelisch sermon, quhair the said Johnne satt uponne the left syde of the pulppett, narrest him; And the sermon being endit, he came doune and tuke the said Johnne be the hand; and led him widderschinnis[63] about.'

In 'A True Discourse of the apprehension of Sundrie Witches lately taken in Scotland,' etc., 1591, is the following 'Item. The said Agnis Tompson (Sampson) was after brought againe before the Kinges Majestie and his Councell, and beeing examined of the meetings and detestable dealings of those witches, she confessed, that upon the night of Allhollow Even last, shee was accompanied, as well with the persons aforesaide, as also with a great many other witches, to the number of two hundreth, and that all they together went to Sea, each one in a riddle or cive, and went into the same very substantially, with flaggons of wine, making merrie and drinking by the way, in the same riddles or cives, to the Kirk of North Barrick in Lowthian; and that after they had landed, tooke handes on the lande, and daunced this reill or short daunce, singing all with one voice,

"'Commer goe ye before, commer goe ye,
Gif ye will not goe before, commer let me."

'At which time shee confessed, that this Geillis Duncane did goe before them, playing this reill or daunce, uppon a small trumpe, called a Jewe's trump, untill they entred into the Kirk of North Barrick.'

This Agnes Sampson was tried on January 27, 1591, for conspiring the King's death, witchcraft, sorcery, incantation, etc., and her ultimate fate was 'to be tane to the Castle (hill) of Edinburgh, and thair bund to ane staik and werreit (strangled), quhill sche wes deid; and thairefter her body to be brunt in assis.'

'Item, fylit and convict, ffor as mekle as sche confest before his Maiestie, That the Dewill, in mannis liknes, mett hir going out in the fieldis frome hir awin hous att Keyth, betwix fyve and sax at ewin, being hir allane; and commandit hir to be at North Bervick Kirk the nixt nycht; And she passit thair on horsbak, and lychtit at the Kirk yaird. Or a lytill before sche come to itt, about ellewin houris att ewin, they danceit alangis the Kirk yaird, Gelie Duncan playit to thame one a trump.'

She then gives the names of many who were present. 'Quhairof thair wes sax men, and all the rest wemen. The wemen maid fyrst thair homage, and nixt the men. The men wer turnit nyne tymes widderschinnes about, and the wemen sax tymes. Johnne Fien blew up the duris, and blew in the lychtis, quhilkis wer lyke mekle blak candillis, stiking round about the pulpett. The Devill start up himselff in the pulpett, lyke are mekle blak man, and callit ewerie man be his name, and ewerie ane ansuerit: "Heir, Mr." The fyrst thing he demandit, was "Gif thay kepit all promeis, and bene guid servandis?" and "Quhat thay had done since the last tyme thay had convenit?"--One his command, thay opnit up the graves, twa within and ane without the kirk, and tuik of the jountis of thair fingaris, tais and neife,[64] and partit thame amangis thame: and the said Agnes Sampsoune gatt for hir pairt, ane windene scheit and twa jountis, quhilk sche tint negligentlie. The Devill commandit thame to keip the jountis upoun thame, quhill thay wer dry, and thane to mak ane powder of thame, to do ewill withall. Then he commandit thame to keip his commandmentis, quhilkis war, to do all the ewill they could.'

Their initiation was similar to their English sisters', as the aforesaid Agnes Sampson affirms. 'The fyrst tyme sche begane to serue the Dewill, was eftir the death of hir husband; and that he apperit to hir, in liknes of ane man, quha commandit hir to acknowledge him as hir maister, and to renunce Chryste; quhairunto sche grant it, being movit be pouertie and his promesis, that sche and hir bairnis sould be maid ritch, and sould gif hir power to be revangeit of hir inimeis; and eftir that, he appointit tyme and place for thair nycht meting; and that tyme, in signe that sche wes becum his seruand, he markit hir in the rycht kne, quhilk mark sche belevit to haif bene ane hurt ressavit be hir fra ane of hir bairnies that wes lyand in the bed with hir; quhilk hurt wes nocht haill for half ane yeir.'

Before finishing with this lady, I must give another portion of her most extraordinary confession. 'Moreover she confessed, that, at the time when his Majestie was in Denmarke, shee being accompanied by the parties before speciallie named, took a cat, and christened it, and afterwards bounde to each part of that cat, the cheefest part of a dead man, and severall joyntis of his bodie: And that, in the night following, the saide cat was convayed into the middest of the sea by all these witches, sayling in their riddles or cives, and so left the saide cat right before the towne of Leith in Scotland. This doone, there did arise such a tempest in the sea, as a greater hath not beene seene.'

This was the way they baptized the cat: 'In the wobstaris[65] hous, in maner following: Fyrst, twa of thame held ane fingar,[66] in the ane syd of the chimnay cruik, and ane uther held ane uther fingar in the uther syd, the twa nebbis[67] of the fingaris meeting togidder; than thay patt the catt thryis throw the linkis of the cruik, and passit itt thryis under the chimnay.'

The confession of Issobell Gowdie, May 3, 1662, although it is somewhat mutilated, gives us a good insight into the manners and customs of Scotch witches:

'Efter that tym ther vold meit bot sometymes a Coven, somtymes mor, somtymes les; bot a Grand Meitting vold be about the end of ilk Quarter. Ther is threttein persones in ilk Coven; and ilk on of us has a Spirit to wait wpon us, quhan ve pleas to call wpon him. I remember not all the Spritis names; bot thair is on called Swein, quhilk waitis wpon the said Margaret Wilson in Aulderne; he is still[68] clothed in grass grein; and the said Margret Wilson hes an niknam called Pikle neirest the Wind. The nixt Sprit is called Rorie who waitis wpon Bessie Wilsone, in Aulderne; he is still clothed in yallow; and hir nikname is Throw the Corne yaird. The third Sprit is called The Roring Lyon, who waitis wpon Issobell Nicoll in Locklow; and [he is still clothed] in sea grein; her niknam is Bessie Rule. The fowrth Sprit is called Mak Hector, qwho waitis wpon Jean Martein, dawghter to the said Margaret Wilson; he is a yowng-lik Devill, clothed still in grass [green. Jean Martein is] Maiden to the Coven that I am of; and hir nikname is Over the Dyke with it, becaws the Divill [alwayis takis the] Maiden in his hand nix him, quhan ve daunce Gillatrypes, and quhan he vold lowp from ...[69] he and she will say, "Ower the dyk with it." The name of the fyft Sprit is Robert the [Rule and he is still clothed in] sadd dun, and seimis to be a Comander of the rest of the Spiritis; and he waittis wpon Margret Brodie, in Aulderne. [The name of the saxt Spirit] is called Thieff of Hell wait upon hir selfe, and he waitis also on the said Bessie Wilson. The name of the sevinth [Sprit is called] The Read Reiver, and he is my owin Spirit, that waittis on my selfe, and is still clothed in blak. The aught Spirit [is called] Robert the Jackis, still clothed in dune, and seimes to be aiged. He is ane glaiked gowked Spirit! The woman's [nikname] that he waitis on, is Able and Stowt! The nynth Spirit is called Laing, and the womans nikname that he vaitis wpon is Bessie Bauld. The Tenth Spirit is named Thomas a Fearie, &c.--Ther wil be many uther Divellis, waiting wpon [our] Maister Divell; bot he is bigger and mor awfull than the rest of the Divellis, and they all reverence him. I will ken them all, on by on, from utheris, quhan they appeir lyk a man.

'Quhan we rease the wind, we tak a rag of cloth, and weitts[70] it in water; and we take a beetle[71] and knokis the rage on a stone, and we say thryse ower:

"'I knok this ragg wpon this stane,
To raise the wind, in the Divellis name;

It sall not lye,[72] untill I please againe!"

'[Whan] we wold lay the wind, we dry the ragg, and say [thryse ower]:

"We lay the wind in the Divellis name,
[It sall not] ryse quhill we lyk to rease it again!"

'And if the wind will not lye instantlie [after we say this] we call wpon owr Spirit, and say to him:

"Thieffe! Thieffe! conjure the wind, and caws it to [lye ...]"

'We haw no power of rain, bot ve will rease the wind quhan ve pleas.--He maid us beliew [...] that ther wes no God besyd him.
'As for Elf-arrow-heidis, the Diuell shapes them with his awin hand, and syne deliueris thame to Elf-boyes, who whyttis and dightis[73] them with a sharp thing lyk a paking neidle; bot [quhan I was in Elfland?] I saw them whytting and dighting them. Quhan I wes in the Elfes howssis, they will haw werie ... them whytting and dighting: and the Diwell giwes them to ws, each of ws so many, quhen.... Thes that dightis thaim ar litle ones, holow, and boss baked![74] They speak gowstie[75] lyk. Quhen the Divell giwes them to ws, he sayes:

"Shoot thes in my name,
And they sall not goe heall hame!"

'And quhan we shoot these arrowes we say:

"I shoot yon man in the Divellis name,
He sall not win heall hame!
And this sal be alswa trw;
Thair sall not be an bit of him on lieiw."[76]

'We haw no bow to shoot with, but spang[77] them from the naillis of our thowmbes. Som tymes we will misse, bot if thay twitch[78] be it beast, or man, or woman, it will kill, tho' they haid an jack[79] wpon them. Qwhen we goe in the shape of an haire, we say thryse owr:

"I sall goe intill ane haire,
With sorrow, and sych, and meikle caire;
And I sall goe in the Divellis nam,
Ay whill I com hom [againe]!"

'And instantlie we start in an hair, And when we wold be owt of that shape, we vill say:

"Haire [haire, God send the caire!]
I am in an hairis liknes just now,
But I sal be in a womanis liknes ewin [now]!"

'When we vold goe in the liknes of an Cat, we say thryse ower:

"I sall go [intill ane catt,]
[With sorrow, and sych, and a blak] shot!
And I sall goe in the Divellis nam,
Ay quhill I com hom again!"

'And if ve [wold goe in ane Craw,[80] then] we say thryse ower:

"I sall goe intill a craw,
With sorrow and sych, and a blak [thraw!
And I sall goe in the Divellis nam,]
Ay quhill I com hom again!"

'And quhen ve vold be owt of thes shapes, we say:

"Catt, catt, (or craw, craw,) [God] send the a blak shott! (or thraw)
   I wes a catt (or craw) just now,
   Bot I sal be [in a woman's liknes evin now.]
Catt, catt, (or craw, craw,) God send the a blak shot! (or thraw)."

'Giff we in the [shape of an catt, an craw, an] haire, or ony uther liknes, &c., go to any of our neighbouris howssis, being Witches, we will [say]:

"[I (or we) conjure] the Goe with ws (or me)!"

'And presentlie they becom as we ar, either cats, hearis, crowes, &c., and goe [with ws whither we wold. Quhan] we wold ryd, we tak windlestrawes, or bean stakes,[81] and put them betwixt owr foot, and say thryse:

"'[Horse] and hattok, horse and goe,
Horse and pellatis, ho! ho!"

'And immediatlie we flie away whair [evir we wold]; and least our husbandis sould miss vs owt of owr beddis, we put in a boosom,[82] or a thrie [leggit stoole besyde thame] and say thryse ower:

"I lay down this boosom (or stooll) in the Devillis name
Let it not steir ... [Quhill I] com again!"

'And immediatlie it seimis a voman, besyd our husbandis.
'Ve can not turn in the lik[nes of ...] Quhen my husband sold beeff, I used to put a swellowes feather in the hyd of the beast, and [say thryse]:

"[I] putt out this beeff in the Divellis nam,
That meikle silver and good pryce com hame!"

'I did ewin so [quhenevir I putt] furth either horse, noat,[83] vebs,[84] or any uther thing to be sold, and still put in this feather, and said the [samin wordis thryse] ower, to caws the comodities sell weill.

"Our Lord to hunting he [is gone]
   ... marble stone,
He sent vord to Saint Knitt...."

Quhan we vold heall ony sor or brokin limb, we say thryse ower

"He pat the blood to the blood, Till all up stood!
The lith to the lith, Till all look with;
Owr Ladie charmed her deirlie Sone, with hir tooth and her townge,
And her ten fingeris----
In the name of the Father, the Son, and the Halie Ghaist!"

'And this we say thryse ower, straiking[85] the sor, and it becomes heall.
'2{dli} For the Bean-straw,[86] or pain in the heaunce,[87] Wee ar heir thrie Maidens charming for the bean-straw; y{e} man of the Midle-earth, blew beaver, land-feaver, maneris of stooris, The Lord fleigged[88] the Feind with his holy candles and yeird foot stone!--Thair she sittis, and heir she is gon!-- Let hir nevir com heir again!
3{dli} For the Feaveris, we say thrise ower, I forbid the qwaking-feavers, the sea-feaveris, the land-feaveris, and all the feaveris that ewir God ordained, owt of the head, owt of the heart, owt of the bak, owt of the sydis, owt of the kneyis, owt of the thieghes, fra the pointis of the fingeris, to the nebes[89] of the toes; owt fall the feaveris goe, [som] to the hill, som to the hap, som to the stone, som to the stok. In Saint Peiteris nam, Saint Paullis nam, and all the Saintis of Hevin: In the nam of The Father, the Sone, and The Halie Gost!
'And when we took the frwit of the fishes from [the] fisheris, we went to the shore, before the boat wold com to it; and we wold say, on the shore syd, thrie seuerall tymes ower,

"'The fisheris ar gon to the sea,
And they vill bring hom fishe to me;

They will bring them hom intill the boat,
Bot they sall get of thaim bot the smaller sort!"

So we either steall a fish, or buy a fish, or get a fish from them [for nowght] an or ma.[90] And with that we haw all the fruit of the heall fishes in the boat; and the fishes that the fishermen thamselues will haw, will be bot froath &c.

'The first woyag that ewer I went with the rest of owr Covens wes to Plewghlandis; and thair we shot an man betwixt the plewgh-stiltis, and he presentlie fell to the ground, wpon his neise and his mowth; and then the Divell gaw me an arrow, and cawsed me shoot an voman in that fieldis; quhilk I did, and she fell down dead. In Winter 1660, quhen Mr. Harie Forbes, Minister at Aulderne, was seik, we maid an bagg of the gallis, flesh, and guttis of toadis, pickles of bear,[91] pairingis of the nailis of fingeris and toes, the liewer of ane hair, and bittis of clowtis. We steipit this all together, all night among watter, all haked[92] throw uther. And whan we did put it among the water, Satan wes with ws, and learned ws the wordis following, to say thryse ower. They ar thus.

"'He is lying in his bed,--he is lyeing seik and sair;
Let him lye intill his bed two monethes and [thrie] dayes mair!
2{li}. Let him lye intill his bed--let him lye intill it seik and sore;
Let him lye intill his bed, monthis two and thrie dayes mor!
3{li}. He sall lye intill his bed, he sall lye in it seik and sore;
He sall lye intill his bed, two monethis and thrie dayes mor!"

'Quhan we haid learned all these wordis from the Devill, as said is, we all fell down [wpon owr] kneis, with owr hear down ower owr showlderis and eyes, and owr handis lifted wp, and owr eyes [stedfastlie fixed wpon] the Divell; and said the forsaidis wordis thryse ower to the Divell, striktlie, against Maister Harie Forbes [his recowering from the said seiknes]. In the night tym we cam into Mr. Harie Forbes chalmer, quhair he lay, with owr handis all smeared [... out] of the bagg to swing it upon Mr. Harie, quhair he wes seik in his bed; and, in the day tyme [... ane of owr] nwmber, quho wes most familiar and intimat with him, to wring or swing the bagg wpon the said Mr. Harie, as we could not prevaill in the night tym against him; quhilk wes accordinglie done.'

'Johne Taylor and his wyff, Bessie, and Margret Wilsones, and I, maid a pictur for the Laird of Parkis maill children. Johnne Taylor brought hom the clay in his plaid newk;[93] his wyff sifted it; we poured in water in a cówg[94] amongst it, and wrought it sor,[95] and maid a pictor of it, lyk a child, als big as a pow. It vanted no mark of the imag of a bairn, eyes, nose, mouth, little lippies, and the hands of it folded down by its sydis. The vordis, quhan we maid it, ver thes:

"'We put this water among this meall,
For long divining,[96] and ill heall;
We put it intill the fyr,
To burn them up both stik and stour,
That be burnt with our will,
As any stikill[97] on a kill!"

The Divell sitton on an blak kist. Ve wer al on owr kneyis, and owr hair about our eyes, looking on the Divell stedfastlie, and our handis lifted up to him, saying the vordes ower. And by this the bairnis died.'

CHAPTER XXII

Early Witchcraft in Scotland--Lady Glamys--Bessie Dunlop--Lady Foulis--Numerous Cases.

Witchcraft in Scotland began early, for we hear of some dozen or more people being burnt at Edinburgh in 1479, for attempting to bewitch the King, James III., to death, by means of a waxen image. In the proclamation of 1510, for regulating the proceedings at circuit courts the judges are instructed to ask the question, 'Gif thair be ony Wichecraift or Soffary wsit in y{e} realme?' but it was not until the passing of the Act of 1563 that the regular persecution of these deluded people began.

The first recorded case of witchcraft that I can find in Pitcairn's 'Criminal Trials in Scotland,' is that of Lady Glamys, where we read:

'31 Jan. 1532. Jonet, Lady Glammys found John Drummond of Innerpeffery as surety for her appearance at the next Justice-aire of Forfar, to underly the law for art and part of the Intoxication of John, Lord Glammys, her husband.'

That considerable sympathy was felt with her is shown by the number of gentlemen who preferred being fined to giving evidence in her case. But this can scarcely be called a case of witchcraft. She was certainly accused of trying to poison her husband by means of charmed drinks, but the chief accusation brought against her at her trial in 1537, by the malice of her husband's brother, was attempting to poison the King, a charge which she disposed of easily in her defence. Said she:

'I am here accus'd for purposing to kill the King; and, to make my pretended crime appear more frightful, it is given out that the way was to be by poison. With what strange impudence can any accuse me of such wickedness who never saw any poison, nor know I anything about the preparation of it? Let them tell where I bought it, or who procur'd it for me? Or, though I had it, how could I use it, since I never come near the King's person, his table, nor Palace? It is well known, that, since my last marriage with this unfortunate gentleman, I have liv'd in the country, at a great distance from the Court. What opportunity could I have to poison the King?'

But it was of no avail, she was to die, and this is her sentence:

'For the quhilkis tressonable crymes, the said Jonet, Lady of Glammys hes foirfallit to oure souerane lord, hir life, hir landis, gudis movable and unmovable: And that scho sall be had to Castell hill of Edinburghe, and their BRYNT in ane fyre to the deid, as ane Traytour. And that I gif for Dome.'

An historian[98] says: 'She heard the sentence pronounced without the least signe of terrour or concern. On the day appointed for her Execution, she suffered on the Castle-Hill of Edinburgh, where she appear'd with so much beauty and little concern, that all the spectators were so deeply afflicted for her, that they burst out with tears and loud lamentations for her untimely end, and were so confident of her Innocence, that they design'd to rescue her. But the King's Officers and Guards being present, hinder'd their attempting anything that way.'

The foregoing is evidently more a political case than one of witchcraft, the earliest of which existing in the records of the High Court of Justiciary in Scotland is June 26, 1563: 'Agnes Mullikine, alias Bessie Boswell, in Dunfermeling, wes Banist and exilit for Witchcraft.' The next is December 29, 1572: 'Jonet Boyman, spous to Williame Steill, Delatit of diuerse crymes of Witchcraft. Convict and Brint.'

The next is most interesting, although it savours more of Elfland than of diablerie, and is dated November 8, 1576:

'Elizabeth, or Bessie Dunlop, spous to Andro Jak in Lyne.[99] Dilatit of the using of Sorcerie, Witchcraft, and Incantatione of spretis of the devill; continewand in familiaritie with thame, at all sic tymes as sche thocht expedient: deling with charmes, and abusing the peple with devillisch craft of sorcerie foresaid, be the meanis after specefeit; usit thir diuerse geiris bypast; specialie, at the tymes and in the maner following.

'In the first, That fforsamekle as the said Elizabeth being demandit, be quhat art and knaulege sche could tell diuerse personnes of thingis thai tynt, or was stollin away, or help seik personnes? Ansuerit and declarit, that sche hirself had na kynd of art nor science swa to do; but diuerse tymes, quhen onye sic personnes come ather to hir, sche wald inquire at ane Thome Reid, quha deit at Pinkye,[100] as he himselff affirmit; wha wald tell hir, quhen euer sche askit.--

'(2) Item. Sche being inquirit, quhat kynd of man this Thom Reid was? Declarit, he was ane honest wele elderlie man, gray beardit, and had ane gray coitt with Lumbart slevis of the auld fassoun; ane pair of gray brekis, and quhyte schankis, gartanit aboue the kne: ane blak bonet on his heid, cloise behind and plane befoir, with silkin laissis drawin throw the lippis thairof; and ane quhyte wand in his hand.

'(3) Item. Being interrogat, how and in quhat maner of place the said Thome Reid came to hir? Ansuerit, as sche was gangand betwix hir awin hous, and the yard of Monk castell, dryvand hir ky to the pasture; and makand hevye sair dule[101] with hir self, gretand[102] verrie fast for hir kow that was deid, hir husband and chyld, that wer lyand seik in the land, and sche new rissine out of gissane.[103] The forsaid Thom mett her by the way, healsit[104] hir, and said, "Gude day, Bessie;" and sche said, "God speid yow, gude man." "Sancta Marie" saide he, "Bessie quhy makis thow sa grit dule and sair greting for ony warldlie thing?" Sche ansuerit, "Allace! haif I nocht grit caus to mak grit dule? ffor our geir is trakit;[105] and my husband is on the point of deid, and ane babie of my awin will nocht leve; and myself at ane waik point; haif I nocht gude caus thane to haif ane sair hart?" But Thom said, "Bessie, thow hes crabit[106] God, and askit sum thing you suld nocht haif done; and, thairfor, I counsell thee to mend to him: for I tell thee thy barne sall die, and the seik kow, or you cum hame; thy twa scheip sall de to; bot thy husband sall mend, and be als haill and feir as euir he was." And, than, I was sum thing blyther, fra he tauld me that my gudeman wald mend. Than Thome Reid went away fra me, in throw the yard of Monk castell; and I thocht he gait in at ane naroware hoill of the dyke, nor ony erdlie man culd haif gane throw, and swa I was sum thing fleit.[107]

'(4) Item. The thrid [? second] tyme, he apperit to hir, as sche was gangand betwix hir awin hous and the Thome of Damwstarnok, quhair he tareit ane gude quhyle with hir, and sperit at hir, "Gif sche wald nocht trow[108] in him?" Sche said, "Sche wald trow in ony bodye did her gude." And Thom promeist hir baith geir, horsis, and ky, and uther graith, gif scho wald denye hir Christindome, and the faith sche tuke at the funt stane?[109] Quhairunto sche ansuerit, "That gif sche suld be revin[110] at horsis-taillis sche suld neuir do that:" bot promeist to be leill and trew to him in onye thing sche culd do. And, forder, he was sumthing angrie with hir that sche wald nocht grant to him that quhilk he spak.

'(5) Item. The ferd tyme he apperit in hir awin hous to hir, about the XII hour of the day, quhair thair was sittand thre tailyeouris, and hir awin gudeman; and he tuke hir apperoun and led hir to the dure with him, and sche followit, and geid[111] up with him to the kill end, quhair he forbaid hir to speik or feir for ony thing sche hard or saw; and quhene thai had gane ane lytle pece fordwerd, sche saw twelf personnes, aucht wemene and four men: The men wer clad in gentlemennis clething, and the wemene had all plaiddis round about thame, and wer verrie semelie lyke to se; and Thome was with theme: And demandit, "Gif sche knew ony of thame?" Ansuerit, "Nane, except Thom." Demandit, "What said thai to hir?" Ansuerit, "Thai baid hir sit doun, and said, Welcome Bessie, will thow go with ws?" Bot sche ansuerit nocht; because Thom had forbidden hir. And, forder, declarit, That sche knew nocht quhat purpois thai had amangis thaime, onlie sche saw thair lippis move; and within a schort space thai pairtit all away; and ane hiddeous uglie sowche of wind followit thame; and sche lay seik quhill Thom came agane bak fra thame.

'(6) Item. Sche being demandit, Gif sche sperit at Thom quhat personnes thai war? Ansuerit, That thai war the gude wychtis that wynnit in the Court of Elfame,[112] quha come thair to desyre hir to go with thame; and, forder, Thom desyrit hir to do the sam; quha ansuerit, "Sche saw na proffeit to gang thai kynd of gaittis, unles sche kend quhairfor!" Thom said, "Seis thow nocht me, baith meit-worth, claith-worth, and gude enough lyke in personn; and he suld make hir far better nor euer sche was?" Sche ansuerit, "That sche duelt with hir awin husband and bairnis, and culd nocht leif thame." And swa Thom began to be verrie crabit with hir, and said, "Gif swo sche thocht, sche wald get lytill gude of him."

'(7) Interrogat. Gif sche had socht ony thing at Thom, to help hir self, or ony uther with? Ansuerit, That quhen sundrie personnes cam to hir to seik help for thair beist, their kow, or yow,[113] or for ane barne that was tane away with ane evill blast of wind, or elf-grippit, she gait[114] and sperit at Thom, Quhat mycht help thame? And Thom wald pull ane herb, and gif hir out of his awin hand; and baid hir scheir[115] the samin with onye uthir kynd of herbis, and oppin the beistis mouth, and put thame in, and the beist wald mend.'

Altogether, she seems to have been a kindly-disposed and beneficent witch; but that did not save her from the sentence--'Convict and Brynt.'

The annals of Scotch witchcraft are tame until we come to the case of Katherine Ross, Lady Foulis, July 22, 1590, who had enough to answer for, as she was accused of witchcraft, incantation, sorcery, and poisoning, her object being to poison her stepson, Robert Munro, then Lord Foulis, and Margery Campbell, wife to George Ross, Lord of Balnagowan. Several of her confederates had been tried and burnt, confessing the plot, before Lady Foulis's trial; but she had great interest, and both she and her stepson Hector Munro were acquitted. Her accusation is very long, so that I must leave all mention of the poisoning, and only take a portion of that relating to the witchcraft:

'Thou art now accusit, for the making of twa pictouris of clay, in company with the said Cristiane Roiss and Marionne Neyne M{c}Allester, alias Loskie Loucart, in the said Cristian Roissis westir chalmer in Canorth; the ane, maid for the distructioune and consumptioune of the young Laird of Fowlis, and the uthir for the young Ladie Balnagoune; to the effect that the are thairof sould be putt at the Brigend of Fowles, and the uther at Ardmoir, for distructioun of the saidis young Laird and Lady: And this sould haif bene performit at Allhallow-mes, in the year of God I{m}V{c}lxxvij yeiris: Quhilkis twa pictouris, being sett on the north syd of the Chalmer, the said Loskie Loucart tuik twa elf arrow heides, and delyuerit ane to you Katherene, and the uther, the said Cristian Rois Malcumsone held in her awin hand; and thow schott twa schottis with the said arrow held, att the said Lady Balnagowne, and Loskie Loucart schott thrie schottis at the said young Laird of Fowlis. In the meanetyme, baith the pictouris brak, and thou commandit Loskie Loucart to mak of new uthir twa pictouris thereaftir, for the said personnes: quhilk the said Loskie Loucart tuik upon hand to do.... Thou art now accusit, for assisting the said Thomas, Cristaine Malcomsone and Marionne Nieyn M{c}Allaster, upoun the secund day of Julij, anno threscoir sevintene yeiris, for making of ane pictur of butter to the said young Robert Munro, Laird of Fowlis, in the said house of Caynort, be the devyse and consultatioune of the said Donald and Williame M{c}Gilleuerie, and the said pictur of buttir, aftir it wes maid, wes set at the wall-syd, in the vester chalmer of the said hous of Coynard, and wes schot at with ane elf-arrow-heid be the said Marionne Neyuen M{c}Alester, alias Loske Loucart, aucht tymes; quhilk pictur scho mist, and haid hit no pairt thairof: And thow and Cristane Malcomsoune being present in the said chalmer, att the schotting of the said pictur, thinkand gane[116] the pictur were hit, it wald be for the distructioune of the young Laird of Fowlis: Lykas,[117] said Thomas was convict for the samin, and sufferit the deid.

'Als. thow art accusit, for being in cumpanie with Cristaine Malcomsonne and Marionne Neyn M{c}Allester, alias Loske Loucart, with the deuyse and consultatioune of Donald and William M{c}Gilliourois, made ane uther pictur of clay to the said Robert Munro, young Laird of Fowlis, in the said hous of Conord; and so it was maid upoune the morne, the vj day of Julij anno lxxvij yeiris; They sat the pictur at the wall-syd of the chalmer of the said hous, and wes schott be the said Loske Loucart, with the said elf-arrow, tuelf tymes, and mist the said pictur: And persauing that ye mist the samin efter euerie schott, and maid the said picture diuerse and sindrie tymes, yit the samin tuk nocht effect to their purpoise; thow and the said tua womene, thy collegis, being present for the tyme, and uising[118] ane takin of the samin; the said Cristaine Ross Malcomsoune haid provydeit thre quarteris of fine linning claithe for the picturis, gif thay haid bene hit with the elf-arrow-heid, and the linning to be bound about the said picturis, and the picturis to haue bene erdit[119] under the Brig end of the Stauk of Fowlis, fornent the get,'[120] etc.

The Scotch stories of witchcraft are quite as many as the English, and the so-called witches executed are far more numerous; the last one being burnt, as I have said, in 1727. In June, 1736, the Acts anent witchcraft were repealed; but I much fear that there is still a hankering after belief in it in many parts of Scotland.

CHAPTER XXIII

Witchcraft in America--In Illinois: Moreau and Emmanuel--In Virginia: Case of Grace Sherwood--In Pennsylvania: Two Swedish Women--In South Carolina--In Connecticut: Many Cases--In Massachusetts: Margaret Jones; Mary Parsons; Ann Hibbins; Other Cases.

North America has been colonized by the British long enough to have enjoyed the visitations of the Devil. And the present Americans, judging by the amount of literature written thereon,[121] seem rather proud of his having dwelt among them; it gives an air of antiquity, and an old-world tone, to the favoured States, which is sadly lacking, and not otherwise procurable, in those unvisited by his Satanic Majesty. As far as I know, there have been but six or seven States troubled with witchcraft: Virginia, Pennsylvania, South Carolina, Massachusetts, Connecticut, and Illinois.

The latter is somewhat remarkable, as it was only received into the Union, as a State, in 1818; yet I read, in 'The Pioneer History of Illinois,' by ex-Governor John Reynolds (Bellville, Ill., 1852), pp. 142, 143, the following:

'In early times the inhabitants of Illinois were in a small degree tinctured with the absurdity and nonsense of witchcraft and fortune-telling; but in after-days this ignorant superstition has entirely disappeared.... It was the belief of some people, and families, that an old woman living on Silver Creek, Illinois, had the power of witchcraft, to take milk from her neighbours' cows, without seeing or touching them....

'In Cahokia, about the year 1790, this superstition [witchcraft] got the upper hand of reason, and several poor African slaves were immolated at the shrine of ignorance for this imaginary offence. An African negro, named Moreau, was hung for this crime on a tree not far south-east of Cahokia. It is stated that he had said, "he poisoned his master, but his mistress was too strong for his necromancy." Another slave, Emmanuel, was shot, in Cahokia, for this crime, and an old woman, Janette, was supposed to have the power to destroy persons and property by her incantations. Many grown people, and all the children, were terrified at her approach.'

These two cases are verified by extracts from the 'Record Book' of Colonel John Todd, Lieutenant-Commandant of the County of Illinois, under Governor Patrick Henry, of the Commonwealth of Virginia:

'Illinois to wit.

'To Richard Winston, Esq{re}, Sheriff in chief of the District of Kaskaskia.

'Negro Manuel, a Slave, in your custody, is condemned by the Court of Kaskaskia, after having made honorable fine at the door of the church, to be chained to a post at the water side, and then to be burnt alive, and his ashes scattered, as appears to me by record. This sentence you are hereby required to put in execution, on tuesday next at 9 o'clock in the morning, and this shall be your warrant.

'Given under my hand and seal at Kaskaskia, the 13{th} day of June, in the 3{rd} year of the Commonwealth.'

'To Cap{t}. Nicolas Janis.

'You are hereby required to call upon a party of your militia to guard Moreau, a slave condemned to execution, up to the town of Kohos. Put them under an officer. They shall be entitled to pay, rashions and refreshment during the time they shall be upon duty, to be certified hereafter by you.

'I am, Sir, your hble servant,
 'JOHN TODD.

'15{th} June 1779.'

Virginia, I believe, can only boast of one witch, and her case is not very widely known. Princess Anne is the southernmost county of Virginia, bounded on the north by Chesapeake Bay, and on the east by the Atlantic. Lynhaven Bay is on the Chesapeake River; and there lived, in the days of 'good Queen Anne,' a young woman named Grace Sherwood, who was somewhat shy in her dealings with her neighbours, probably because they invested her with uncanny powers, and even said that she had voyaged across the Atlantic, as far as the Mediterranean, in an eggshell; that on her arrival, at the end of her journey, she had been so pleased with the smell of the rosemary she had found growing there, that she brought back some of the plants with her, and set them about her cottage. These evil rumours were brought to the ears of the authorities, and Grace Sherwood was haled before the justices assembled at Princess Anne Court House; and the entry of her examination, etc., in the court record is as follows:

'Princess Annes.

'At a Court held y{e} 10th July 1706.

Present
{ Col{o} Moseley   Capt. Moseley   }
{ Cap{t} Woodhouse   Jno. Cormick   } Justices.
{ Capt. Chapman   Capt. W{m} Smyth }
   Richason--come late.

[Sidenote: Grace Sherwood to be Ducked.]

'Whereas Grace Sherwood being Suspected of Witchcraft--have a long time waited for a fit opportunity for a further Examination--and by her Consent, & Approbation of y{e} Court, it is ordered y{t} y{e} Sherr take all such Convenient assistance of boats and men, as shall be by him thought fit to meet & at John Harper's plantation, in order to take y{e} said Grace Sherwood forthwith, & put her into water above man's Debth & try her how she swims. Therein always having Care of her life to preserve her from Drowning & as soon as she comes Out y{t} he request as many Ancient and Knowing women as possible to come to Serch her Carefully for teat spotts and marks about her body not usual on Others & y{t} as they find y{e} same to make report on Oath To y{e} truth ther of to the Court; and, further, it is ordered y{t} Four women be requested to Shift and Serch her before she goo into y{e} water y{t} she carry nothing about her to cause any further Suspicion.

[Sidenote: Order XX.]
[Sidenote: Grace Sherwood Ducked, etc.]

'Whereas on Complaint of Luke Hill in behalf of her Majesty y{t} now is ag{t} Grace Sherwood for a person Suspected of Witch craft & having had Sundry Evidences sworn ag{t} her, proving many Circumstances to which She could not make any Excuse, Little or Nothing to say in her own behalf, only Seamed to Rely on w{t} y{e} Court should doo, and there upon Consented to be tryed in y{e} Water, & Like-wise to be Serched again Bodily. Experiment being tried, She swiming w{en} therein, and bound Contrary to Custom & y{e} judg{t} of all y{e} Spectators, & afterward, being Serched, & five Ancient weomen who have all Declared on Oath y{t} she is not like y{em} nor noo Other women y{t} they know of ... all w{ch} Circumstances y{e} Court weighing in their Consideration, Doo there fore ord{r} y{t} y{e} Sherr take y{e} s{d} Grace Into his custody, and to comm{t} her body to ye Common Gaol of this County, there to secure her by irons or other Wise, there to Remain till Such time as shall be otherwise Directed in order for her comming to y{e} Common Gaol of y{e} County, to be brought to a future tryall there.

'Edw{d} Moseley & 'Jno Richason.'

As nothing more can be found respecting her, she was probably let go.

As a justice of the peace, William Penn had to sit in judgment upon two Swedish women who were indicted as witches, and true bills were found against them; but they got off, owing to some flaw in the indictment. And this, as far as I know, is the sole instance of a trial for witchcraft in Pennsylvania.

Drake, in 'Annals of Witchcraft,' p. 215, says: 'About this period [1712], in the Colony of South Carolina, some suspected of witchcraft were seized upon by a sort of ruffianly Vigilance Committee, and condemned to be burnt, and were actually roasted by fire, although we do not learn that the injuries thus inflicted proved fatal. The parties so tortured, or their friends, brought action in the regular courts, for the recovery of damages; but the jury gave them nothing.'

In the early days of Connecticut there were twelve crimes punishable by death, according to the 'Capitall Lawes, established by the General Court the First of December 1642,' the second of which is: 'Yf any man or woman be a witch (that is) hath, or consulteth w{th} a familliar spirit, they shall be put to death. Ex. xxii. 18. Lev. xx. 27. Deu. xxvij. 10, 11.'[122] And they had not to wait long for a victim, for the last entry in John Winthrop's Journal for 1646 is, 'One ... of Windsor arraigned and executed at Hartford for a witch,' Nothing more is certainly known of this case, which is memorable as being the first execution for witchcraft in New England.

The Connecticut Legislature also applied the same law, somewhat modified, to the Pequot Indians, on May 31, 1675:[123] '(2) That whosoever shall powau, or use witchcraft, or any worship to the divill, or any fals god, shall be convented and punished.'

The following are the known cases of witchcraft in Connecticut; but, as far as I can see, none present any particular features of interest for the reader.[124]

1646	Winthrop's 'One ... of Windsor'	executed
1648	Mary Jonson, of Hartford or Wethersfield	do.
1651	Mr. and Mrs. Carrington, of Wethersfield	do.
	Goody Bassett, of Stratford	do.
1653	Goody Knapp, of Fairfield	do.
1658	Goody Garlick, of Easthampton, L.I.	acquitted
1661	Mr. and Mrs. Jennings, of Laybrook	freed by disagreement of jury
1662	Mr. and Mrs. Greensmith, of Hartford	executed
1663	Mary Barnes, of Farmington	d0.
	Mrs. Elizabeth Seager, of Hartford (?)	acquitted
	Mrs. Elizabeth Seager, of Hartford (2nd trial)	do.
1665	Mrs. Elizabeth Seager, of Hartford (3rd trial)	convicted, but freed by the court
1670	Katharine Harrison, of Wethersfield	convicted; the court refused to sentence, and dismissed the accused
1692	Mrs. Staples, of Fairfield	acquitted
	Goody Miller, of Fairfield	do.
	Elizabeth Clawson, of Fairfield	do.
	Mercy Disborough, of Fairfield	convicted, but probably pardoned by the general court
1697	Mrs. Denham and daughter	acquitted, perhaps accused only before the grand jury

But it was in Massachusetts that witchcraft was rampant. The Pilgrim Fathers when they landed at Plymouth, on December 22, 1620, brought with them from England the belief in witchcraft and the personality of the Devil, which was then the creed of the majority of those living in the mother country, and therefore they were no worse than their brethren or parents. So that we must not blame them if we find among their early records, dated New Plymouth, November 15, 1636, that they considered witchcraft a capital crime, and enumerated as such directly after treason and murder; and they defined the crime so punishable as 'Solemne compaction, or conversing with the divell, by way of witchcraft, conjuration, or the like.'

The Devil, however, had got somehow into Massachusetts, for we read in Governor Winthrop's Journal that in 1639 'The Indians near Aquiday being pawwawing in this tempest, the Devil came and fetched away five of them. Query.'

The first instance of witchcraft in this Colony is recorded in Winthrop's Journal in 1648, but he gives no specific date of the court being held, but most likely it was that of May 13, 1648, of which a record remains: 'That This Court, being desirous that the same Course which hath been taken in England for the discovery of witches, by watching, may also be taken here, with the witch now in question, and therefore do order that a strict watch be set about her, every night, and that her husband be confined in a private room, and watched also.'

The entry in the Journal is as follows: 'At this Court, one Margaret Jones of Charlestown was indicted and found guilty of witchcraft, and hanged for it. The evidence against her was: 1. that she was found to have such a malignant touch, as many persons (men, women and children), whom she stroaked or touched with any affection or displeasure, or etc., were taken with deafness, or vomiting, or other violent pains or sickness. 2. The practising physic, and her medicines being such things as (by her own confession) were harmless, as aniseed, liquors, &c., yet had extraordinary violent effects. 3. She would use to tell such as would not make use of her physic, that they would never be healed, and, accordingly, their diseases and hurts continued, with relapse against the ordinary course, and beyond the apprehension of all physicians and surgeons. 4. Some things which she foretold, came to pass accordingly; other things she could tell of (as secret speeches, etc.) which she had no ordinary means to come to the knowledge of. 5. She had, upon search, an apparent teat, as fresh as if it had been newly sucked, and, after it had been scanned; upon a forced search, that was withered, and another began on the opposite side. 6. In the prison, in the clear daylight, there was seen, in her arms, she, sitting on the floor, and her clothes up, etc., a little child, which ran from her into another room, and the officer following it, it was vanished. The like child was seen in two other places, to which she had relation; and one maid that saw it, fell sick upon it, and was cured by the said Margaret, who used means to be employed to that end. Her behaviour at her trial was very intemperate, lying notoriously, and railing upon the jury and witnesses, etc., and in the like distemper she died. The same day and hour she was executed, there was a very great tempest in Connecticut, which blew down many trees, etc.'

The next authentic instance is that of Mary Parsons, whose case seems to have been somewhat urgent, as on May 8, 1651, there is a minute on the court records:[125] 'The Court, understanding that Mary Parsons, now in prison, accused for a witch, is likely, through weakness to die before trial, if it be deferred, do order, that on the morrow, by eight o'clock in the morning, she be brought before and tried by the General Court, the rather that Mr. Pynchon may be present to give his testimony in the Case.'

This 'Mr. Pynchon' came from England with Governor Winthrop in 1630, and was named in the charter granted by Charles II. to Massachusetts, as one of the Governor's eighteen assistants. He returned to England in 1652, settled at Wraysbury, Bucks, where he died October 29, 1662. Hutchinson says of him: 'Mr. Pynchon was a gentleman of learning, as well as religion. He laid the foundation of Roxbury, but soon removed to Connecticut River; was the father of the town of Springfield, where his family hath flourished ever since.'

For some reason, she was not brought before the court till May 13, when the following is recorded: 'Mary Parsons, wife of Hugh Parsons of Springfield, being committed to prison for suspicion of witchcraft, as also for murdering her own child, was, this day, called forth, and indicted for Witchcraft. "By the name of Mary Parsons, you are here, before the General Court, charged, in the name of this Commonwealth, that, not having the fear of God before your eyes, nor in your heart, being seduced by the Devil, and yielding to his malicious motion, about the end of February last at Springfield, to have familiarity, or consulted with, a familiar spirit, making a covenant with him; and have used divers devilish practices by witchcraft, to the hurt of the persons of Martha and Rebecca Moxon, against the Word of God, and the laws of this jurisdiction, long since made and published." To which indictment she pleaded "Not guilty." All evidences brought in against her being heard and examined, the Court found the evidences were not sufficient to prove her a witch, and therefore she was cleared in that respect.'

But she was indicted for the murder of her child, found guilty, and sentenced to be hanged; it is doubtful, however, whether the sentence was ever carried out. Her husband, 'One Hugh Parsons of Springfield, was tried in 1652 for witchcraft, and found guilty by the jury. The Magistrate refused to consent to the verdict, and the case, as the law provided, came to the General Court, who determined that he was not legally guilty of witchcraft.'[126]

'The most remarkable occurrence in the Colony in the year 1655 was the trial and condemnation of Mrs. Ann Hibbins for witchcraft. Her husband, who died in the year 1654, was an agent for the Colony in England, several years one of the assistants, and a merchant of note in the town of Boston; but losses in the latter part of his life had reduced his estate and increased the natural crabbedness of his wife's temper, which made her turbulent and quarrelsome, and brought her under church censures; and, at length, rendered her so odious to her neighbours, as to cause some of them to accuse her of witchcraft. The Jury brought her in guilty, but the magistrates refused to accept the verdict, so the cause came to the General Court, where the popular clamour prevailed against her, and the miserable old woman was condemned and executed. Search was made upon her body for tetts, and in her chests for puppets, images, etc., but there is no record of anything of that sort being found. Mr. Beach, a minister in Jamaica, in a letter to Doctor Increase Mather in the year 1684, says, "You may remember what I have sometimes told you your famous Mr. Norton once said at his own table, before Mr. Wilson the pastor, elder Penn and myself and wife, etc., who had the honour to be his guests. That one of your magistrate's wives, as I remember, was hanged for a witch, only for having more wit than her neighbours. It was his very expression, she having, as he explained it, unhappily guessed that two of her persecutors, whom she saw talking in the street, were talking of her; which, proving true, cost her her life, notwithstanding all he could do to the contrary, as he, himself, told us."[127]

'It fared with her as it did with Joan of Arc in France; some counted her a saint, and some a witch, and some observed solemn marks of Providence set upon those who were very forward to condemn her, and to brand others upon the like ground, with the like reproach. This was the second instance upon record of any persons being executed for witchcraft in New England. She was not executed until June, 1656. She disposed of her estate by will executed May 27, 1656, and a codicil June 16. She appointed several of the principal gentlemen overseers, and hoped they would show her so much respect, as to see her decently interred. There was no forfeiture of goods for felony.'

There was a case of witchcraft in Hartford in 1662, when three women were condemned, and one, at least, executed. In 1669 Susanna Martin, of Salisbury, was tried on this charge, 'but escaped at that time.' Another case at Groton in 1671, and yet another at Hampton in 1673. In 1658, in Essex County, an attempt was made to convict one John Godfrey, of Andover, as a witch, and at the County Court of Salem, June 29, 1659, he was bound in one hundred pounds to appear when called upon. But he turned the tables against his accusers, bringing actions against them for slander. In one case he got twopence damages and twenty-nine shillings costs, in another ten shillings damages and costs fifty shillings.

In November, 1669, Goody Burt, a widow, was prosecuted, but acquitted. In 1673 Eunice Cole, of Hampton, was tried, but her sentence was 'to depart from, and abide out of, this jurisdiction.' On November 24, 1674, at Salem, which even then was coming to the fore with its witches, Christopher Browne was had up before the County Court, for 'having reported that he had been treating or discoursing with one whom he apprehended to be the Devil, which came like a gentleman, in order to his binding himself to be a servant to him. Upon his examination, his discourse seeming inconsistent with truth, etc., the Court giving him good counsel and caution, for the present dismiss him.'

On March 30, 1680, Caleb Powell was brought before the court at Ipswich, under an indictment of witchcraft, in molesting one William Morse, of Newbury, stones being thrown, furniture behaving abnormally, bedclothes snatched off, and many other inconveniences; but it could not be proved, and the wind-up of the affair was: 'Though this court cannot find any evident ground of proceeding against the said Caleb Powell, yet we determine that he hath given such ground of suspicion of his so dealing, that we cannot so acquit him, but that he justly deserves to bear his own share, and the costs of the prosecution of the complaint.' Elizabeth Morse, wife of the above, was next, on May 20, 1680, tried and convicted of witchcraft. On May 27 she was sentenced to death, was twice reprieved, and ultimately allowed to return home.

CHAPTER XXIV

Cotton and Increase Mather--The Case of Goodwin's Daughter--That of Mr. Philip Smith--The Story of the Salem Witchcrafts--List of Victims--Release of Suspects--Reversal of Attainder, and Compensation.

We now come to the time of Cotton Mather, whose name is a 'household word' in connection with witchcraft in Massachusetts. He was the son of Increase Mather, D.D., one of the early presidents of Harvard College, was born in 1633, studied at Harvard, and at the age of twenty was appointed copastor with his father at Boston. He begins his first witch story thus: 'There dwells at this time, in the south part of Boston, a sober and pious man, whose name is John Goodwin, whose Trade is that of a Mason, and whose Wife (to which a Good Report gives a share with him in all the Characters of Virtue) has made him the Father of six (now living) Children. Of these Children, all but the Eldest, who works with his Father at his Calling, and the Youngest, who lives yet upon the Breast of its mother, have laboured under the direful effects of a no less palpable than stupendous WITCHCRAFT.'[128]

As the reader will see that it is impossible to quote Cotton Mather very much at length, on account of his excessively rotund style, I must tell the story as briefly as possible. Sometimes these unhappy children would be by turns either deaf, dumb, or blind, or all three at once, their jaws be dislocated, and then close sharply with a loud snap. 'They would bark at one another like Dogs, and again purr like so many Cats.... Yea they would fly like Geese; and be carried with an incredible Swiftness thro' the air, having but just their Toes now and then upon the ground, and their Arms waved like the Wings of a Bird. One of them, in the House of a Kind Neighbour, flew the length of the Room, about 20 foot, and flew into an Infant's high armed Chair; none seeing her feet all the way touch the floor.'

Cotton Mather took the eldest daughter home to live with them, in order that he 'might be furnished with Evidence and Argument as a Critical Eye Witness, to confute the Saducism of this debauched Age.' For some days all went well, but on November 20 she was once more possessed. She tried to fly, to dive, her eyes sunk into her head, so that they thought they would never return to their normal position, and she complained that Goody Glover, a poor crazy Irish woman, had put an invisible but very potent chain round her leg. She could not read the Bible, but a Quaker book she was able to read, with the exception of the names of God and Christ. Queer books, like the 'Oxford Jests' and 'Cambridge Jests,' she could read well enough, but could only pronounce the words 'Devils' or 'Witches' with extreme difficulty.

'Every now and then an Invisible Horse would be brought unto her by those whom she only called them, and, Her Company: upon the Approach of Which, her eyes would be still closed up; for, (said she) They say I am a Tell-Tale, and, therefore, they will not let me see them. Upon this would she give a Spring as one mounting an Horse, and Settling her self in a Riding Posture, she would, in her Chair be agitated as one sometimes Amble-ing sometimes Trotting, and sometimes Galloping very furiously.'

This state of things would not do, so divers ministers and devout friends fell to a-praying, but all to no purpose, her invisible adversaries on one occasion dragging her to an oven which was heating, and another time choking her, till she was black in the face, with an invisible rope and noose; she even began to torment good Mr. Mather. 'When I had begun to study my Sermon, her Tormentors again seized upon her; and all Fryday and Saturday did they manage her with a special Design, as was plain, to disturb me in what I was about. In the worst of her extravagancies, formerly, she was more dutiful to myself than I had reason to Expect, but, now, her whole carriage to me, was with a Sauciness that I had not been us'd to be treated with. She would knock at my Study Door, affirming That some below would be glad to see me; when there was none that ask't for me. She would call to me with multiplyed Impertinences, and throw small things at me, wherewith she could not give me any hurt. Shee'd Hector me at a strange rate for the work I was at, and threaten me with I know not what mischief for it.'

By dint of energetic prayer she began to amend, but she had one more very bad breakout. 'Moreover, Both she at my house, and her Sister at home, at the time which they call Christmas, were by the Dæmons, made very drunk, though they had no strong Drink (as we are fully sure) to make them so. When she began to feel herself thus drunk, she complain'd, O, they say they will have me to keep Christmas with them! They will disgrace me when they can do nothing else! And, immediately the

Ridiculous Behaviour of one drunk, were with a wonderful exactness represented in her Speaking, and Reeling, and Spewing, and anon Sleeping, till she was well again.'

The next example Cotton Mather gives us is that of 'Mr. Philip Smith, aged about Fifty years, a Son of eminently vertuous Parents, a Deacon of the Church at Hadley, a Member of our General Court, an Associate in their County Court, a Select-man for the affairs of the Town, a Lieutenant in the Troop; and, which crowns all, a man for Devotion and Gravity, and all that was Honest, exceeding exemplary. Such a man, in the Winter of the year 1684 was murdered with an hideous Witchcraft, which filled all those parts with a just astonishment.

'He was concerned about Relieving the Indigencies of a wretched woman in the Town; who, being dissatisfied at some of his just cares about her, expressed her self unto him in such a manner, that he declared himself apprehensive of receiving mischief at her hands; he said he doubted she would attempt his Hurt.'

In the beginning of the following January he fell sick, and took to his bed; but he could not rest, he was delirious and spoke in sundry voices and languages, and felt hundreds of pins pricking him all over. Sometimes there was a strange smell of musk about the place. As, in his agony, he called upon the supposed witch, his kind friends 'did three or four times in one Night go and give Disturbance to the Woman that we have spoken of: all the while they were doing of it, the good man was at ease, and slept as a weary man; and these were all the times they perceived him to take any sleep at all.'

Sometimes fire was seen on the bed, but when attention was called to it, it vanished. Something as big as a cat moved in the bed, but no one could catch it; and 'a discreet and sober Woman, resting on the Bed's Feet, felt as it were, a Hand, the Thumb and the Finger of it, taking her by the side and giving her a Pinch; but turning to see What it might be, nothing was to be seen.' Many more marvels occurred, and at last the poor man died, yet even then his bed moved of itself more than once, and at night, when they were preparing for his funeral, noises were heard in the room 'as though there had been a great Removing and Clattering of stools and chairs.' I cannot find that the witch was punished.

He next gives an instance of a boy at Tocutt, who held a great deal of communication with the Devil without absolutely resigning his soul to him, and who must have lived a very uncomfortable existence. 'He speaks of men coming to him before they come in Sight; and, once, two being with him, their Backs turned, the Devil carried him away, they knew not how, and after search, they found him in a Cellar, as dead, but, after a little space, he came to Life again. And another time, threw him up into a Chamber, stopped him up into a Hole where they after found him. Another time, he carried him about a Bowshot, and threw him into a Hog-Stye amongst Swine, which ran away with a terrible noise.'

He gives two more instances of possession by the Devil; but they are mild cases which yielded to prayer. There are other minor cases of witchcraft which I have omitted, because I would fain have space to tell of the works of the Devil at Salem in 1692.

Salem was then a small village, about sixteen miles north-east of Boston, and its minister was the Rev. Samuel Parris, born in London in 1653. He entered Harvard College, but could not take a degree, went to Barbados, where he engaged in mercantile pursuits, and finally turned religious, and was ordained minister of Salem congregation in 1689, naturally taking a leading part in the little community.

At his house, during the winter of 1691-92, a society of girls met, curiously enough, for the purpose of practising palmistry, fortune-telling, necromancy, magic, and spiritualism; and they soon became so far advanced in these arts as to be seized with unnatural spasms, falling insensible on the floor, writhing in agony, and uttering piercing cries. As this conduct was decidedly abnormal, as was their amusement, it was settled that they were bewitched, and they were sympathized with as being 'afflicted Children.' Fasting and prayer were tried, but with no good result. On being questioned as to who had bewitched them, they answered 'Good,' 'Osborn,' and 'Tituba.' Sarah Good was a woman generally disliked, Sarah Osborn was a bed-ridden woman who did not bear a very good character, and Tituba was an Indian woman in Mr. Parris' service.

On March 1, 1692, they were brought before the court charged with bewitching the children. One indictment must serve as a specimen for all:

'The Jurors for our Sovereigne Lord & Lady King William & Queen Mary Doe present: That Sarah Good, ye wife of William Good of Salem Village, In the County of Essex, husbandman, upon y{e} first day of March in y{e} fourth year of y{e} Reigne of our Sovereigne Lord & Lady W{m} & Mary, by y{e} Grace of God, of England, Scotland, ffrance & Ireland King & Queen, defend{rs} of y{e} faith etc & Divers other days & times as well before as after, Certaine Detestable Arts, Called Witchcrafts & Sorceries, wickedly & ffeloniously hath used, practised & Exercised at & within y{e} Township of Salem aforesaid, In, upon & against An Puttman, Single woman of Salem Village, by which said Wicked arts, the said An Puttman y{e} said first day of March, in y{e} fourth year abovesaid & divers other other days & times, as well before as after, was & is hurt, Tortured, afflicted, Pined, Consumed, wasted & Tormented, & also for Sundry acts of Witchcraft by said Good Committed & done before & since that time against y{e} peace of our Soveraigne Lord & Lady y{e} King &

Queen Their Crowne & dignity & against y{e} forme of Statues In that Case made & provided.

'Witness. Ann Putman. Jurat. Eliz. Hubbard. Abigail Williams. Jurat.'

On examination, Good and Osborn denied the accusation in toto, but Tituba, the Indian woman, gave damning evidence against them, and it is worthy of being given in extenso:

'THE EXAMINATION OF TITIBE.

'Titibe what evil Spirit have you familiarity with?--None.
'Why do you hurt these children?--I do not hurt them.
'Who is it then?--The Devil for ought I know.
'Did you never see the Devil?--The Devil came to me and bid me serve him.
'Who have you seen?--Four women sometimes hurt the children.
'Who were they?--Goode Osburn and Sarah Good, and I doe not know who the other were. Sarah Good and Osburne would have me hurt the children, but I would not. She further saith there was a tall man of Boston that she did see.
'When did you see them?--Last night at Boston.
'What did they say to you?--They said, hurt the children.
'And did you hurt them?--No, there is 4 women and one man. They hurt the children, and they lay all upon me, and they tell me if I will not hurt the children, they will hurt me.
'But you did not hurt them?--Yes, but I will hurt them no more.
'Are you not sorry you did hurt them?--Yes.
'And why then doe you hurt them?--They say hurt children or wee will doe worse to you.
'What have you seen?--An man come to me and say serve me.
'What service?--Hurt the children; and, last night, there was an appearance that said kill the children; and if I would not go on hurting the children, they would do worse to me.
'What is this appearance you see?--Sometimes it is like a hog, and sometimes like a great dog; this appearance shee saith shee did see 4 times.
'What did it say to you?--It, the black dog said, serve me, but I said, I am afraid. He said, if I did not, he would doe worse to me.
'What did you say to it?--I will serve you no longer; then he said he would hurt me; and then he looked like a man, and threatened to hurt me. Shee said that this man had a yellow bird that kept with him, and he told me he had more pretty things that he would give me if I would serve him.
'What were those pretty things?--He did not show me them.
'What, also, have you seen?--Two rats--a red rat and a black rat.
'What did they say to you?--They said, serve me.
'When did you see them?--Last night, and they said, serve me, but I would not.
'What service?--Shee said, hurt the children.
'Why did you goe to Thomas Putnams last night, and hurt his child?--They pull and hall me, and make me goe.
'And what would they have you doe?--Kill her with a knife.
'Left. Fuller and others said at this time when the child saw these persons, and was tormented by them, that she did complayn of a knife, that they would have her cut her head off with a knife.
'How did you go?--We ride upon stickes, and are there presently.
'Do you goe through the trees, or over them?--We see nothing, but are there presently.
'Why did you not tell your Master?--I was afraid they would cut off my head if I told.
'Would you have hurt others if you could?--They said they would hurt others, but they could not.
'What attendants hath Sarah Good?--A yellow bird, and she would have given me one.
'What meate did she give it?--It did suck between her fingers.
'Did you not hurt Mr. Currin's child?--Goode Good and Goode Osborn told [me] that they did hurt Mr. Curren's child, and would have me hurt him too, but I did not.
'What hath Sarah Osburn?--Yellow dog. Shee had a thing with a head like a woman, with 2 legges, and wings. Abigail Williams that lives with her Uncle Parris said that she did see the same creature, and it turned into the shape of Goode Osburn.
'What else have you seen with Osburn?--Another thing, hairy; it goes upright like a man; it hath only 2 legges.
'Did you not see Sarah Good upon Elizabeth Hubbard, last Satterday?--I did see her set a wolfe upon her to afflict her. The persons with this maid did say that she did complain of a wolfe. Shee further saith that she saw a cat with Good, at another time.
'What cloathes doth the man go in?--He goes in black cloathes, a tal man with white hair, I think.
'How doth the woman go?--In a white whood, and a black whood with a top knot.
'Doe you see who it is that torments these children now?--Yes, it is Goode Good, shee hurts them

The Devil, in Britain and America
in her own shape.

'And who is it that hurts them now?--I am blind now, I cannot see.'

In the end, all three were sent to gaol. Mrs. Osburn died in gaol on May 16. Sarah Good was hanged, and Tituba lay in prison for thirteen months, and was then sold to pay her gaol fees.

Evidently the taste for notoriety in the 'afflicted children' was developing. One of them, Ann Putnam, denounced one Martha Corey for pricking and tormenting her. Mrs. Corey seems to have been a harmless church-member, and denied all the imputations of witchcraft cast on her; but even her husband bore testimony against her anent an ox which he thought had been bewitched. She was hanged. Her husband was afterward arrested on a similar charge, and his was a most singular case. By law, if found guilty, his goods, etc., were forfeited. He had the singular courage to defeat the law by the law itself. He caused a deed to be drawn up, duly witnessed, etc., by which he left his property to two out of his four sons-in-law, who befriended his wife (the other two gave witness against her). He then refused to plead either guilty or not guilty. He was had up the legal three times before the judge, but as he continued dumb he was sentenced to the Peine forte et dure, that of 'pressing' until he pleaded or died. If he died under the punishment his goods were not forfeited.

The punishment was that he was stretched out upon his back, his arms and legs drawn out by cords and fastened to the four corners of his dungeon. A board, or plate of iron, was laid upon his stomach, and upon this was placed a certain weight. Next day he was given, at three different times, three little morsels of barley bread, and nothing to drink. The next day, three little glasses of water, and nothing to eat, and if he continued obstinate and dumb, he was left uncared for till he died. Corey begged them to add weights until they killed him, and they mercifully did so. Verily, he expiated his testimony against his wife.

It would be impossible to give, within the limits of this volume, an account of all the trials of the Salem witches. Suffice it to say that the little clique who met at the house of the Rev. S. Parris continued to accuse their neighbours all round. The following is a list taken from the 'Records of Salem Witchcraft, copied from the original Documents. Privately printed for W. Elliot Woodward, Roxbury;' Massachusetts, 1864. Those in italics were hanged; the fate of the others except in two or three instances I know not:

Sarah Good,* Sarah Osburn (died in gaol), Tituba, Indian (sold), Martha Corey,* John Procter,* Dorcas Good, Rebecca Nurse,* Elizabeth Procter,* (pleaded she was enceinte), Mary Warren, Bridget Bishop, Abigail Hobbs,* Sarah Wilds,* Philip English, Susannah Martin, Elizabeth Hart, Dorcas Hoar,* George Jacobs,* John Willard,* Ann Pudeater, Rebecca Jacobs, Roger Toothaker, Mary Eastey,* Sarah Procter, Susannah Roots, Benjamin Procter, Martha Carrier,* Elizabeth How,* William Procter, Wilmott Reed, Elizabeth Fosdick, Elizabeth Paine, Mary Ireson, George Burroughs,* Abigail Faulkner,* Ann Foster, Mary Lacey,* Rebecca Eames,* Samuel Wardwell,* Mary Parker,* Mary Bradbury,* Giles Corey,* (pressed to death), Alice Parker, Margaret Scot.

Who can say, after reading the above list, that, if the Devil were in anyone at Salem, he was not in that precious lot of 'afflicted children'? In fact, people began to fight shy of them; they even accused a member of Increase Mather's family, and made charges against Mrs. Hale, wife of the Minister of the First Church in Beverley, so that their testimony at last received no credence. After the Sessions of September 22, no one was hanged, even if convicted; and in April, 1693, the Governor-General, by proclamation, gave freedom to all suspects that were in confinement, and in 1711 a reversal of attainder was granted in those cases marked with an asterisk, and compensation made to their representatives to the amount of £578 12s.

APPENDIX

LIST OF BOOKS CONSULTED AND USED IN THIS WORK.

Harl. MSS., 1766, f. Dan John Lydgate's Translation (or Paraphrase) of John Boccace de Casu Principum, in English Verse: done by the command of Duke Humfrey, about the beginning of the Reign of Henry the Sixth.

Tboeck van den leuen ons heeren ihesu christi. Gheraert de leeu. Tantwerpen, 1487, 4to.

Von den unholden oder hexen. Molitor (Ulrich). Rütlingen, 1489, 4to.

Registrum hujus operis libri cronicarum in figuris et ijmagibus ab inicio mūdi. Schedel (Hartmannus), A. Koberger. Nuremberge, 1493, fol.

Introductio in Chaldaicam Linguā, Syriacā, atq Armenicā, & decē alias linguas. Characterum Differentiū Alpha beta, circiter quadraginta, & eorūdem innicem cōformatio. Mystica et Cabalistica quā plurima scitu digna. Et descriptio ac simulachrū Phagoti Afranij. Theseo Ambrosio ex Comitibus Albonesii IV. Doct. Papieñ. Canonico Regulari Lateranensi, ac Sancti Petri in Cælo Aureo. Papiæ Præposito Authore. 1539.

Hexen Meysterey. Dess ... Fürsten ... Sigmunds von Ostereich mit U. (Ulrich) M. (Molitor) und C. Schatz, wielandt Burgermeister zu Costentz ... ein schön Gesprech von den Onholden ... Weitleuffiger mit mer Exempeln der Alten, dann vor nie kains aussgangen, &c. Costentz, 1545.

Historia de Gentibus Septentrionalibus, earum que diversis statibus, conditionibus, moribus, ritibus, superstitionibus, disciplinis, exercitiis, regimine, victu, bellis, structuris, instrumentis, ac mineris metallicis, & rebus mirabilibus, nec non universis penè animalibus in Septentrione de gentibus eorumque natura ... Autore Olao Magno Gotho Archiepiscopo Upsalensi. Suetiæ & Gothiæ Primate. Romæ, 1555.

The Examination of John Walsh before Master Thomas Williams, Commissary to the Reverend father in God, William, bishop of Excester, upon certayne Interrogatories touchyng Wytchcrafte and Sorcerye, in the presence of diuers gētlemen and others. The xx of August, 1566. Imprynted at London by John Awdely, dwelling in litle Britain streete without Aldersgate 1566. The xxiij of December.

The disclosing of a late counterfeyted possession by the deuyl in two maydens within the Citie of London. Printed at London by Richard Watkins. 1574.

A Dialogue of Witches, in foretime named Lottellers, and now commonly called Sorcerers. Wherein is declared breefely and effectually, what soeuer may be required, touching that argument. A treatise very profitable, by reason of the diuerse and sundry opinions of men in this question, and right necessary for Judges to understande, which sit upon lyfe and death. Written in Latin by Lambertus Danæus, And now translated into English. Printed by R. W. 1575.

A most strange and rare example of the iust iudgement of God executed upon a lewde and wicked Coniurer the xvij day of Januarie 1577. In the parish church of S. Mary Overis in Southwark, in the presence of divers credible and honest persons. Imprinted at London by Henrie Bennyman.

A Rehearsall both straung and true, of hainous and horrible actes committed by Elizabeth Stile, Alias Rockingham, Mother Dutten, Mother Deuell, Mother Margaret. Fower notorious Witches apprehended at Winsore in the Countie of Barks, and at Abbington arraigned, condemned and executed, on the 26 daye of Februarie last, Anno 1579. Imprinted at London for Edward White at the little North-doore of Paules, at the signe of the Gun, and are there to be sold.

A Detection of damnable driftes practized by three Witches arraigned at Chelmissforde in Essex, at the laste Assizes there holden, whiche were executed in Aprill 1579. Set forthe to discouer the Ambushementes of Sathan, whereby he would surprise us, lulled in securitie, and hardened with contempte of God's vengeance threatened for our offences. Imprinted at London for Edward White at the little North-doore of Paules.

De la Demonomanie des Sorciers ... par J. Bodin. Angevin. A Paris, Chez Jacques du Puys Libraire Juré, à la Samaritaine. 1580.

A true and iust Recorde of the Information, Examination and Confession of all the Witches, taken at S. Oses, in the countie of Essex: whereof some were executed, and other some entreated according to the determination of lawe. Wherein all men may see what a pestilent people Witches are, and how unworthy to lyue in a Christian Commonwealth. Written orderly, as the cases were tryed by evidence. By W. W. Imprinted in London at the three Cranes in the Vinetree by Thomas Dawson. 1582.

The Discouerie of witchcraft. Wherein the lewde dealing of witches and witchmongers is notablie detected, the knauerie of coniurors, the impietie of inchantors, the folie of soothsaiers, the impudent falshood of cousenors, the infidelitie of atheists, the pestilent practises of Pythonists, the curiositie of figure casters, the varietie of dreamers, the beggerlie art of Alcumystrie, the abhomination of idolatrie, the horrible art of poisoning, the vertue and power of naturall magicke, and all the conueiances of Legierdemaine and iuggling are deciphered: and many other things opened, which haue long lien hidden, howbeit verie necessarie to be knowne. Hereunto is added a treatise upon the nature and substance of spirits and diuels, &c.: all latelie written by Reginald Scot Esquire, 1 John 4. 1. 'Beleeue not euerie spirit, but trie the spirits, whether they are of God; for manie false prophets are gone out into the world,' &c. 1584.

A true and most Dreadfull discourse of a woman possessed with the Deuill: who in the likeness of a headlesse Beare fetched her out of her Bedd, and in the presence of seuen persons, most straungely roulled her thorow three Chambers, and downe a high paire of staiers, on the fower and twentie of May last, 1584. At Dichet in Sommersetshire. A matter as miraculous as euer was seen in our time. Imprinted at London for Thomas Nelson.

IIII Livres des Spectres ou Apparitions et Visions d'Esprits, Anges et Demons se monstrans sensiblement aux hommes. Par Pierre le Loyer Cōseiller au Siege presidial d'Angers. A Angers, pour Georges Nepuen, Libraire demeurant à la Chauss{e} Sainct Pierre. 1586.

A Discourse of the subtill Practises of Deuilles by Witches and Sorcerers. By which men are and haue bin greatly deluded: the antiquitie of them: their diuers sorts and Names. With an Aunswer unto diuers friuolous Reasons which some doe make to prooue that the Deuils did not make those Aperations in any bodily shape. By G. Gyfford. Imprinted at London for Toby Cooke. 1587.

A true Discourse, Declaring the damnable life and death of one Stubbe Peeter, a most wicked Sorcerer, who, in the likenes of a Woolfe, committed many murders, continuing this diuelish practise 25 yeeres, killing and deuouring Men, Women and Children. Who for the same fact was taken and executed the 31 of October last past in the Towne of Bedbur neer the Cittie of Collin in Germany. Trulye translated out of the high Duch according to the Copie printed in Collin, brought ouer into England by George Bore's ordinary Poste, the xj daye of this present Moneth of June 1590, who did both see and heare the same. At London: Printed for Edward Venge, and are to be sold in Fleet-street, at the signe of the Vine.

The most strange and admirable discouerie of the three Witches of Warboys, arraigned, conuicted and executed at the last Assizes at Huntington for the bewitching of the fine daughters of Robert Throckmorton Esqre., and diuers other persons, with sundrie Diuellish and grieuous torments. And also for bewitching to death of the Lady Crumwell, the like hath not been heard of in this age. London: Printed by the Widdowe Owin, for Thomas Man, and Iohn Winnington, and are to be solde in Paternoster Rowe, at the signe of the Talbot. 1593.

A True Discourse, upon the matter of Martha Brossier of Romorantin, pretended to be possessed by a Deuill. Translated out of French into English by Abraham Hartwell. Ecclesiastie 19. 'He that is hastie to giue credite, is light minded; and shall be held as one that sinneth against his owne Soule.' London: Imprinted by Iohn Wolfe, 1599.

Malleus Maleficarum: De lamiis et strigibus, et sagis aliisque Magis & Demoniacis, eorumque arte, potestate, & poena ... Tractatus aliquot tam veterum quam recentiorum auctorum, &c. 2 tom. Francofurti, 1600, 8vo.

A true Narration of the strange and grevous vexation by the Devil of 7 persons in Lancashire, and William Somers of Nottingham. Wherein the doctrine of Possession and Dispossession of Demoniakes out of the word of God, is particularly applyed unto Somers and the rest of the persons controuerted: together with the use we are to make of these workes of God. By Iohn Darrell, Minister of the word of God. 'He that is not with me, is against me: and he that gathereth not with me, scattereth.' Matth. xii. 30. Printed 1600.

A Dialogue concerning Witches and Witchcrafts. In which is layed open how craftily the Diuell deceiueth not onely the Witches, but many other, and so leadeth them awrie into manie great errours. By George Giffard, Minister of God's word in Maldon. London: Printed by R. F. and F. K. and are to be sold by Arthur Iohnson, at the signe of the Flower-de-Luce and Crowne in Paules Church-Yard. 1603.

Demonologie. In forme of a Dialogue. Diuided into three books. Written by the High and mightie Prince, Iames, by the grace of God, King of England, Scotland, France and Ireland. Defender of the Faith, &c. London: Printed by Arnold Hatfield for Robert Wald-graue. 1603.

A Treatise of Specters or Straunge Sights, Visions and Apparitions appearing sensibly unto men. Wherein is deliuered the Nature of Spirites, Angels and Divels: their power and properties: as also of Witches, Sorcerers, Enchanters and such like.... Newly done out of French into English. London;

Printed by Val. S. for Mathew Lownes. 1605.

Discours, et Histoires des Spectres, Visions et Apparitions des Esprits, Anges, Demons et Ames, se monstrans visibles aux hommes. Divisez en huict livres. Esquels par les Visions Merveilleuses, et prodigieuses Apparitions avenuës en tous siecles, tirees et recuillies des plus celebres autheurs tant Sacrez que Prophanes ... Aussi est traicté des Extases et rauissements &c. Par Pierre le Loyer, Conseiller du Roy au siege Presidial d'Angers. A Paris, Chez Nicolas Buon, demeurant au mont Sainct Hilaire a l'enseigne Sainct Claude. 1605.

A Full and True Account Both of the Life; and also of the Manner and Method of carrying on the Delusions, Blasphemies and Notorious Cheats of Susan Fowls, as the same was Contrived, Plotted, Invented, and Managed by wicked Popish Priests, and other Papists, with a Design to scandalize our Church and Ministers, by insinuating that the Virtue of Casting out Devils, and Easing Persons Possess'd was only in the Power of their Church. As also, Of her Tryal and Sentence at the Old Baily, the 7th of this instant May, for blaspheming Jesus Christ, and cursing the Lord's Prayer. London: Printed for J. Read in Fleet Street. 1608.

Strange and Wonderful News. Being a True, tho' Sad Relation of Six Sea Men (Belonging to the Margaret of Boston) who Sold Themselves to the Devil, And were Invisibly Carry'd away. With an Account of the said Ship being Sunk under Water, where She continued full Eleuen Weeks: All which Time, to Admiration, the rest of the Ship's Crew Liv'd, and Fed upon Raw Meat, and Live Fish that Swam over their Heads. The Names of the Three Persons that were, (thro' Mercy) Preserv'd so long under water, were William Davies (a Man very well known to the Merchants in London) Mr. William Kadner, and Mr. William Bywater. There was only One Boy Drowned. The Truth of which Strange and Miraculous Relation will be Attested at Mr. Loyd's Coffee House, near the General Post Office in Lombard-Street: where the original Letter, at large, will be shewn to any Person that desires to be further satisfy'd in the Truth hereof; and by several Eminent Merchants upon the Exchange. London: Printed for H. Marston in Cornhill. No date.

A Discourse of the damned Art of Witchcraft, so farre forth as it is reuealed in the Scriptures and manifest by true experience. By William Perkins. O. Legge, Cambridge, 1608, 8vo.

Discours des Sorciers, avec six Advis en faict de Sorcelerie. Et une Instruction pour un Iuge en semblable matiere: Par Henry Boguet Dolanois, grand Iuge en la terre S. Oyan de Ioux, ditte de S. Claude, au Comte de Bourgongne.... Seconde Edition. A Lyon, Chez Pierre Rigaud en ruë Merciere, au coing de ruë Ferrandiere, a l'Horloge. 1608.

The wonderful discouerie of Elizabeth Sawyer, a Witch, late of Edmonton, her conuiction and condemnation and Death. Together with the relation of the Diuels accesse to her, and their conference together. Written by Henry Goodcole, Minister of the Word of God, and her continuall Visiter in the Gaole of Newgate. London: Printed for William Butler, and are to be sold at his Shop in Saint Dunstons Church Yard Fleet Street. 1611.

The Witches of Northamptonshire. Agnes Browne, Joane Vaughan, Arthur Bill, Hellen Ienkenson, Mary Barber, Witches. Who were all executed at Northampton the 22 of Iuly last 1612. London: Printed by Tho: Purfoot, for Arthur Iohnson. 1612.

The Wonderfull Discouerie of Witches in the Countie of Lancaster. With the Arraignment and Triall of Nineteene notorious Witches, at the Assizes and generall Gaole deliuerie, holden at the Castle of Lancaster, upon Munday, the seuenteenth of August last 1612. Before Sir Iames Altham, and Sir Edward Bromley, Knights; Barons of his Maiesties Court of Exchequer: And Justices of Assize, Oyer and Terminer, and generall Gaole deliuerie in the Circuit of the North Parts. Together with the Arraignment and Triall of Iennet Preston, at the Assizes holden at the Castle of Yorke, the seuen and twentieth day of Iulie last past, with her Execution for the murther of Master Lister, by Witchcraft. Published and set forth by the Commandement of his Maiesties Iustices of Assize in the North Parts. By Thomas Potts, Esquier. London: Printed by W. Stansby for Iohn Barnes, dwelling neare Holborne Conduit. 1613.

Tableau de l'Inconstance des Mauvais Anges et Demons. Ou il est amplement traicté des Sorciers, et de la Sorcellerie. Livre tres-utile et necessaire, non seulement aux Iuges, mais à tous ceux qui viuent sous les loix Chrestiennes. Avec un Discours contenant la Procedure faite par les Inquisiteurs d'Espagne et de Nauarre, à 53 Magiciens, Apostats, Iuifs et Sorciers, en la ville de Logrogne en Castille, le 9 Novembre 1610. En laquelle on voit combien l'exercice de la Iustice en France, est plus iuridiquement traicté, et auec de plus belles formes qu'en tous autres Empires, Royaumes, Republiques et Estats. Par Pierre de Lancre, Conseiller du Roy au Parlement de Bordeaux ... A Paris, Chez Nicolas Buon, ruë sainct Iacques, à l'enseigne de sainct Claude, et de l'Homme Sauuage. 1613.

A True and Feareful Vexation of one Alexander Nyndge: being most horribly tormented with the Deuill, from the 20 day of Ianuary to the 23 of Iuly. At Lyeringswell in Suffocke; with his Prayer after his Deliuerance. Written by his owne brother, Edward Nyndge Master of Arts, with the Names of the Witnesses that were at his Vexature. ¶ Imprinted at London for W. B. and are to bee sold by Edward

Wright at Christ Church Gate. 1615.

Le Fleau des Demons et Sorciers par J. B. (Bodin). Angevin. Derniere Edition, à Nyort, par Dauid du Terroir. 1616.

The Triall of Witch-craft, shewing the true and right methode of the Discouerie: with A Confutation of Erroneous wayes. By Iohn Cotta, Doctor in Physicke. London: Printed by George Purslowe for Samuel Rand, and are to be solde at his shop neere Holburne-Bridge. 1616.

A Treatise of Witchcraft. Wherein sundry Propositions are laid downe, plainely discouering the wickednesse of that damnable Art, with diuerse other speciall points annexed, not impertinent to the same, such as ought diligently of euery Christian to be considered. With a true Narration of the Witchcrafts which Mary Smith, wife of Henry Smith, Glouer, did practise: Of her contract vocally made between the Deuill and her, in solemn termes, by whose meanes she hurt sundry persons whom she enuied: Which is confirmed by her owne confession, and also from the publique Records of the Examination of diuerse upon their oathes: And, lastly, of her death and execution, for the same, which was on the twelfth day of Ianuarie last past. By Alexander Roberts, B.D. and Preacher of Gods Word at Kings-Linne in Norffolke.... London: Printed by N. O. for Samuel Man, and are to be sold at his Shop in Pauls Church-Yard, at the signe of the Ball. 1616.

The Merry Devil of Edmonton. As it hath beene sundry times Acted by his Maiesties Seruants, at the Globe on the Bankside. At London. Printed by G. Eld, for Arthur Iohnson, dwelling at the signe of the white-Horse in Paules Church-yard, ouer against the great North Doore of Paules. 1617.

The Mystery of Witchcraft. Discouering the Truth, Nature, Occasions, Growth and Power thereof. Together with the Detection and Punishments of the same. As Also, the seuerall Stratagems of Sathan, ensnaring the poore Soule by this desperate practize of annoying the bodie: with the seuerall Uses thereof to the Church of Christ. Very necessary for the redeeming of these Atheisticall and secure (sic) times. By Thomas Cooper. London: Printed by Nicholas Okes. 1617.

The Wonderful Discouerie of the Witchcrafts of Margaret and Philip Flower, daughters of Ioan Flower, neere Beuer Castle, Executed at Lincolne March 11, 1618. Who were specially arraigned and condemned before Sir Henry Hobart, and Sir Edward Bromley, Iudges of Assise, for confessing themselues actors in the destruction of Henry, Lord Rosse, with their damnable practises against others the Children of the Right Honourable Francis, Earle of Rutland. Together with the seuerall Examinations and Confessions of Anne Baker, Ioan Willimot, and Ellen Greene, Witches in Leicestershire. Printed at London by G. Eld for I. Barnes, dwelling in the long Walke, neere Christ-Church. 1619.

The Boy of Bilson: or a true Discovery of the late notorious Impostures of certaine Romish Priests in their pretended Exorcisme, or expulsion of the Diuell out of a young Boy, named William Perry, sonne of Thomas Perry of Bilson in the County of Stafford, Yeoman. Upon which occasion, hereunto is premitted A briefe Theologicall Discourse, by way of Caution, for the more easie discerning of such Romish Spirits; and iudging of their false pretences, both in this, and the late Practises ... at London. Imprinted by F. K. for William Barret. 1622.

The Infallible and Assured Witch: or the Second Edition of the Tryall of Witch craft. Shewing the right and true methode of the discouerie; with a confutation of erroneous waies carefully reviewed and more fully cleared and Augmented. By Iohn Cotta, Doctor in Physicke. London: Printed by I. L. for R. H. and are to be sold at the signe of the Grey hound in Pauls Church Yard. 1625.

The late Lancashire Witches. A well received Comedy, lately Acted at the Globe on the Banke-side, by the King's Majesties Actors. Written by Thom Heywood, and Richard Broome Aut prodesse solent, aut delectare. London: Printed by Thomas Harper for Benjamin Fisher, and are to be Sold at his Shop at the Signe of the Talbot, without Aldersgate. 1634.

A Relation of the Devill Balams departure out of the body of the Mother Prioresse of the Ursuline Nuns of Loudun. Her fearefull motions and contorsions during the Exorcisme, with the Extract of the Proces verball, touching the Exorcismes wrought at Loudun, by order of the Bishop of Poictiers, under the authority of the King. Printed at Orleans 1635. Or the first part of the Play acted at Loudun by two Divels, a Frier, and a Nun. Faithfully translated out of the French Copie, with some Observations for the better illustration of the Pageant. London: Printed by R. B. and are to be sold in S. Pauls Church-yard, and in S. Dunstans Church Yard in Fleet Street, at the Shop turning up to Clifford's Inn. 1636.

A Dog's Elegy, or Rupert's Tears, for the late Defeat given him at Marston moore, neer York by the Three Renowned Generalls: Alexander, Earl of Leven, Generall of the Scottish Forces. Fardinando Lord Fairfax, and the Earle of Manchester, Generalls of the English Forces in the North. Where his beloved Dog, named Boy, was killed by a Valiant Souldier, who had skill in Necromancy. Likewise the strange breed of this Shagg'd Cavalier, whelp'd of a Malignant Water Witch; With all his Tricks and Feats.

'Sad Cavaliers, Rupert invites you all

That doe survive, to his Dogs Funerall.
Close mourners are the Witch, Pope, & Devill,
That much lament yo'r late befallen evill.'

Printed at London, for G. B. July 27, 1644.

A true and exact Relation of the severall Informations, Examinations, and Confessions of the late Witches, arraigned and executed in the County of Essex. Who were arraigned and condemned at the late Sessions, holden at Chelmesford before the Right Honorable Robert Earle of Warwicke, and severall of his Majesties Justices of Peace, the 29 of July 1645. Wherein the severall murthers, and devillish Witchcrafts committed on the bodies of men, women and children, and divers cattell, are fully discovered.... London: Printed by M. S. for Henry Overton and Benj. Allen, and are to be sold at their Shops in Popes head Alley. 1645.

The Lawes against Witches and Coniuration, and Some brief Notes and Observations for the Discovery of Witches. Being very usefull for these Times, wherein the Devil reignes and prevailes over the soules of poor Creatures, in drawing them to that crying Sin of Witchcraft. Also the Confession of Mother Lakeland, who was arraigned and condemned for a Witch, at Ipswich in Suffolke.... London: Printed for R. W. 1645.

The Examination, Confession, Triall and Execution of Joane Williford, Joan Cariden, and Jane Hott: Who were executed at Feversham in Kent, for being Witches, on Munday the 29 of September 1645. Being a true Copy of their evill lives and wicked deeds, taken by the Maior of Feversham and Jurors for the said Inquest. With the Examination and Confession of Elizabeth Harris, not yet executed. All attested under the hand of Robert Greenstreet, Maior of Feversham. London: Printed for J. G., October 2, 1645.

The Discovery of Witches in answer to severall Queries, lately delivered to the Judges of Assize for the County of Norfolk, and now published M. [Matthew] H. [Hopkins] Witch finder, for the benefit of the whole Kingdom. London, 1647, 4to.

The full Tryals, Examination and Condemnation of Four Notorious Witches, At the Assizes held at Worcester, on Tuseday the 4th of March. With the manner, how they were found guilty of Bewitching several Children to Death. As also, Their Confessions, and last Dying Speeches at the Place of Execution; with other Amazing Particulars concerning the said Witchcraft.... London: Printed by I. W., near Fleet-street. No date.

The Woodstock Scuffle, or, Most Dreadfull Apparitions that were lately seene in the Mannor-House of Woodstock, neere Oxford, to the great Terror and wonderfull Amazement of all there that did Behold them. Printed in the yeere 1649.

Wonderfull News from the North, or a true Relation of the sad and grievous Torments Inflicted upon the Bodies of three Children of Mr. George Muschamp, late of the County of Northumberland, by Witchcraft; and how miraculously it pleased God to strengthen them, and to deliver them. As also the prosecution of the sayd Witches, as by Oaths, and their own Confessions will appear, and by the indictment found by the Jury against one of them, at the Sessions of the Peace held at Alnwick, the 24 day of April, 1650.... London: Printed by T. H., and are to be sold by Richard Harper, at his shop in Smithfield. 1650.

Doctor Lamb Revived, or Witchcraft condemn'd in Anne Bodenham, a Servant of his, who was Arraigned and Executed the Lent Assizes last at Salisbury, before the Right Honourable the Lord Chief Baron Wild, Judge of the Assise. Wherein is set forth her strange and wonderful Diabolical usage of a Maid, Servant to Mr. Goddard, as also, hir attempt against his Daughters, but by Providence delivered. Being necessary for all good Christians to Read, as a Caveat to look to themselves that they be not seduced by such Inticements. By Edmond Bower, an eye and ear Witness of her Examination and Confession. London: Printed by T. W. for Richard Best and John Place, and are to be Sold at their Shops at Grays Inn Gate and Furnival's Inn Gate in Holburn. 1653.

An Advertisement to the Jury-men of England touching Witches. Together with a Difference between an English and Hebrew Witch. London: Printed by I. G. for Richard Royston. At the Angel in Ivie-lane. 1653.

A Compendious History of the Goths, Swedes and Vandals and Other Northern Nations. Written by Olaus Magnus, Arch-Bishop of Upsall, and Metropolitan of Sweden. London: Printed by I. Streeter, and are to be sold by Humphrey Mosely, &c. 1658.

Strange and Terrible Newes from Cambridge, being A true Relation of the Quakers bewitching of Mary Philips out of the Bed from her Husband in the Night, and transformed her into the shape of a Bay Mare, riding her from Dinton towards the University. With the manner how she became visible again to the People in her own Likeness and Shape, with her sides all rent and torn, as if they had been spur-gal'd, her hands and feet worn as black as a Coal, and her mouth slit with the Bridle Bit. Likewise, her Speech to the Scholars and Country-men, upon this great and wonderful Change, her Oath before the

Judges and Justices, and the Names of the Quakers brought to tryal on Friday last at the Assises held at Cambridge. With the Judgment of the Court. As also, the Devil's snatching of one from his Company, and hoisting of him up into the Air, with what hapned thereupon. London: Printed for C. Brooks, and are to be sold at the Royal Exchange in Cornhill. 1659.

The Just Devil of Woodstock, Or, A True Narrative of the Several Apparitions, the Frights and Punishments inflicted upon the Rumpish Commissioners Sent thither, to Survey the Mannors and Houses belonging to his Majestie. London: Printed in the Year 1660.

A Philosophical Endeavour towards the Defence of the Being of Witches and Apparitions. In a letter to ... R. Hunt. Esq. By a Member of the Royal Society. J. G. [Glanvill] London, 1666.

Some Philosophical Considerations Touching the Being of Witches and Witchcraft written in a Letter to the much Honour'd Robert Hunt Esq: By J. G. a Member of the Royal Society. London: Printed by E. C. for James Collins at the King's Head in Westminster Hall. 1667.

A Blow at Modern Sadducism. In some Philosophical Considerations about Witchcraft. And the Relation of the Famed Disturbance at the House of M. Mompesson, with Reflections on Drollery, and Atheisme. The Fourth Edition Corrected and Inlarged. By Jos Glanvill. Fellow of the Royal Society. London: Printed by E. Cotes for James Collins at the King's Head in Westminster Hall. 1668.

The Question of Witchcraft Debated; Or, a discourse against their Opinion that affirm Witches.... London: Printed in the Year 1669.

The Opinion of Witchcraft Vindicated. In an Answer to a Book Intituled the Question of Witchcraft Debated. Being a letter to a Friend by R. T. London: Printed by E. O. for Francis Haley, and are to be sold at his Shop at the corner of Chancery Lane in Holborn. 1670.

The Witch of the Woodlands, Or, The Coblers New Translation. Written by L. P.

'Here Robin the Cobler for his former evils
Was punisht worse than Faustus with his devils.'

Printed by A. P. for W. Thackeray at the Angel in Duck Lane neer West Smithfield. 1670?

The Question of Witchcraft debated. Or a Discourse against their Opinion that affirm Witches, considered and enlarged. The Second Edition. By the Author John Wagstaffe.... London: Printed for Edw. Millington, at the Pelican in Duck Lane. 1671.

The Dæmon of Burton. Or a true Relation of Strange Witchcrafts or Incantations lately practised at Burton in the Parish of Weobley in Herefordshire. Certified in a Letter from a Person of Credit in Hereford. London: Printed for C. W. in the year 1671.

A Treatise proving Spirits, Witches and Supernatural Operations, by Pregnant Instances and Evidences: Together with other Things worthy of Note. By Meric Casaubon D.D. London: Printed for Brabazon Aylmer, at the Tree Pigeons in Cornhill. 1672.

A Pleasant Treatise of Witches, Their Imps, and Meetings, Persons bewitched, Magicians, Necromancers, Incubus, and Succubus's, Familiar Spirits, Goblings, Pharys, Specters, Phantasms, Places Haunted, and Devillish Impostures. With the difference between Good and Bad Angels, and a true Relation of a good Genius. By a Pen near the Covent of Eluthery. London: Printed by H. B. for C. Wilkinson at the Black Boy in Fleet street, and Tho. Archer and Tho. Burrell under St. Dunstan's Church. 1673.

The Wonder of Wonders, or Strange News from Newton in York-shire. Being a True and Perfect Relation of a Gentleman turn'd into a statue of Stone, which Statue stands now in the Garden of Goodman Wilford, a sufficient Farmer living in the same Town. Together With the occasion of the Fright upon Himself, Wife, and Maid, by four Persons, upon the 12th of May 1675. Set forth to prevent Surreptitious Reports. Printed in the Year 1675.

The Displaying of supposed Witchcraft, Wherein is affirmed that there are many sorts of Deceivers and Impostors, and Divers persons under a passive Delusion of Melancholy and Fancy. But that there is a Corporeal League made betwixt the Devil and the Witch, Or that he sucks on the Witches Body, has Carnal Copulation, or that Witches are turned into Cats, Dogs, raise Tempests, or the like, is utterly denied and disproved. Wherein also is handled, The Existence of Angels and Spirits, the truth of Apparitions, the Nature of Astral and Sydereal Spirits, the force of Charms and Philters; with other abstruse matters. By John Webster, Practitioner in Physick.... London: Printed by J. M. and are to be sold by the Booksellers in London. 1677.

Wonderful News from Buckinghamshire, or a perfect Relation How a young Maid hath been for Twelve years and upwards, possest with the Devil; And continues so to this very day in a Lamentable Condition. With an Account of several Discourses with the said Evil Spirit, and his Answers: attested by Ear-witnesses; and other strange Circumstances from time to time relating there unto. Published for the Awaking and Convincing of Atheists and modern Sadducees, who dream that there is neither Angel nor Spirit. Licensed according to Order. London: Printed for D. M. 1677.

A Discovery of the Impostures of Witches and Astrologers.... By John Brinly, Gent. London: Printed for John Wright, at the Crown on Ludgate Hill, and sold by Edward Milward, Book Seller in Leitchfield. 1680.

Melampronœa: or a Discourse of the Polity and Kingdom of Darkness. Together With a Solution of the chiefest Objections brought against the Being of Witches. By Henry Hallywell, Master of Arts, and sometime Fellow of Christs Colledge in Cambridge.... London: Printed for Walter Kettilby, at the Bishops Head in S. Paul's Church Yard. 1681.

Strange and wonderful News from Yowel in Surry; Giving a True and Just Account of One Elizabeth Burgiss, Who was most strangely Bewitched and Tortured at a sad rate, having several great lumps of Clay pulled forth from her Back, full of Pins and Thorns, which pricked so extreamly, that she cry'd and roar'd in a vehement and outragious manner, to the great amazement of all the Beholders. As also. How great Stones, as big as a Man's Fist, were thrown at her in the Dwelling House of Mr. Tuers, which came flying into the House, and that none of the Family was any ways hurt, but this Maid; Also how the Bellows was thrown at her. Mr. Tuers. her Master, finding his House thus troubled, after some time, sent her home to her Mothers House at Asteed, about three Miles off from Yowel, where by the way She was most strangely assaulted with Stones as before; and after She came to her Fathers House, the throwing of the Pewter Dishes, Candlesticks, and other clattering of Household-Goods at her, besides the displacing of a Musical Instrument, hanging up her Grand Fathers Breeches on the top of the Sealing. With many more strange and miraculous things, filling the Spectators with Wonder and amazement. Printed for J. Clarke, Seignor; at the Bible and Harp in West Smithfield. 1681.

The Tryal, Condemnation and Execution of three Witches, viz: Temperance Floyd, Mary Floyd, and Susanna Edwards. Who were Arraigned at Exeter on the 18th of August 1682. And, being prov'd Guilty of Witch Craft, were Condemned to be Hang'd, which was accordingly Executed in the view of many Spectators, whose strange and much to be lamented Impudence, is never to be forgotten. Also, how they Confessed what Mischiefs they had done, by the assistance of the Devil, who lay with the above named Temperance Floyd, nine nights together. Also, how they Squeezed one Hannah Thomas to death in their Arms; How they also caused several Ships to be cast away, causing a Boy to fall from the top of a Main Mast into the Sea. With many Wonderful Things, worth your Reading. Printed for J. Deacon at the sign of the Rainbow, a little beyond St. Andrews Church in Holborn. 1682.

A Tryal of Witches at the Assizes held at Bury St. Edmonds for the County of Suffolk; on the Tenth day of March, 1664. Before Sir Matthew Hale, Kt. then Lord Chief Baron of his Majesties Court of Exchequer. Taken by a Person then Attending the Court. London: Printed for William Shrewsbery at the Bible in Duck Lane. 1682.

A Strange, True, and Dreadful Relation of the Devil's appearing to Thomas Cox, a Hackney Coach-Man; Who lives in Cradle Alley in Baldwin's Garden, First in the habit of a Gentleman with a Roll of Parchment in his hand, and then in the shape of a Bear, which afterwards vanish'd away in a flash of Fire, at Eight of the Clock on Friday Night. October the 31st, 1684. London: Printed by E. Mallet. 1684.

Pandemonium, or the Devil's Cloyster, Being a further Blow to Modern Sadduceism, Proving the Existence of Witches and Spirits, in A Discourse deduced from the Fall of the Angels, the Propagation of Satan's Kingdom before the Flood; The Idolatry of the Ages after, greatly advancing Diabolical Confederacies. With an Account of the Lives and Transactions of several Notorious Witches. Also A Collection of several Authentick Relations of Strange Apparitions of Dæmons and Spectres, and Fascinations of Witches, never before Printed. By Richard Bovet, Gent., London. Printed for J. Walthoe, at the Black Lion, Chancery Lane, over against Lincoln's Inn. 1684.

Satan's Invisible World discovered; or A choice Collection of Modern Relations, proving evidently against the Saducees and Atheists of this present Age, that there are Devils, Spirits, Witches, and Apparitions, from Authentick Records, Attestations of Famous Witnesses, and undoubted Verity. To all which is added, The Marvellous History of Major Weir, and his Sister; with two Relations of Apparitions at Edinburgh. By Mr. George Sinclar, late Professor of Philosophy in the Colledge of Glasgow.... Edinburgh: Printed by John Reid. 1685.

A Discourse, proving by Scripture and Reason, And the Best Authours, Ancient and Modern, that there are Witches: and How far their Power extends to the doing of Mischief both to Man and Beast: And likewise the Use and Abuse of Astrology laid open.... London: Printed by J. M. and sold by John Weld, at the Crown in Fleet Street, between the Two Temple Gates. 1686.

News from Pannier Alley: or, a True Relation of Some Pranks the Devil hath lately play'd with a Plaster-Pot there. London: Printed and Publish'd by Randal Taylor. 1687.

Memorable Providences, Relating to Witchcrafts and Possessions. A Faithful Account of many Wonderful and Surprising Things, that have befallen several Bewitched and Possessed Persons in New-England. Particularly, A Narrative of the marvellous Trouble and Releef Experienced by a pious Family in Boston, very lately and sadly molested with Evil Spirits. Whereunto is added A Discourse delivered unto a Congregation in Boston, on the Occasion of that Illustrious Providence. As also A Discourse delivered unto the same Congregation, on the occasion of an horrible Self-Murder Committed in the Town. With an Appendix in vindication of a Chapter in a late Book of Remarkable Providences, from the Calumnies of a Quaker at Pen-silvania. Written by Cotton Mather, Minister of the Gospel, And Recommended by the Ministers of Boston and Charleston. Printed at Boston in N. England by R. P. 1689. Sold by Joseph Brunning, at his Shop at the Corner of the Prison Lane next the Exchange.

The Certainty of the World of Spirits, fully evinced by unquestionable Histories of Apparitions and Witchcrafts, Operations, Voices, &c. Proving the Immortality of Souls, the Malice and Misteries of the Devils and the Damned, and the Blessedness of the Justified. Written for the Conviction of Sadduces and Infidels by Richard Baxter.... London: Printed for T. Parkhurst at the Bible and Three Crowns in Cheapside; and J. Salusbury at the Rising Sun over against the Royal Exchange. 1691.

The Wonders of the Invisible World. Observations As well Historical as Theological, upon the Nature, the Number, and the Operations of the Devils. Accompany'd with (I.) Some Accounts of the Grevious Molestations, by Dæmons and Witchcrafts, which have lately annoy'd the Countrey: and the Trials of some eminent Malefactors Executed upon occasion thereof: with several Remarkable Curiosities therein occurring. (II.) Some Counsils, Directing a due Improvement of the terrible things, lately done, by the Unusual and Amazing Range of Evil Spirits, in Our Neighbourhood: and the methods to prevent the Wrongs which those Evil Angels may intend against all sorts of people among us; especially in Accusations of the Innocent. (III.) Some Conjectures upon the great Events likely to befall the World in General, and New England in Particular; as also upon the Advances of the Time when we shall see Better Dayes. (IV.) A short Narrative of a late Outrage committed by a knot of Witches in Swedeland, very much Resembling, and so far Explaining, That under which our parts of America have laboured! (V.) The Devil discovered: In a Brief Discourse upon those Temptations, which are the more Ordinary Devices of the Wicked One. By Cotton Mather. Boston: Printed by Benj. Harris for Sam Phillips. 1693.

A further Account of the Tryals of the New-England Witches. (Collected by D. [Deodat] L. [Lawson]) ... To which is added Cases of Conscience concerning Witchcrafts, and Evil Spirits personating Men. Written ... by I. [Increase] Mather. 2 parts, London. 1693.

A Collection of Modern Relations of Matter of Fact, concerning Witches and Witchcraft Upon the Persons of People. To Which is prefixed a Meditation concerning the Mercy of God, in preserving us from the Malice and Power of Evil Angels. Written by the late Lord Chief Justice Hale upon Occasion of a Tryal of several Witches before him, Part 1. London: Printed for John Harris, at the Harrow in the Poultry. 1693.

A Faithful Narrative of the Wonderful and Extraordinary Fits which Mr. Tho. Spatchet (Late of Dunwich and Cookly) was under by Witchcraft: or A Mysterious Providence in his even Unparalleled Fits. With an Account of his first Falling into, Behaviour under, and (in part) deliverance out of them. Wherein are several Remarkable Instances of the Gracious Effects of Fervent Prayer. The whole drawn up and written by Samuel Petto, Minister of the Gospel at Sudbury in Suffolk, who was an Eye-witness of a great part. With a Necessary Preface.... London: Printed for John Harris at the Harrow in the Poultrey. 1693.

Miscellanies. Collected by J. Aubrey, Esqre. London: Printed for Edward Castle next Scotland Yard Gate, by Whitehall. 1696.

A Sad, Amazing, and Dreadful Relation of a Farmer's Wife, near Wallingford in Barkshire, who Abusing her Husband for selling Corn cheap to the Poor, and wishing the Devil might Thrash, the next Day found him Thrashing in the Barn, and was, by him, thrown on the Mow, remaining there in a pitious manner, not to be removed, feeding on the Ears of Corn, and refusing all other Food. With her Description of the Devil; how he vanished from her, and a great Quantity of Corn he had Thrashed was found black and burned. London: Printed and Sold by J. W. 1697.

A Relation of the Diabolical Practices of above Twenty Wizards and Witches of the Sheriffdom of Renfrew in the Kingdom of Scotland, contain'd in their Tryalls, Examinations, and Confessions; And for which several of them have been Executed this present Year, 1697. London: Printed for Hugh Newman, at the Grasshopper in the Poultry.

Sadducismus Debellatus: Or a True Narrative of the Sorceries and Witchcrafts exercis'd by the Devil and his Instruments upon Mrs. Christian Shaw, Daughter of Mr. John Shaw of Bargarran in the County of Renfrew in the West of Scotland, from Aug. 1696 to Apr. 1697. Containing the Journal of her Sufferings, as it was Exhibited and Prov'd by the Voluntary Confession of some of the Witches, and other Unexceptionable Evidence, before the Commissioners Appointed by the Privy Council of Scotland to Enquire into the same. Collected from the Records. Together with Reflexions upon Witchcraft in General, and the Learned Arguments of the Lawyers on both Sides, at the Trial of Seven of those Witches, who were Condemned; And some Passages which happened at their Execution.... London: Printed for H. Newman, and A. Bell, at the Grasshopper in the Poultry, and at the Cross Keys and Bible in Cornhill near Stocks Market. 1698.

The Second Part of the Boy of Bilson; or, a True and Particular Relation of the Impostor Susanna Fowles, Wife of John Fowles of Hammersmith, in the County of Middlesex, who pretended her self Possess'd with the Devil. Giving an Exact Account of the Beginning, Progress, Conferences, Discovery, Commitment, Confession, &c., of the said Impostor.... London: Printed, and are to be sold by E. Whitlock, near Stationers Hall. 1698.

A Strange and True Relation of One Mr. John Leech, Who lived in Huntington-Shire, at a place called Ravely, not farre distant from Huntington Town, who was (about ten dayes agoe) Carried twelve miles in the Ayre, by two Finnes, and also of his sad and lamentable death.... London. 1700?

The History of Witches and Wizards: Giving a True Account of all their Tryals in England, Scotland, Sweedland, France, and New England; with their Confession and Condemnation.... By W. P. London. 1700?

More Wonders of the Invisible World. Display'd in Five Parts. Part I. An Account of the Sufferings of Margaret Rule, Written by the Reverend Mr. C. [Cotton] M. [Mather]. P. II. Several Letters to the Author, &c. And his Reply relating to Witchcraft. P. III. The Differences between the Inhabitants of Salem Village and Mr. Parris their Minister, in New England. P. IV. Letters of a Gentleman uninterested, Endeavouring to prove the received Opinions about Witchcraft to be Orthodox. With short Essays to their Answers. P. V. A short Historical Account of Matters of Fact in that Affair. To which is added A Postscript relating to a Book intitled The Life of Sir William Phips. Collected by Robert Calef, Merchant, of Boston in New England.... London: Printed for Nath. Hillar, at the Princes Arms, in Leaden-Hall Street, over against St. Mary Ax, and Joseph Collyer at the Golden Bible on London Bridge. 1700.

Magnalia Christi Americana: or, the Ecclesiastical History of New England from its First Planting in the Year 1620 unto the Year of our Lord 1698. In Seven Books.... By the Reverend and Learned Cotton Mather, M.A. And Pastor of the North Church in Boston, New-England. London: Printed for Thomas Parkhurst at the Bible and Three Crowns in Cheapside. 1702.

A True and Full Relation of the Witches at Pittenweem. To which is added by way of Preface, An Essay for proving the Existence of Good and Evil Spirits, relating to the Witches at Pittenween, now in Custody, with Arguments against the Sadducism of the Present Age. Edinburgh: Printed by John Reid Junior, and are to be Sold at his Printing House in Libertouns Wynd. 1704.

A Full and True Relation of the Discovering, Apprehending and taking of a Notorious Witch, who was carried before Justice Bateman in Well-Close, on Sunday July the 23d. Together with her Examination and Commitment to Bridewell, Clerkenwel. London: Printed by H. Hills in Blackfryars near the Waterside. 1704.

Christ's Fidelity the only Shield against Satan's Malignity. Asserted in a Sermon Delivered at Salem-Village the 24th of March, 1692. Being Lecture-day there, and a time of Publick Examination, of some Suspected for Witchcraft. By Deodat Lawson, Minister of the Gospel. The Second Edition.... Printed at Boston in New England, and Reprinted in London by R. Jockey for the Author; and are to be sold by T. Parkhurst, at the Bible and Three Crowns in Cheapside; and F. Lawrince at the Angel in the Poultry. 1704.

An Exact Narrative and many Surprizing Matters of Fact Uncontestably wrought by an Evil Spirit or Spirits in the House of Master Jan Smagge, Farmer in Canvy-Island near Leigh in Essex, upon the 10th, 13th, 14th, 15th and 16th of September last, in the Day-time: In the Presence of The Reverend Mr. Lord Curate to the said Island, Jan Smagge, Master of the House, and of several Neighbours, Servants and Strangers, who came at different times, as Mr. Lord's particular Care to discharge his Duty, and their Curiosity led them to this place of Wonders. Together with a Short Account of some of the Extraordinary Things credibly said to have formerly disturb'd the House, both before and since Mr. Smagge came into it: The utmost Caution being used not to exceed the Truth in the minutest Circumstance. In a Letter from Maiden in Essex to a Gentleman in London London: Printed and Sold by John Morphew near Stationer's Hall. 1709.

A Terrible and seasonable Warning to young Men; Being a very particular and True Relation of one Abraham Joiner, a young Man about 17 or 18 Years of Age.... London, 1710?

A Full and Impartial Account of the Discovery of Sorcery and Witchcraft Practised by Jane Wenham of Walkerne, in Hertfordshire, upon the Bodies of Anne Thorn, Anne Street, &c. The Proceedings against Her from Her being first Apprehended, till she was Committed to Gaol by Sir Henry Chauncy. Also Her Tryal at the Assizes at Hertford before Mr. Justice Powell, where she was found Guilty of Felony and Witchcraft, and receiv'd Sentence of Death for the same. March 4, 1711-12.... London: Printed for E. Curll at the Dial and Bible against St. Dunstan's Church in Fleet street. 1712.

Witchcraft Farther Display'd. Containing I. An Account of the Witchcraft practis'd by Jane Wenham of Walkerne in Hertfordshire, since her Condemnation, upon the Bodies of Anne Thom, and

Anne Street, and the deplorable Condition in which they still remain. II. An Answer to the most general Objections against the Being and Power of Witches: With some remarks upon the Case of Jane Wenham in particular, and on Mr. Justice Powel's Procedure therein. To which are added The Tryals of Florence Newton, a famous Irish Witch, at the Assizes held at Cork, Anno 1661: as also of two Witches at the Assizes held at Bury St. Edmunds, in Suffolk, in 1664, before Sir Matthew Hale (then Lord Chief Baron of the Exchequer) who were found guilty and executed.... London: Printed for E. Curll, at the Dial and Bible against St. Dunstans Church in Fleet street. 1712.

A full Confutation of Witchcraft: More particularly of the Depositions Against Jane Wenham, Lately Condemned for a Witch, at Hertford. In which the Modern Notion of Witches are overthrown, and the Ill Consequences of such Doctrines are exposed by Arguments; proving that Witchcraft is Priestcraft.... In a Letter from a Physician in Hertfordshire, to his Friend in London. London: Printed for J. Baker, at the Black-Boy in Pater-Noster Row. 1712.

The Case of the Hertfordshire Witchcraft consider'd. Being an Examination of a Book entitled A Full and Impartial Account of the Discovery of Sorcery and Witchcraft, Practis'd by Jane Wenham of Walkern, upon the Bodies of Anne Thom, Anne Street, &c. London: Printed for John Pemberton, at the Buck and Sun against St. Dunstan's Church in Fleet-street. 1712.

The Impossibility of Witchcraft. Plainly proving from Scripture and Reason That there never was a Witch, and that it is both Irrational and Impious to believe there ever was. In which the Depositions against Jane Wenham, Lately Try'd and Condemned for a Witch at Hertford, are Confuted and Expos'd.... London: Printed and Sold by J. Baker at the Black-Boy in Pater-Noster-Row. 1712.

The Belief of Witchcraft Vindicated: proving from Scripture, there have been Witches; and from Reason that there may be Such still. In Answer to a late Pamphlet, Intituled, The Impossibility of Witchcraft: Plainly proving that there never was a Witch, &c. By G. R., A.M. London: Printed for J. Baker, at the Black-Boy in Pater-Noster-Row. 1712.

A Compleat History of Magick, Sorcery and Witchcraft: Containing I. The most Authentick and best attested Relations of Magicians, Sorcerers, Witches, Apparitions, Spectres, Ghosts, Dæmons, and other preternatural Appearances. II. A Collection of several very scarce and valuable Tryals of Witches, particularly that famous one, of the Witches of Warboyse. III. An Account of the first Rise of Magicians and Witches; shewing the Contracts they make with the Devil, and what Methods they take to accomplish their Infernal Designs. IV. A full Confutation of all the Arguments that have ever been produced against the Belief of Apparitions, Witches, &c, with a Judgment concerning Spirits, by the late Learned Mr. John Locke. 2 vols. London: Printed for E. Curll at the Dial and Bible, J. Pemberton at the Buck and Sun, both against St. Dunstan's Church in Fleet Street and W. Taylor at the Ship in Pater-Noster-Row. 1715.

An historical essay concerning Witchcraft with observations ... tending to Confute the Vulgar errors about that point. As also two sermons: one [on John xv. 24] in proof of the Christian Religion: the other [on Ps. cxlviii. 2] concerning ... good and evil angels by Francis Hutchinson Bishop of Down and Connor. London, 1718.

British Magazine for 1747.

The History of the Colony of Massachusets-Bay, from the first settlement thereof in 1628. Until its Incorporation with the Colony of Plimouth, Province of Main, &c, by the Charter of King William and Queen Mary in 1691.... By Mr. Hutchinson Lieutenant Governor of the Massachusets Province. Boston, New England: Printed by Thomas and John Fleet at the Heart and Crown in Cornhill. 1749.

An Authentic, Candid, and Circumstantial Narrative of the Astonishing Transactions at Stockwell in the County of Surry. On Monday and Tuesday, the 6th and 7th Days of January 1772. Containing A Series of the most surprising and unaccountable Events that ever happened, which continued from first to last, upwards of Twenty Hours, and at different Places.... The Second Edition. London: Printed for J. Marks, Bookseller, in St. Martin's Lane. 1772.

A Narrative of the Sufferings and relief of a Young Girl; Strangely Molested by Evil Spirits and their Instruments, in the West: Collected from Authentic Testimonies, with a Preface and Postscript. Containing Reflections on what is most Material or Curious, either in the History or Trial of the Seven Witches who were Condemned and Burnt in the Gallow Green of Paisley.... Paisley: Printed and Sold by Alexander Weir. 1775.

A Tragi-Coomodie called The Witch, Long since acted by His Ma{ties} Servants at the Black-Friers. Written by Tho Middleton. 1778. [The following note in pen and ink will explain how a play by a contemporary of Massinger, Ben Jonson, etc., bears this date; for until this copy the play was never printed: 'This play was given me by Mr. Reid, who printed 100 Copies for the use of his friends, from a M.S. in Mr. Pearsons[129] library.']

A Collection and Abridgement of Celebrated Criminal Trials in Scotland, from A.D. 1536 to 1784, with Historical and Critical Remarks. By Hugo Arnot, Esq., Advocate.... Edinburgh: Printed for the Author by William Smellie. 1785.

A Journal of the Transactions and Occurrences in the Settlement of Massachusetts and other New-England Colonies, from the year 1630 to 1644. Written by John Winthrop, Esq., First Governor of Massachusetts; and now first published from a correct copy of the original Manuscript. Hartford: Printed by Elisha Babcock. 1790.

A Narrative of some extraordinary things that happened to Mr. Richard Giles's Children, at the Lamb, without Lawford's Gate, Bristol; supposed to be the effect of Witchcraft. By the late Mr. Henry Durbin, Chymist, Who was an Eye and Ear Witness of the principal Facts herein related. To which is added A Letter from the Rev. Mr. Bedford, late Vicar of Temple, to the Bishop of Gloucester, Relative to one Thomas Perks of Mangotsfield, who had Dealings with Familiar Spirits. Bristol: Printed and Sold by R. Edwards, Broad Street; Sold also by T. Hurst and W. Baynes, Paternoster Row, London; and by Hazard and Browne, Bath. 1800.

The Magus, or Celestial Intelligencer, being a complete system of Occult Philosophy.... By Francis Barrett, F.R.C.... London: Printed for Lackington, Allen and Co., Temple of the Muses, Finsbury Square. 1801.

A Collection of Scarce and Valuable Tracts, on the most Interesting and Entertaining Subjects: but chiefly such as relate to the History and Constitution of these Kingdoms. Selected from an infinite number in print and manuscript, in the Royal, Cotton, Sion, and other public, as well as private, Libraries; particularly that of the late Lord Somers. The Second Edition, revised, augmented, and arranged by Walter Scott, Esqre.... London: Printed for T. Cadell and W. Davies, Strand; W. Miller, Albemarle Street; R. H. Evans, Pall Mall; J. White and J. Murray, Fleet Street; and J. Harding, St James's Street. 1809.

Newes from Scotland, Declaring the damnable life of Doctor Fian, a notable Sorcerer, who was burned at Edenborough in Ianuarie last 1591. Which Doctor was register to the deuill, that sundrie times preached at North Baricke Kirke, to a number of notorious Witches. With the true examinations of the said Doctor and witches, as they uttered them in the presence of the Scottish king. Discouering how they pretended to bewitch and drowne his Maiestie in the sea comming from Denmarke, with such other wonderfull matters as the like hath not bin heard at anie time. Published according to the Scottish copie. Printed for William Wright. [This is a reprint of a rare tract by H. Freeling, for the members of the Roxburghe Club, 1816.]

Memorialls, or The Memorable Things that fell out within this island of Brittain from 1638 to 1684. By the Rev. Mr. Robert Law. Edited from the MS. by Charles Kirkpatrick Sharpe, Esqre.... Edinburgh: Printed for Archibald Constable and Co. 1818.

The History and Antiquities of the Parish of Edmonton in the County of Middlesex.... By William Robinson Gent, F.S.A.... London: Printed for the Author.... 1819.

A Collection of Rare and Curious Tracts on Witchcraft and the Second Sight; with an Original Essay on Witchcraft. Edinburgh: Printed for D. Webster, 35, West College Street. 1820.

Letters on Demonology and Witchcraft, addressed to J. G. Lockhart, Esqre., by Sir Walter Scott, Bart. London: John Murray, Albemarle Street. 1830.

Lectures on Witchcraft. Comprising a History of the Delusion in Salem in 1692. By Charles W. Upham, Junior Pastor of the First Church in Salem. Boston: Carter, Hender and Babcock. 1831.

Criminal Trials in Scotland, from A.D. 1488 to 1624. Embracing the entire Reigns of James IV. and V., Mary, Queen of Scots, and James VI. Compiled from the Original Records and MSS., with Historical Notes and Illustrations, by Robert Pitcairn, Esq., Writer to his Majesty's Signet, F.S.A. Scot, and Hon. F.S.A. Perth, etc. Edinburgh: William Tait, Princes Street; and Longman, Rees, Orme, Brown, Green, and Longman, London. 1833.

The Darker Superstitions of Scotland, illustrated from History and Practice. By John Graham Dalyell, F.A.S.E. Edinburgh: Waugh and Innes; W. Curry Junior and Co., Dublin; and Whittaker and Co., London. 1834.

A Collection of Rare and Curious Tracts relating to Witchcraft in the Counties of Kent, Essex, Suffolk, Norfolk and Lincoln, between the years 1618 and 1664. Reprinted verbatim from the Original Editions.... London: John Russell Smith, 4, Old Compton Street, Soho. 1838.

Memoirs of Extraordinary Popular Delusions. By Charles Mackay.... London: Richard Bentley, New Burlington Street.... 1841.

The Public Records of the Colony of Connecticut.... By J. Hammond Trumbull.... Hartford: Brown and Parsons. 1850.

The Pioneer History of Illinois, containing the Discovery, in 1673, and the History of the Country to the Year 1818, when the State Government was organized. By John Reynolds. Belleville, Ill.: Published by N. A. Randall. 1852.

The History of New England, from 1630 to 1649. By John Winthrop, Esq., First Governor of the Colony of the Massachusetts Bay, from his Original Manuscripts, with Notes.... By James Savage, President of the Massachusetts Historical Society. Boston: Little, Brown and Co. 1853.

Domestic Annals of Scotland, from the Reformation to the Revolution. By Robert Chambers.... W. and R. Chambers, Edinburgh and London. 1858.

Witch Stories. Collected by E. Lynn Linton.... London: Chapman and Hall, 193, Piccadilly. 1861.

La Sorcière. J. Michelet. Deuxième Édition, revue et augmentée. Bruxelles et Leipzig: A. Lacroix, Verboeckhoven et Cie, Éditeurs, Rue Royale, 3, Impasse du Parc. 1863.

La Sorcière: The Witch of the Middle Ages. From the French of J. Michelet, by L. J. Trotter.... London: Simpkin, Marshall and Co., Stationer's Hall Court. 1863.

Records of Salem Witchcraft. Copied from the Original Documents. Privately printed for W. Elliot Woodward. Roxbury, Mass. 1864.

Salem Witchcraft; with an Account of Salem Village, and a History of Opinions on Witchcraft and Kindred Subjects. By Charles W. Upham. Boston: Wiggin and Lunt. 1867.

Some Miscellany Observations on our present Debates respecting Witchcrafts, in a Dialogue between S. and B. By P. E. and J. A. Philadelphia: Printed by William Bradford for Hezekiah Usher. 1692. Boston Congregational Quarterly reprints, No 1. 1869. [This tract is by the Rev. Samuel Willard, of the Old South Church, Boston. S. and B. probably stand for Salem and Boston. S. takes the part of the magistrates, B. that of the clergy. This tract is mentioned by Calef in his 'More Wonders of the Invisible World.']

Cotton Mather and Witchcraft. Two Notices of Mr. Upham his Reply. [By Charles Wentworth]. Boston: T. R. Marvin and Son, 131, Congress Street; London, Henry Stevens, 4, Trafalgar Square. May, 1870.

Demonology and Devil Lore. By Moncure Daniel Conway, M.A.... London: Chatto and Windus, Piccadilly. 1879.

The Mysteries of All Nations: Rise and Progress of Superstition, Laws against, and Trials of, Witches, Ancient and Modern Delusions, together with Strange Customs, Fables, and Tales relating to Mythology, Days and Weeks, Miracles, Poets and Superstition, Monarchs, Priests and Philosophers, Druids, Demonology, Magic and Astrology, Divination, Signs, Omens and Warnings, Amulets and Charms, Trials by Ordeal, Curses and Evil Wishes, Dreams and Visions, Superstition in the Nineteenth Century. By James Grant. Leith: Reid and Son, 35, Shore; Edinburgh: W. Paterson; London: Simpkin, Marshall and Co. 1880.

Bibliographical Notes on Witchcraft in Massachusetts. By George H. Moore, LL.D., Superintendent of the Lenox Library. Read before the American Antiquarian Society, April 25th, 1888. Worcester: Printed for the Author. 1888.

Scottish Review, October, 1891, Edinburgh.
Boston Monthly Magazine, vol. i., p. 251.
Congregational Quarterly, vol. x., p. 154.
Putnam's Monthly Magazine, vol. ii., p. 249; vol. vii., p. 505; vol. xiv., p. 207.
The Galaxy, vol. xix., p. 358.
Christian Examiner, vol. xi., p. 240.
American Monthly Review, vol. i., p. 140.
American Whig Review, vol. iii., p. 60.
North American Review, vol. cvi., p. 176.
New England Historical and Genealogical Register, vol. xiii., p. 193.
Southern Review, N.S., vol. iii., p. 306.
The Hesperian, vol. i., p. 191.
Congregational Review, vol. ix., p. 201.
Harper's Magazine, vol. lxix., p. 99.
Magazine of American History, vol. xiv., p. 458.
New Englander, vol. xliv., p. 788.

THE END.

BILLING AND SONS, PRINTERS, GUILDFORD.

FOOTNOTES:

1. The old writers and the old maps probably meant mosquitoes when they said 'Here be Divells.'
2. 'A Discourse of the Subtill Practises of Deuilles by Witches and Sorcerers,' etc. By G. Gyfford. Lond., 1587.
3. Chap. iv.
4. 'The Discouerie of Witchcraft, etc., by Reginald Scot, Esq{re},' 1584, p. 377.
5. 'The Just Devil of Woodstock; or, a True Narrative of the Several Apparitions, the Frights and Punishments, inflicted upon the Rumpish Commissioners Sent thither, to Survey the Mannors and Houses belonging to His Majestie.' London; printed in the year 1660.
6. 'The Woodstock Scuffle; or Most Dreadfull Apparitions that were lately seene in the Mannor-House of Woodstock, neere Oxford, to the great Terror and Wonderful Amazement of all there, that did Behold them.' 1649.
7. 'Palpable Evidence of Spirits and Witchcraft, in an Account of the Fam'd Disturbance by the Drummer, in the House of M. Mompesson, etc.' London, 1668.
8. The writer was the Rev. Joseph Glanville, M.A., F.R.S., Chaplain in Ordinary to King Charles II., Rector of the Abbey Church, Bath, and a Prebendary of Worcester.
9. 'The Dæmon of Burton; or, A True Relation of Strange Witchcrafts, or Incantations, lately practised at Burton, in the Parish of Weobley, in Herefordshire. Certified in a Letter from a Person of Credit in Hereford.' London, 1671.
10. Herefordshire.
11. Ewell.
12. 'Strange and Wonderful News from Yowel in Surry, giving a True and Just Account of One Elizabeth Burgiss, who was most strangely Bewitched,' etc. London, 1681.
13. 'Discours des Sorciers,' by Henry Boguet (Lyon, 1608), p. 417.
14. Whooping.
15. Shriek.
16. A sheaf or bundle.
17. Table.
18. Hiccoughing.
19. Or bannocks, oat cakes.
20. A hump.
21. A hedgehog.
22. Sleight, cunning.
23. These extracts are from an English translation of Olaus Magnus, 1658.
24. A Finn is even now reckoned to be a very uncanny person on board ship, and to be able to control the weather.
25. The same selling of winds used to be done both in the Isle of Man and the Orkneys.
26. 'Demonologie,' lib. ii., cap. v.
27. 'The Discouerie of Witchcraft,' lib. i., cap. iii.
28. The Spectator, No. cxvii.
29. Lib. iii., cap. i.
30. A bat.
31. Lib. i., cap. iv.
32. 'A Dialogue concerning Witches and Witchcrafts,' by George Giffard. London, 1603.
33. 'The Discovery of Witches,' etc., by Matthew Hopkins, Witch-finder. London, 1647.
34. Bairns, or children.
35. Warts.
36. Gyves or fetters.
37. Torture.
38. Notes and Queries, Series IV., vol. viii., p. 44.
39. Gentleman's Magazine, 1759, p. 93.
40. Ed. 1730, p. 187.

41. A dove or wood-pigeon.

42. 'A Rehearsall both Straung and true, of hainous and horrible acts committed by Elizabeth Stile, alias Rockingham, Mother Dutten, Mother Deuell, Mother Margaret, Fower notorious Witches, apprehended at Winsore in the Countie of Barks, and at Abbington arraigned, condemned and executed on the 26 daye of Februarie last, Anno 1579.'

43. 'A true and iust Recorde of the Information, Examination and confession of all the Witches, taken at S. Oses in the Countie of Essex: whereof some were executed, and other some entreated according to the determination of lawe,' etc. London, 1582.

44. A mole.

45. 'The Wonderful Discouerie of Elizabeth Sawyer, a Witch, late of Edmonton,' etc. London, 1621.

46. 'A Treatise of Witchcraft,' etc., by Alex. Roberts, B.D. London, 1616.

47. Ay.

48. 'The full Tryals, Examination, and Condemnation of four Notorious Witches at the Assizes held at Worcester on Tuseday the 4th day of March,' etc. London, 1647.

49. 'A Collection of Modern Relations of Matter of Fact concerning Witches and Witchcraft upon the Persons of People,' etc. London, 1693.

50. 'Doctor Lamb revived; or, Witchcraft condemned in Anne Bodenham.' London, 1653.

51. 'The History of Witches and Wizards,' etc., by W. P. London, 1700 (?).

52. 'The History of Witches and Wizards,' etc., by W. P. London, 1700 (?).

53. 'A Collection of Modern Relations of Matter of Fact concerning Witches and Witchcraft upon the Persons of People,' etc. London, 1693.

54. 'Witchcraft Farther Display'd.' London, 1712.

55. A solar was an upper chamber.

56. Patrick Adamsone, Archbishop of St. Andrew's.

57. Fever and ague.

58. Palpitation of the heart.

59. Weakness of the back and loins.

60. Flux.

61. A salve.

62. Large clasp-knives.

63. Contrary to the course of the sun.

64. Hand.

65. Weaver's.

66. Paw.

67. Tips.

68. Always.

69. Mutilated.

70. Wet.

71. A piece of flat wood, somewhat like a cricket bat, with which, in washing, the clothes are beaten.

72. Be allayed.

73. Shapes and trims.

74. Hollow-backed.

75. Gruffly.

76. Alive.

77. Jerk.

78. Touch.

79. A coat of mail.

80. Crow.

81. Bean-straws.

82. Besom.

83. Cattle.

84. Webs of cloth.

85. Stroking or rubbing.

86. Sciatica.

87. Haunch.

88. Frightened.

89. Ends.

90. One or more.

91. Grains of barley.

92. Chopped up together.
93. In a fold of his plaid.
94. A quaigh, or cup.
95. Hard.
96. Lingering sickness.
97. Stubble.
98. 'History of Scotland,' by David Scott. London, 1727.
99. Lyne, or Linne, in Ayrshire.
100. Battle of Pinkie, September 10, 1547.
101. Grieving much.
102. Weeping.
103. Child-bed; in old French, gisante, a woman that lies in.
104. Hailed.
105. Dwindled away.
106. Provoked.
107. Frightened.
108. Trust.
109. In baptism.
110. Riven, drawn asunder.
111. Went.
112. Fairyland.
113. Ewe.
114. Went.
115. Sift or strain.
116. Thinking if.
117. Likewise.
118. Wishing.
119. Buried.
120. Gate.
121. I have before me at this present writing seventeen volumes of American magazines containing articles on witchcraft in America, and that is not an exhaustive list.
122. 'The Public Records of the Colony of Connecticut, prior to the Union with New Haven Colony, May, 1665,' by J. Hammond Trumbull (Hartford, 1850), vol. i. p. 77.
123. 'Records,' vol. ii., p. 575.
124. The New Englander, November, 1885, p. 817.
125. For this and much else relating to witchcraft in Massachusetts, I am indebted to that most exhaustive book, 'Salem Witchcraft,' etc., by Charles W. Upham (Boston, 1867).
126. Hutchinson, 'History of Massachusetts Bay,' 1767, vol. i., p. 179.
127. Hutchinson, 'History of Massachusetts Bay,' 1767, vol. i., p. 187.
128. 'Memorable Providences Relating to Witchcrafts and Possession,' etc., by Cotton Mather (Boston, 1689), p. 1.
129. Major Pearson, at the sale of whose library the British Museum acquired the 'Roxburghe Ballads.'

www.ingramcontent.com/pod-product-compliance
Lightning Source LLC
Chambersburg PA
CBHW071857070526
44583CB00016B/1735